PRINCIPLES OF LEGISLATION

PRINCIPLES
OF
LEGISLATION

THE USES OF POLITICAL AUTHORITY

BY MICHAEL D. BAYLES

UNIVERSITY OF KENTUCKY

WAYNE STATE UNIVERSITY PRESS

DETROIT 1978

Library of Congress Cataloging in Publication Data

Bayles, Michael D.
    Principles of legislation.

    Bibliography: p
    Includes index.
    1. Authority. 2. Legitimacy of governments.
I. Title.
JC571.B39   328'.01   78-3220
ISBN 0-8143-1599-2

TO JAN, FOR THE GOOD TIMES

CONTENTS

ACKNOWLEDGMENTS

Several people have aided in the writing of this book, often unknowingly. The most direct influence was Joel Feinberg, in a series of lectures given during the summer of 1969 at the Conference on Political and Legal Philosophy at the University of California-Irvine, sponsored by the Council for Philosophical Studies. Alan Perreiah, Kenneth Henley, and James Smith read early drafts of parts of the book and made helpful suggestions. My students have also argued these topics with me, and I profited from the discussions. Jacqueline Beir, Pat Harris, and especially Lori Miller transformed a frequently illegible copy into an accurately typed manuscript. My daughter Melanie also aided in its preparation. The book has also profited greatly from the editing of Jean Owen. Finally, the University of Kentucky Research Foundation helped finance the cost of the research and preparation of the manuscript.

Parts of this book have appeared earlier, usually in considerably different form. Chapter VI is a revised and expanded version of "Criminal Paternalism," in *The Limits of Law: Nomos XV*, ed. J. Roland Pennock and John W. Chapman (New York: Lieber-Atherton, 1974), pp. 174-88. Parts of Chapters V and VII are from "Rationales for Environmental Legislation," in *Law and the Ecological Challenge: Amintaphil II*, ed. Eugene Dais (Buffalo, N.Y.: Wm. S. Hein, Jay Stewart Publications, 1978). The much expanded version in this book profited from the comments of my respondents, James Nickel and Wade Robison. "Civil Disobedience," in Chapter IX, is a revised version of part of "The Justifiability of Civil Disobedience," *Review of Metaphysics* 24 (1970):3-20. These materials are used with permission.

9

We the People of the United States, in Order to form a more perfect Union, establish Justice, insure domestic Tranquility, provide for the common defence, promote the general Welfare, and secure the Blessings of Liberty to ourselves and our Posterity, do ordain and establish this Constitution for the United States of America.

Preamble, Constitution of the United States of America

INTRODUCTION

In the early 1970s many voices, some shrill and frantic, others deep and meditative, described a worldwide crisis of authority. Governmental, religious, and educational authority seemed to be crumbling throughout the world. During the 1960s, mass demonstrations against racial discrimination and the war in Vietnam occurred, and then, in the spring of 1970, college campuses all over the United States erupted in protest over the "incursion" into Cambodia. The 1968 Papal encyclical *Humanae Vitae*, with its condemnation of most forms of contraception, brought an outcry and outright rejection from Catholics around the world. In the same year, students rioted in the streets of Paris and in the buildings of Columbia University, and the age of the modern student strike began.

In contemporary crisis-oriented culture, new crises quickly supersede old ones as the focus of attention. Yet whatever may be the case in religion and education, the crisis of political authority has deepened. Public confidence in political authority withers around the world. The governments of Great Britain and Italy appear incapable of effectively managing depressed economies with concomitant rapid inflation. Proposed mandatory sterilization in India leads to rioting and the fall of Indira Gandhi. In the United States, a Sargasso Sea of government regulations, the blatant ineffectiveness of federal programs, both old and new, and the Watergate and Congressional scandals erode confidence in the federal government. This erosion may become a landslide as voters witness a Congress unable to enact an effective energy program despite the urging of two presidents. Similar examples of governmental ineptitude come with every newspaper. In a recent survey of public confidence

11

in persons in various occupations, congressmen ranked next to last, just ahead of used-car salesmen.

This book has been provoked by, and is addressed to, the present political situation. Its fundamental premise is that governments may justifiably claim the allegiance of their citizens only if they pursue substantive purposes which citizens have sound reasons to accept. Much of the present loss of confidence in political authority results from discontent with the purposes of government. Some citizens do not accept present governmental purposes because they do not believe these purposes are to their benefit. Others expect governments to solve problems beyond their competence; that is, they want governments to adopt what are in fact unrealizable purposes. Yet other citizens are discontented because much legislation is not well-designed to further appropriate purposes.

This book sets out those purposes which average citizens have good reason to agree that political authorities should pursue and values which they have good reason to agree that political authorities should respect. These purposes and values provide good reasons for and against legislation. Consequently, they are presented as legislative principles, those principles which specify reasons for and against legislation. However, there are different legal techniques or kinds of legislation. In considering legislative principles, the appropriate legal techniques are specified. The combinations of acceptable principles and appropriate legal techniques constitute the uses of political authority, for they indicate what political authorities should do, and only if political authorities do what they ought will citizens owe allegiance to the state.

In two respects, this book differs from much traditional political philosophy. First, while most political philosophies rest upon ethical theory, I claim that political philosophy is independent of ethical theory. My arguments are based on appeals to self-interest and, when necessary, to limited benevolence, without assuming ethical principles. Second, while most political philosophy emphasizes political procedures or the forms of government—democracy, aristocracy, etc.—the focus here is on substantive purposes. The forms of government are ignored, on the assumption that no particular form will guarantee the right results. If political authorities generally succeed in pursuing and respecting acceptable purposes and values, the procedures by which they are selected and make decisions are of little importance. The fundamental issue is what government ought to do, for only when one knows what *ought* to be done can one determine the procedures most likely to result in its *being* done.

Fruitful discussion of the uses of political authority requires examining various social problems and possible legislation to deal with them. No definitive recommendations for legislation are provided. My intention is to illustrate plausible approaches to problems. Social problems involve questions of both facts and values, and the brief discussions here cannot adequately reflect that complexity. Their purpose is merely to provide a general framework of acceptable principles on the basis of which specific solutions may be sought.

This book does not consider all possible legislative principles, only the basic ones. If the arguments put forth are sound, the principles developed here supply the foundation for a reasonable legislative policy which provides citizens with good reasons for political allegiance. However, there is much room for disagreement with respect to specific legislation. Moreover, convincing authorities that legislation must be evaluated and enacted on the basis of these principles is a difficult but critical task. Its accomplishment will require a determined effort by all concerned citizens.

I
POLITICAL
AUTHORITY

For many people, political authority is puzzling. They want to know what political authority is and what it is for. Before one can determine what political authority is for, one needs to have a general conception of it. If the purpose of political authority is considered before it is defined, functions ill-suited to it may be suggested. For example, when he campaigned for the Democratic presidential nomination in 1968, Senator Eugene McCarthy suggested that one of the primary functions of a president is to be a moral example for the nation. However, the office of the president may be a poor environment for a moral example.

One must distinguish between the uses which political authority was originally intended to have and those which it might have. Some people assert that political authority cannot be used for any purposes other than those for which it was originally intended. Such a contention is usually couched in the rhetoric of "the purposes of the Founding Fathers." However, there is no a priori reason why political authority cannot be used in ways for which it was not originally intended, but what these might be depends in part upon its nature—what it is.

Moreover, political authority may not have originally been intended for anything. Political authority is not an invention like the automobile but something which evolved in the relations among people. Thus appeals to the original purposes or intentions may be somewhat misleading. Nonetheless, one can consider the purposes or uses which the designers of specific political systems had in mind, for example, those of the drafters of constitutions.

The usefulness of political authority cannot reside in its useless-
ness. If political authority cannot do anything, or if it cannot do
anything as well as or better than other things can, then it is useless. If it is useless, then retaining it merely so that men will reflect
upon the utility or value of other institutions is too great a burden:
some educational equipment is not worth the price. But before one
scraps political authority, one must determine what it is and see
whether or not it might have any uses.

POWER AND COERCION

Philosophers have disagreed about political authority. Some have
held that it is simply a kind of power. Others have held that
authority and power are incompatible and, therefore, that political
authority cannot be power. Still others suggest that it is all of these,
and other things as well. For example, it might be held that political authority sometimes involves power, sometimes influence, and
sometimes other forms of control.

One must distinguish between the possessive and active uses of
terms such as 'power', 'influence', and 'authority'. In Aristotelian
terminology, the possessive use refers to the potentiality and the
active use to the exercise of the potentiality. The possessive use
involves expressions such as 'has power, influence, authority', i.e.,
those using the auxiliary verb 'to have'. The active use involves
either a verb form of the term, e.g., 'influences', or an auxiliary
verb such as 'exercise', e.g., 'exercises authority'.

It is useful to have a term designating all the ways in which one
person may affect the behavior of another. Sometimes 'power' has
been used for this purpose: a person, X, has power over another, Y,
with respect to behavior of type A if and only if (a) X can do B, and
(b) should X do B, Y would be more likely to do A. To exercise such
power on a particular occasion, X must actually affect Y's behavior.
Thus, for X to exercise such power over Y with respect to behavior
A, at least the following conditions are required: (1) X does B; (2)
Y does A; and (3) had X not done B, Y would have been less
likely to do A. However, there is no need to use 'power' in this
sense because there is already an ordinary English expression for it,

namely, 'X's behavior causally affects Y's behavior'. In short, X's doing A can (does) cause Y to do B.

A more interesting concept pertains to the class of X's behavior in which, for any reason, he intends to affect Y's behavior. Sometimes 'power' is used to refer only to this subclass of behavior which affects that of others. However, since 'power' is used in so many different ways, it is best to avoid it whenever possible. For that reason, 'control' is used here for that behavior of X in which he intentionally affects Y's behavior. Hence, for 'control' in both the possessive and active uses, another condition must be added to those required for X's behavior to affect Y's causally. For the active use, the condition is that (4) X intends that Y do A. For the possessive use, the condition is that (c) X knows that Y's doing A depends on his (X's) doing B. This knowledge enables X to affect Y's behavior if for any reason he chooses to do so.

The difference between causally affecting another's behavior and actually controlling that behavior may be illustrated by the following simple examples. Suppose X sets a garbage can on the sidewalk and Y detours around it as he walks along. Then X's behavior causally affects Y's, but X does not control Y's behavior. Suppose, however, that X sets the garbage can near the curb in order to make Y walk closer to the alley where X is waiting to mug him. Then, if Y detours around the garbage can, X has not merely causally affected Y's behavior but has controlled it.

Control over another person may be of two basic kinds. X's control over Y's conduct may depend upon his having the ability (or upon Y's thinking that he does) to affect Y in ways which Y considers desirable or undesirable; that is, X's control over Y depends upon his ability to do something for or to Y if he does or does not do A. X's control over Y depends upon his giving or proposing to give Y benefits or harms. For example, if X controls Y by bribing him, X is promising to benefit Y for doing something. Likewise, if X controls Y by blackmailing him, he is threatening to harm Y if he does not act as X directs. Strictly speaking, what X proposes need not be an actual benefit or harm, but only what Y believes to be a benefit or harm. A person may be benefited or harmed in ways which he does not consider either desirable or undesirable. Hence, the essential condition is that X shall affect or propose to affect Y in a way which Y thinks desirable or undesirable. 'Benefit' and 'harm' will be used to mean what the recipient thinks desirable or undesirable. Although they ordinarily have an objectivity of meaning which is not captured in this use, there do not appear to be any more convenient terms.

In the second kind of control over others, X's ability to control Y's conduct does not depend upon benefits and harms—on doing something for or to Y. Rational persuasion is probably the clearest example of this sort of control. X may simply be able to present arguments which convince Y that he should or should not do A. Many other sorts of control, such as that by propaganda or love, are of this sort. There are, of course, borderline cases; for example, it is not clear how to classify control which depends on the giving or withholding of approval. In part, how it is ordinarily classified depends upon how much Y values X's approval. If Y greatly values X's approval, the withholding of it may be very undesirable to him, and X's control would then be said to be of the first sort. However, for theoretical purposes, it seems best to classify control over others which depends solely upon giving or withholding approval as of the second sort, since it does not involve X *doing* anything except approving or disapproving. If the giving or withholding of approval entails further benefits or harms, e.g., a job promotion, then it is of the first sort. Here, after approving or disapproving, X takes further action affecting Y based upon his approval or disapproval.

The ordinary concept of power over another person is a form of control of the first type. It is unclear whether all control over others which involves benefits or harms is 'power'. 'Power' tends to be restricted to control which depends upon harm. But if X can bribe Y, it would appear to be appropriate to say X has power over Y. The moral acceptability of the control also seems to affect whether 'power' is appropriate in ordinary discourse. The term tends to be used for that control which is not morally acceptable. However, it is certainly linguistically permissible to use 'power' when one thinks the control is morally acceptable.

For purposes of analyzing political systems, one of the most important types of power is coercion. At least two kinds or varieties of coercion may be distinguished. In one type, physical force is directly applied to cause another person to behave in a certain way. For example, one may clasp someone's hand and force his finger down on the trigger of a gun. Such 'occurrent coercion' takes place infrequently and does not require much analysis. It is what is sometimes called the use of "raw" power. Such coercion counts as power because it is assumed the victim does not want to behave as he is made to behave. Thus, the coercer does something to him, affects him, in a way he judges to be undesirable.

In the second variety, 'dispositional coercion', one person (the agent) threatens another (the victim) with a sanction (harm) if the latter fails to act as requested. This type of coercion occurs more frequently than the other and has been the topic of considerable controversy among philosophers. A rather common analysis of the usual cases of dispositional coercion contains the following elements: (1) person X intends that Y do A; (2) X further intends to harm Y if he does not do A; (3) X threatens Y with harm if Y does not do A; (4) Y does do A; (5) Y would have done otherwise had he so chosen; (6) Y would have chosen otherwise had he not been threatened. This analysis covers only standard or core cases; various modifications and additions must be made for non-standard ones.[1] It is not necessary for each of these conditions to be fulfilled in every case of coercion. However, normally they are all present.

These various factors require some comment in order to make the conception clear.[2] Condition (1) distinguishes coercion from force, restraint, compulsion, constraint, and mere threats. Physical conditions may force or compel a person to act as he would not have otherwise acted, but they do not coerce him. Likewise, chains may constrain or restrain a person, but they do not coerce him. Coercion must result from the activities of a personal agent. Moreover, in a mere threat, the threatener does not intend that the victim act in any specific way. "I'm going to kill you!" is a threat but does not involve coercion.

'Coercion' is an achievement word; it signifies success. If the victim does not act as the agent intends, then he was not coerced; however, the agent did try to coerce him. Conditions (4), (5), and (6) ensure that the victim was in fact coerced. They indicate that the victim did act as the agent intended and that it was the agent's threat that made him so act.

Conditions (2) and (3) are subject to considerable dispute. Some philosophers have claimed that coercion need not involve the threat of harm but may result from the offer of tremendous benefits.[3] Much of this dispute turns upon the analysis of threats, offers, and harms. For example, suppose a slaveowner beats his slaves daily. Further suppose that one day he proposes not to beat slave Y if he does A. Has the slaveowner offered not to beat the slave if he does A, or has he threatened to beat him if he does not do A? Such cases, and there are many other puzzling ones, make it difficult to decide whether or not all dispositional coercion involves threats.

There are two possible ways in which the above analysis may be defended. One is to claim that the loss of legitimately expectable benefits may constitute a harm, so that a proposal not to provide such a benefit is a threat of harm. However, it is difficult to determine what counts as a legitimately expected benefit. If one simply bases it on what usually happens, then the slave in the above example cannot legitimately expect not to be beaten. Hence, he would be offered a benefit and not coerced to do A. However, one may also base legitimate expectations on what a person is morally entitled to have. Thus, one might take something like the following position: if something is essential for a person's health, is not readily obtainable elsewhere, and can and should be provided (at least on easier terms), then its denial is a harm. On some such grounds one might hold that the slave is entitled not to be beaten, so the slaveowner is threatening to deprive him of something he can legitimately expect and, hence, coercing him to do A.[4]

While this approach best fits the ordinary use of 'coercion', it creates a difficulty when one is considering what political authority ought to do. For example, suppose the government proposes to provide welfare payments to mothers with dependent children on condition that they not have sexual intercourse with men. On this approach, whether or not the government is coercing the mothers not to have intercourse depends upon whether the women can legitimately expect such welfare payments without this condition. If they can, then they are being threatened and coerced; if they cannot, then they are being made an offer and not being coerced. However, whether government ought to do something depends in part on whether it involves coercing people. Coercion is undesirable, so it is more difficult to justify policies which involve coercion than those which do not. But on this approach, the decision that coercion is involved depends upon one's judgement of what the government ought to do. Hence, one cannot use the fact that coercion is involved to decide what the government ought to do. One must be able to determine whether coercion is involved prior to, and independent of, determining what the government ought to do. Consequently, this way of defending the above analysis of coercion is unsatisfactory when one's purpose is to determine what government ought to do. It puts the cart before the horse, since it requires one to determine what government ought to do before deciding whether it is coercing people.

The second way to defend the above analysis of coercion is simply to be hard-nosed about the definition of coercion. One does not count the denial of legitimately expectable benefits as a harm. On this approach, a threat and, hence, coercion, are involved if X will do something to Y if Y does not do as X wants and if Y views his situation as worse after the proposal than it in fact was before the proposal. The condition that Y views his situation as worse than "it in fact was before the proposal" excludes cases where Y is mistaken about what he could do before the proposal. For example, suppose Y thinks he can buy a loaf of bread for forty-five cents, but when he goes to the bakery the baker offers to sell him a loaf for sixty-five cents, which is the actual current price. Now Y may think that the baker's proposal made his situation worse than it was. Y is assuming that he can buy bread for forty-five cents a loaf, but in fact, he cannot do so. So unless one requires that Y be worse off than he *in fact* was just before the proposal, every time prices go up and Y is unaware of it, he is being coerced.[5]

On this hard-nosed approach, difficulties may arise about the timing of a proposal. One clever technique for controlling the behavior of another is to first deprive him of goods and then appear as a benefactor by proposing to provide them if he will act in some specified manner. Immediately prior to the proposal to provide the goods, the person did not have them, so the proposal is an offer. However, this offer is part of an attempt to control the person, so that overall he has not been benefited. If one looks at the entire project, then the person has been coerced, for he has been threatened with a permanent harm. The crucial aspect of these sorts of cases is the intention of the agent at the time the victim is deprived of the goods. If his intention is to take them away so that he can later offer to return them, then the action is coercion. It differs from other types in that the threat is being carried out, and the agent will cease his activities if the victim acts as desired. However, if at the time of depriving the victim of the goods the agent has no intention of later returning them, then the action is not coercion. The definition, in these sorts of cases, is not based on the relation of harm and benefit to the victim but on the specification of the agent's action.

This approach avoids the difficulty of the first one with respect to deciding what political authorities ought to do. One no longer has to determine what political authorities ought to do before deciding whether or not coercion is involved. Hence, one can always argue against a policy or action on the ground that it involves coercion. Nor does this approach have the consequence that one cannot condemn offers such as those to the mothers with dependent children and to the slave. Not all offers need be morally legitimate. The slave is, on this analysis, being made an offer; he sees himself as better off after the master's proposal than he was in fact before. But the master may still be condemned as evil for beating the slave, and the offer may be said to be unjust. The slave is being exploited, taken advantage of, and forced to do A. However, he is not threatened and coerced into doing it. Hence, while this second approach does not fit ordinary usage as well as the first, it will be used here. The chief reason for adopting it is to avoid begging questions about what government ought to do. It should be noted, however, that everything called 'coercion' in this approach is also coercion in the other approach. Consequently, this approach picks out conduct which is incontrovertibly coercion.

Since 'coercion' is an achievement word, 'to coerce' applies only to the exercise of power. There is no possessive expression such as 'to have coerciveness', denoting the ability to coerce. The expression 'coercive power' can be used to denote the ability to coerce. 'Exercise coercive power' then means the same as 'coerce'. The adjectival form of 'coerce', i.e., 'coercive', is used to refer to attempts to coerce. For example, a coercive threat is one used in an attempt to coerce. The attempt need not be successful for the threat to be appropriately described as coercive.

The issue posed at the beginning of this section, the relation between power and authority, can now be settled. The ordinary concept of power over another is of a form of control of the first type, that depending upon the ability to benefit or harm another. Authority with respect to another person is a form of the second type of control over another, which does not depend upon the ability to benefit or harm another. If X has authority with respect to Y, he need not propose harms or benefits to get Y to do something. X can get Y to perform actions by telling, commanding, or ordering him to do them.

Thus, power and authority appear to be mutually exclusive, but it is only the exercise of power and the exercise of authority on a specific occasion which are mutually exclusive. That is, if X proposes to benefit or harm Y in order to get him to do something, then he does not exercise authority. A person may possess or have both authority and power over another; that is, X may be able to get Y to do something either by merely telling him to do it or by threatening him. Usually, power is not exercised if a person has authority, for the use of power is more "costly" than the use of authority. It requires providing benefits or being prepared to harm a person, not merely telling him to do something.

AUTHORITY

One can make a rough distinction between authority over people which concerns conduct and authority which concerns belief.[6] For example, the authority of an expert on Etruscan art is primarily concerned with belief, while that of a policeman is primarily concerned with conduct. This distinction roughly corresponds with that between being *an* authority and being *in* authority. An authority is someone whose judgements about some topic are likely to be true, or at least are more likely to be true than those of a layman. A person in authority is someone whose commands or directives are to be followed.

However, authority over belief and authority over conduct overlap. An authority may be concerned either with knowing that or knowing how. If a person is an authority on, say, how to swim, then his directions are likely to be followed and are worthy of being followed. To be an authority on how to do something, one need not be able to do it. An athletic coach need not ever have played the sport he coaches. A person who knows how to do something will have authority over one's conduct because one thinks his suggestions are likely to be correct. The element of correctness is crucial to the concept of someone being an authority. An authority is someone who either knows about some topic or is more likely than others to be correct about it. Hence, the topic must be one about which judgments may be right or wrong, correct or incorrect. Some people deny that there can be moral authorities because they deny that moral judgments can be true or false, correct or incorrect. To be in authority a person need not be more likely than others to be correct about a topic. Hence, the element of correctness is not relevant to being in authority.

An effort is often made to correlate a person's being *an* authority and a person's being *in* authority; that is, authority over belief is a basis for authority over conduct, and vice versa. At the most elementary level, an authority on Etruscan art may be placed in authority in classes on the topic, for such a person is best able to judge what should be studied and to lead a discussion of the topic. Moreover, being in authority may provide opportunities for becoming an authority. Being in authority, a person may concern himself with a topic so much that he becomes an authority or may receive special information which makes him an authority. For example, it is some-

times said that one should be very cautious about criticizing governmental decisions in foreign affairs, since those who make decisions
have information many people do not have. Possession of such information may make them authorities on the topic. However, it need
not do so, because possession of relevant information does not
guarantee that their judgments are more likely to be correct than
those of others.

Political authority is a type of authority over conduct; it is primarily a species of being in authority. One might object that so
classifying political authority begs several questions. It apparently
rules out the possibility of political authority being exercised over
matters of belief. Yet throughout history political authority has
frequently been exercised in matters of religious belief. Indeed, the
kings and queens of England are still the heads of the Church of
England.

The answer to this objection is relatively simple. Usually, when
political authority is exercised over religious matters, the control is
over conduct, not belief. People may be forced to join certain religious sects and to engage in specified religious practices, but they
do not have to believe the doctrines of those sects. The most that
may be involved is swearing fidelity to, or belief in, certain doctrines. One may, as Galileo did, swear belief in a doctrine without
believing it. Moreover, one can clearly distinguish the political from
the religious positions of the English monarchs. The full title of the
monarch states these positions separately. And, of course, at one
time they held only positions of political authority. The fact that
one person simultaneously holds two different positions of authority does not mean that the two positions are identical.

Another objection may be made to the claim that political authority involves being in a position of authority over conduct. People
frequently control political affairs even though they are not in positions of authority. Both Rasputin and Henry Kissinger (in his days
as a presidential adviser) had great political authority without holding significant positions in government. To answer this objection
one must distinguish authority and influence. 'Influence' may refer
to all the forms of the second type of control over others except
authority. Thus, influence is control over another which does not
depend on benefits or harms, doing something to or for the person
controlled, and is not the use of authority. The difference between
influence and authority is that the exercise of authority need only
involve the issuance of directives or norms in order to get people to

act in specified ways. When a person exercises influence, he must typically do more than merely tell people how to act. For example, in rational persuasion various reasons are offered for acting in some way.

For the most part, people such as Rasputin and Henry Kissinger do not exercise political authority directly but exert influence over those in authority. As a presidential adviser, Kissinger's principal function was to recommend policies to President Nixon, who had the authority to adopt them. However, Kissinger's position as a presidential adviser did entail some authority, and the president delegated to him other authority to carry on negotiations, etc. As secretary of state, Kissinger was perhaps better able to negotiate because he occupied a significant position of authority and could implement more decisions on his own than he could as a presidential adviser.

Since the exercise of authority does not rest upon threats, promises, or reasons, those subject to it must in some sense accept it. A person is an authority because he has a personal characteristic —knowledge about a topic. Similarly, a person is a charismatic authority because he has or is thought to have personal qualities. That is, he is accorded authority because he exemplifies characteristics deemed valuable. Being *in* authority does not depend upon personal characteristics in this way: rather unexemplary people may be in authority. To be in authority is to occupy a position or role of authority which entitles one to issue norms, so this type of authority rests upon acceptance of positions of authority.

Positions of authority are determined by rules specifying various conditions. First, there are usually conditions which a person must meet to hold the position, e.g., be elected or appointed. Second, there may be conditions as to the manner in which authoritative norms are to be issued, e.g., in writing or from the throne. The expression 'authoritative norms' is used here to cover any sort of prescriptive statement, whether general or singular. The chief requirement is that there be some associated concept of persons complying or not complying with the norms. Third, positions of authority usually (maybe always) extend only to certain areas. For example, a union leader has authority over union members' dues and strike conditions, not brands of television sets purchased by those members. Similar conditions apply to the concept of an authority.[7] However, one further condition is involved in the concept of a *position* of authority which need not be involved in that of an authority. This is the purpose(s) for which the position exists. For example, the position of an auditor is created to ensure that the financial records are accurate.

In almost every formal organization, the various conditions for a position of authority are specified by several rules. The constitution or by-laws of a club usually have various rules specifying the functions (purposes) of a secretary and other rules specifying the qualifications for the office and the method of filling it. All these rules can be conceived as parts of one larger rule. Such a device makes it easier to form a clear concept of a position of authority. The general form of such a rule constituting a position of authority is as follows: person X, with qualifications Q, may issue norms N, in a manner M, to persons Y, concerning topic T, for purposes P.

A rule constituting a position of authority is what legal scholars call a power-conferring rule.[8] The concept of power involved here is not the one analyzed above. This sort of power is deontic power and is really identical with authority with respect to a certain kind of topic. 'Deontic' here refers to normative relations dependent on rules rather than promotion of goals, ends, or purposes. There are at least eight basic power concepts: right, duty, privilege, no-right, power, liability, immunity, and disability.[9] These concepts derive from law but can be applied, with little alteration, to any normative system of rules. Deontic power indicates the ability specified by rules to make norms or determine their incidence, for example, to legislate or to perform marriages. To have deontic power is to have the ability to make changes in one or more of the deontic relations of the system. Liability is the correlative of deontic power; it is to be subject (liable) to having applicable norms changed by someone's exercise of deontic power. These conceptions of power and liability must be kept distinct from those of right and duty.

There has been much dispute by philosophers concerning the right of authorities to be obeyed and the duty of their subjects to obey them. This problem arises because some philosophers have treated rules constituting positions of authority as duty-imposing rules (with correlative rights) instead of power-conferring rules.[10] Since the rules constituting positions of authority are not duty-imposing ones with correlative rights, it follows that they do not confer either a right to issue norms or a duty to obey them. All the deontic conceptions and relations may apply to a person in a position of authority,[11] but they apply in different ways, which it is important to keep distinct.

One must distinguish between the deontic concepts and relations pertaining to a position and those pertaining to the person who occupies that position. If X has met the qualifications for occupying a position of authority, then he has a right to that position, and others have a duty to accord him that position. But the position itself does not consist of a right to issue norms with a correlative duty to obey them. Instead, it consists of the deontic power to issue norms and the correlative liability of others to those norms. Some people may have a duty to accord X a position of authority but not be liable (subject) to the norms he issues. For example, a mayor may have a duty to install a man as commissioner but no duty to obey the norms which that commissioner issues.

Positions of authority almost always empower persons to create duties and rights or to vary their incidence. A position of authority which did not empower persons to do these things would be very strange, for the person would only be empowered to empower others to do things, to confer deontic powers on others. This point indicates another way of understanding that positions of authority do not primarily consist of rights and correlative duties. Suppose King Uno of the kingdom of Unomia issues a norm stating that if one citizen destroys the property of another, then he has a duty to pay for its replacement. If Unomian X drives his car over Y's bicycle, then X has a duty to pay Y for it, and Y has a right to be paid. Note, however, that X's duty is to Y, not to King Uno. If, however, a position of authority involved the right to issue norms and a correlative duty to obey, then X would in fact have two duties. Besides his duty to Y, he would also have a duty to King Uno to pay for the replacement of Y's bicycle. Further, King Uno would have a right to X's paying Y. It seems clear, however, that X has only one duty to pay for replacing the bicycle, and that is a duty to Y.

Not all positions are positions of authority. Any position, including one of authority, may involve rights and duties. Such rights are referred to in expressions such as "have the authority to enter a restricted area." One may have the authority, or may be authorized, to do something (other than issue norms) without being in a position of authority. Such authority or authorization must be given by someone in authority, i.e., someone who can issue norms or vary their incidence. Usually a position involves rights to the tools or information without which a person cannot do his job. For example, an auditor may have the right or authority to inspect the account books of all departments of a company, and whoever has charge of the books has a duty to let him do so. An auditor may also have the duty to inform the company president of the yearly balances and net profits and losses. But none of these rights and duties involves an auditor's having authority over others. Auditors, in fact, usually have little authority over others. They have authority over their secretaries, of course, but that is hardly unique to being an auditor.

Even if positions of authority do not carry with them the right to issue norms or the right to be obeyed, it does not follow that one cannot have an obligation to comply with the norms issued by persons in authority. The preceding arguments only show that those in authority do not have a right to be obeyed, and that those subject to persons in positions of authority do not have a duty to obey, which is a duty to the authorities. However, one may have obligations which are not to anyone.[12] The obligation, if any, to comply with the norms issued by authorities must be of this sort. The concept of obligations which are not to anyone is not easy to explain. Before considering it directly, it may help to make a couple of other distinctions about authority.

Authority may be effective or ineffective. Authority is effective if there is in fact general compliance with the norms issued. Consider the hypothetical example of an unruly high school class. The teacher is in a position of authority according to the formal rules of the high school. He may tell the class to be quiet and perform certain tasks, but his directions may be ignored. He does not have effective authority. On the other hand, a student leader may have effective authority over the class. After the class has "acted up" for a while, he may say, "O.K. That's enough. Let's settle down now," and the class may do so.

One may think that this example shows that authority does not depend upon rules; however, that would be a mistake. One must distinguish between the formal or paper rules and the actual or operative rules.[13] According to the formal or paper rule, the teacher has authority over the class. In practice, the class follows another rule which gives the student leader authority over the class. To understand how a system actually operates, one needs to examine the working or operative rules, not the formal ones on an organization chart. This point is a basic insight of realistic jurisprudence and represents the behavioral approach to political science.

One may also distinguish between legitimate and illegitimate authority. Legitimate authority is that granted by the formal or official power-conferring rules. The distinction between legitimate and illegitimate authority must always be made with reference to a set of rules. This set is usually, but not necessarily, the official or formal rules. Thus a judge who renders a decision *ultra vires* exercises illegitimate authority. A person's authority is illegitimate if he has not in fact achieved his position in accordance with the formal or official power-conferring rules, or if he issues norms for persons or on topics beyond the scope encompassed in a power-conferring rule.

It is now possible to show why an obligation to comply with norms issued by an authority, if there is any, must be an obligation which is not to anyone. Suppose the city council passes an ordinance forbidding parking on one side of a street. One may ask where the city council gets the authority to issue such an ordinance. It may be empowered to do so by an act of the state legislature, but where does the legislature get its authority? It may be empowered by the state constitution. The state constitution, however, is a set of power-conferring rules. One may simply stop here and claim that all authority must ultimately come from power-conferring rules. However, some philosophers, like Thomas Hobbes, have been reluctant to say that ultimate authority derives from rules. Authority, they believe, must derive from persons. Thus, they will take the issue one step further and hold that the state constitution is authoritative only because it was adopted by the citizens. However, it is futile to continue this attempt to locate authority in persons, for one may always ask where any person who is asserted to have authority gets such authority. Ultimately, the question as to whether authority stems from persons or rules is a pseudo-problem, because for any person with authority one may specify a rule (formal or operative) which grants it.

The fundamental question about the source of obligation thus concerns the basis of an ultimate power-conferring rule. One must distinguish two different questions about such a rule. One question is whether there is an operative rule which grants authority. This question is essentially one of fact and may be answered on the basis of empirical investigation. Do people in fact act in conformity with such a rule and evaluate one another's behavior in terms of it? If so, then people who occupy positions of authority in conformity with that rule have legitimate authority.

However, the fact that authority is legitimate according to some ultimate power-conferring rule does not imply that one has an obligation to comply with the norms issued by persons in legitimate positions of authority. The basic question is whether or not one ought to comply with or follow the ultimate power-conferring rule. If one ought to do so, then the authority may be called justifiable, and one may claim that one has an obligation to comply with norms issued by justifiable authorities. Sometimes 'legitimate authority' is used to mean that the authority is legitimate (as here defined) and that it is justifiable. However, some term is needed to distinguish between the propriety of exercising authority according to a rule (whether a person acted in conformity to a rule) and the propriety of the rule itself (whether the rule itself is justifiable).

THE STATE

The preceding section analyzed the general concept of authority over conduct, in particular, the concept of being in a position of authority. However, not all authority is political authority, nor does this book focus on all political authority; for instance, the authority of leaders of political parties is not considered. Instead, the crucial questions facing people concern the justifiability of that political authority which pertains to official positions in the state or government. The concept of political authority to be analyzed in this section pertains to this latter, more narrow, concept of political authority.

Political authority is that which is exercised over, or directs the use of, the supreme coercive power in a territory (or population). This definition distinguishes political authority from other kinds, such as economic and religious authority, by the topic concerning which norms may be issued. To understand that supreme coercive power is necessary for political authority, one need only consider the conditions under which a revolution is successful or under which there is a state of civil war. The Chinese political revolution was over when the Communist Party under Mao Tse-tung gained military control over the mainland. It is sometimes said that while Mao had de facto authority in China, he did not have de jure authority. For years Chiang Kai-shek claimed that he was the de jure political authority over Mainland China. There are three points to be considered in understanding this claim. (1) Mao had effective political authority over Mainland China. (2) Mao's political authority was legitimate. For political authority to be legitimate, it must conform to a power-conferring rule. When one considers the *existence* of political authority, one must refer to an ultimate power-conferring rule which is operative. The power-conferring rule in virtue of which Mao had legitimate authority is, in fact, operative. (3) When Chiang and his supporters asserted that Mao did not have de jure political authority, they were not denying that there was an operative power-conferring rule which legitimated his authority; what they were saying was that such a rule must be justifiable. They held that another power-conferring rule which legitimated Chiang's authority was the only justifiable one. Because they defined legitimacy in terms of this inoperative paper rule, they claimed Mao's authority was not legitimate. The term de jure may be used to mean either legitimate or justifiable.

By 'supreme coercive power' is meant the ability to attempt to coerce any person in the territory or to harm any person if the attempt at coercion is not successful. The supreme coercive power is thus usually the property of the military and police of a country. Even if a person is able to evade any attempt at harming him, e.g., by hiding, he is still subject to that political authority. The fact that political authority is exercised over the supreme coercive power does not imply that political authority cannot be exercised concerning other topics, but if persons subject to the norms do not comply, coercion may be used to obtain the desired conduct.

Finally, the fact that political authority is exercised over the supreme coercive power does not imply that there are not other centers of coercive power in the territory. The term 'supreme' would not be needed were there no other persons with coercive power. For example, parents have coercive power over children. The existence of political authority does not exclude such power. But when push comes to shove, the parent's power is less than that of the political authorities; the political authorities can coerce a child into disobeying its parents despite the parents' attempts at counter-coercion, and they can coerce the parents themselves. However, if there is a person who can stand up to such power and win, then the coercive power is not supreme. One must distinguish this case, which shows that the coercive power is not supreme, from cases of escape or hiding, in which it is not possible to bring the coercive power to bear. A person who escapes or hides recognizes that he is confronting a stronger power. One who has fought and won, for example, a guerrilla leader controlling a mountainous region, is simply not under the same system of political authority.

The definition of political authority as being exercised over the supreme coercive power in a territory may appear paradoxical, for power and authority as here defined cannot be simultaneously exercised. The crucial point to note is that the authority and the coercive power are not exercised over the same people upon the same occasion. This point is illustrated by the fact that while armies exercise coercive power, their structure rests upon authority. An officer does not use power to get his subordinates to carry out a task: he merely gives a command. Yet the result may be the exercise of power over other persons. On occasion persons in the army refuse to obey orders. In that case, they too may be coerced into doing something.

A similar point was noted by David Hume. He thought that philosophers should reflect upon the ease with which men obey political authority, and then remarked:

When we inquire by what means this wonder is effected, we shall find that, as force is always on the side of the governed, the governors have nothing to support them but opinion. It is, therefore, on opinion only that government is founded, and this maxim extends to the most despotic and most military governments as well as to the most free and most popular. The sultan of Egypt or the emperor of Rome might drive his harmless subjects like brute beasts against their sentiments and inclination. But he must, at least, have led his *mamelukes* or *praetorian bands*, like men, by their opinion.[14]

For Hume's 'opinion' one should substitute the word 'authority'.

Two points are involved here. First, if anyone is to have considerable coercive power, then he must have authority. Otherwise, his power will be limited to that which he is physically capable of exerting. Of course, with modern weapons it is possible for one person to have considerable coercive power, for example, someone who controls a long-range, nuclear-armed missile. But by and large, it is still true that a person must have authority over others if he is to have much coercive power. Even the person with the missile needs others to service it. Modern weapons have simply made it easier than before for a small number of people to have coercive power temporarily over many others.

Hume's second point is that the governed have more power than the governors, yet in most situations they cannot mobilize that power. For example, one may contest the claim that members of the

army obey authority rather than coercive power. A soldier obeys
his superior because he knows he will be shot or imprisoned if he
does not do so. But he can only be imprisoned or shot if his fellow-
soldiers obey orders. If everyone refused to obey, then there could
be no coercion. This is the underlying idea in the pacifist slogan:
what if they gave a war and nobody came? But someone always
comes because no one can be sure that the others will also refuse.
Each person is afraid that he will be the only one to refuse and then
suffer the consequences. History shows that this fear is justified.
The only real exceptions are the few mutinies scattered throughout
history, greatly feared by the authorities. However, almost always,
mutineers immediately proceed to set up an authority system of
their own.

While political authorities can use the supreme coercive power,
it does not follow that they need do so. Indeed, they prefer not to
use it, since authority is much more efficient. As the exercise of
power and authority are mutually exclusive, authority cannot be
used when coercive power is. Thus, authority may be exercised to
see that the supreme coercive power is not used.

The discussion so far has not distinguished between one rule
establishing a single political authority and a complex set of rules
establishing various positions of political authority. The doctrine
of absolute sovereignty maintains that there is only one rule determining political authority in a society. Thomas Hobbes defines
sovereignty or political authority in terms of various rights (deontic
powers), including those of making war and peace, rewarding and
punishing, deciding controversies, and prescribing the rules of
property. He then concludes that "these are the rights, which make
the essence of sovereignty; and which are the marks, whereby a
man may discern in what man, or assembly of men, the sovereign
power is placed, and resideth. *For these are incommunicable, and
inseparable.*"[15]

This doctrine of absolute sovereignty can be taken as descriptive,
analytic, or prescriptive. In the above quotation, Hobbes seems to
suggest that the doctrine represents a matter of fact. He asserts that
the concurrence of these rights or powers in one person or assembly
is a mark by which one can determine who is sovereign. Yet some
of his other remarks suggest that the claim is an analytic one—that
by definition there is no political authority unless these powers
are united. He may also mean that unless these rights are united
there will be chaos or civil war, which, he thought, should be
avoided at all costs.

Since the purpose of this discussion is to define political authority and the state, the prescriptive interpretation of Hobbes' doctrine will be ignored. There is, in fact, usually no person or assembly of persons who have all the powers or rights which Hobbes says are necessary to sovereignty. For example, in the United States there is no one person or group which has both supreme judicial authority and the right to make war. Only Congress has the power to declare war, yet Congress does not have power over the Supreme Court except indirectly, through the confirmation of appointees and through certain areas of control over the jurisdiction of federal courts. Thus, a system of political authority need not assign any one position complete authority.

While the doctrine of absolute sovereignty is false, a system of political authority must have some unity. This unity is achieved by a hierarchy of political authority. The question of the source of the city council's authority to make traffic ordinances is an example. Authority may be basic or delegated. The state legislature delegated authority to the city council to make traffic ordinances. If one assumes that the state legislature gets its authority directly from the constitution as the ultimate power-conferring rule, then its authority is basic. There may be several basic authorities within a system so long as the topics of their authority differ. These authorities are all part of the same system because their authority derives from the same set of power-conferring rules.

'The state' and 'government' may now be defined. The state is a rather amorphous entity. Historically, it has been defined as everything from a committee for managing the common affairs of the capitalist class to the march of God through the world.[16] However, it is simply a system of political authority. It is not a material thing to which one can point and say, "There it is," or, "There is a corner of it." The land occupied by a state may vary as boundaries are changed; there may be states composed of nomadic groups. To determine whether a territory is part of one state or another, one must know which system of political authority is operative in it. The state cannot be identified with any set of persons because its citizens change. A concept of the state must allow for continuity through time despite changes in membership and territory. Moreover, a state must be distinguished from a nation: a nation may be a group of people with a common culture and economic system, but, as the principle of self-determination of nations presupposes, a nation need not constitute a state.

The state consists of the system of authority positions and relations specified by the set of operative rules determining positions
of basic political authority. If one wishes to include positions and
relations of delegated authority in the state, then not all the rules
specifying the system need be operative; some may only be legitimated by the operative rules defining the basic positions. The unity
of the set of rules stems from the relations among them. Thus, for
example, members of the United States Supreme Court are appointed by the president, subject to confirmation by the Senate. The
rules defining the position of justice of the Supreme Court refer to
rules defining other positions within the system. The question is
how many such rules may be changed while the same state remains.
Amendments to the United States constitution do not affect the
identity of the state because they occur in accordance with another
rule of the system, yet a revolution and a new constitution establish
a new state.

Two other features of this definition should be noted. First, it is
confined to relations specified by operative rules of the basic
political authority. Such a definition keeps clear the distinction between the existence of a state and its justifiability. A state is a
system of authority determined by rules which either are operative
or, in the case of past states, were operative, whether or not such a
system is or was justifiable. Hence, after the Communist revolution
Chiang Kai-shek did not occupy a position of authority in Mainland
China. Second, the state is ideal in one sense, for only the rules for
positions of basic authority need be operative. Frequently, the rules
determining positions of delegated authority are not operative, although the formal or official rules constituting those positions of
authority are in conformity with the operative, ultimate, power-
conferring rules. Consequently, persons who do not occupy positions of authority according to the formal rules may still have effective authority.

There are two definitions of 'government', a broad and a narrow
one. In the broad sense, the 'government' consists of the people
occupying both positions of basic and of delegated political authority. In the narrow sense, the 'government' consists only of those
persons in the positions of basic political authority. For example, in
the broad sense, the government of Great Britain consists of all
members of Parliament and almost all other governmental employees. In the narrow sense, the government primarily consists of
the members of the cabinet. Likewise, in the United States, the

government in the narrow sense consists of the president, the members of Congress, and the justices of the Supreme Court.

The fundamental activities of a system of political authority are determined by the norms established by persons in positions of basic authority. One must distinguish between establishing norms and applying them. The executive and judicial branches of governments are primarily involved in applying (and interpreting) the norms issued by the legislative branch, although both do make new rules. Of course, this distinction between branches of government is a very rough one. In the United States, the president is involved in legislation, and in Great Britain members of the cabinet are also members of Parliament. However, the focus of policy decisions usually lies with the legislature. Hence, the legislature is taken in this account as the focus of attention for determining the uses of political authority. But the considerations to be developed for legislative decisions apply to all policymaking concerned with national affairs. Functionally, to legislate is to issue norms, and the fundamental legislative activity is performed by those occupying the positions of basic authority.

II
JUSTIFICATION

Positions of authority are constituted by rules granting deontic power to persons to issue norms for certain purposes. Political authority is distinguished from other types of authority by the fact that one of its topics is the exercise of the supreme coercive power in society. Thus, if political authority concerning some topic (other than the use of coercive power) is ineffective, coercion can be used.

The state is the system of positions and relations of basic political authority determined by power-conferring rules. Differences among states depend upon the specific conditions of the rules constituting these positions. Rules constituting positions of authority have the following general form: person X, with qualifications Q, may issue norms N, in manner M, to persons Y, concerning topics T, for purposes P. A person who occupies a position of authority has a duty to promote the purposes for which it exists and is held responsible for so doing. While he has some discretion as to what to do in promoting these purposes, the sphere of his discretion and authority is defined by the topics concerning which he may issue norms. The logical scope of topics for norms is all those concerning which specific conduct may further the given purposes, but some topics may be beyond the power of a position to regulate even though norms concerning them might further its purposes: for example, the United States Congress may not make laws (issue norms) abridging freedom of speech. Restrictions on the topics of norms are substantive limits to authority which may protect purposes and values other than those which the authority is to promote. There may also be procedural limits to authority. These limits specify methods for exercising powers; for example, advance warning of changes in norms may have to be given. Moreover, different

37

sorts of qualifications may exist for persons occupying positions of authority. The differences between states depend upon differences in the rules which constitute positions of basic authority. While each system of political authority has several such rules, for simplicity the discussion below is frequently phrased as though there were only one.

AUTONOMY OF POLITICAL ALLEGIANCE

Whether one ought to comply with the norms issued by political authorities depends upon the justifiability of the rules constituting the positions of political authority. The basic question is whether one owes allegiance to, or ought to comply with, the ultimate power-conferring rules. This issue is generally discussed in terms of 'political obligation'. Because there are disputes as to whether 'obligation' is the appropriate term to use in this context, the term 'allegiance' will often be used instead.[1] Further reasons for preferring 'allegiance' to 'obligation' are presented somewhat later.

Obligation or allegiance may be characterized as political for two distinct reasons.[2] First, one may characterize obligations by their subject matter: one may speak of financial, family, or political obligations. Second, one may classify obligations by their grounds or sources as contractual, legal, or moral.

Most philosophical discussions of political obligation concern an obligation to the state. The grounds given for this obligation are usually moral. For example, after distinguishing the two ways of classifying an obligation as political, John Ladd writes, "Since our question is one of ethics, the form [ground] of obligation with which we shall be concerned is moral obligation."[3] Consequently, political philosophy is not treated as an independent branch of thought but a mere subdivision of ethics—like medical ethics.

There are serious practical and philosophical difficulties in treating the question of political obligation or allegiance as an ethical issue. First, if political allegiance rests upon moral obligation, no adequate account of political allegiance can be given until one has developed an adequate ethical theory. This problem is graphically illustrated by the theory of Robert Nozick. He contends that "the moral prohibitions it is permissible to enforce are the source of whatever legitimacy the state's fundamental coercive power has." His general argument for a minimal state rests upon a theory of natural rights, yet, as he admits, his book does not present "a precise theory of the moral basis of individual rights."[4] Since most philosophers reject natural rights theory, Nozick's general argument is undermined in many eyes. One may contend, as Nozick does, that the assumptions of ethical theory concern only basic features which any acceptable ethical theory must contain; however, this defense is very shaky. There is little agreement as to what an acceptable ethical theory must provide. Many people would contend that an ethical theory which cannot justify more than a minimal state is, for that very reason, unacceptable. In particular, Nozick's account of private property includes incidents of ownership which many people would reject, and yet without them much of his argument for a minimal government collapses.

Second, grounding political allegiance on ethical theory seems to imply that there can be no generally accepted basis of political authority in a pluralistic society. Most modern, industrialized societies are pluralistic, that is, their members share very few moral principles. There is, of course, a general agreement about some basic moral principles, for example, that one ought not to commit murder. However, there is little agreement about less basic principles such as whether one should provide food stamps to strikers and students. Moreover, there are strong differences in border areas—for example, the issues of abortion and euthanasia. One standard view has been that although in such societies there are many differences with respect to substantive principles, there may be agreement as to procedures to be followed in making collective decisions. Of course, it could be that different substantive ethical principles would all support allegiance to the same general procedural form of political authority. However, this appears to be very unlikely because a part of the constitutive rules of political authority is concerned with the purposes for which it is to be exercised. If different ethical principles implied the same general purposes, they would be equivalent in practice, but if they are, then there really is no moral pluralism.

Rex Martin has argued that trying to justify political authority on the basis of moral or ethical obligations is merely an instance of a more general mistake, namely, trying to provide an external justification of political allegiance.[5] Since the ground must always be something outside the political system, it can never establish a special obligation to laws as such or to political authority as such. The obligation or allegiance will be to laws or political authority because they are moral, commanded by God, etc. Hence Martin claims that allegiance to political authority must be based within the system. If he means that the system of political authority must contain within itself the obligation to it, then there cannot be any internal justification. The justification of an obligation must always be outside itself. If, however, he means that the justification must refer to the internal structure of the system of political authority, then many moral justifications do that. For example, it is frequently claimed that one has an obligation to a political system only if that system is a democratic one.

Martin's argument does contain a kernel of truth, however. One must distinguish between justifications which appeal to another assumed obligation and those which do not. Any attempted justification of political allegiance which uses as its ground another obligation—to promote the greatest good, to adhere to contracts—does not provide an independent basis of political allegiance. Political allegiance or obligation will always be a species of some other general type of obligation and will be open to all the possible criticisms of that obligation. In short, what one needs is a direct argument for political allegiance which is not based on some other obligation.

One can view justifications of political allegiance as being of three basic types.[6] The first type rests upon special prior assumptions about the world or society, for example, divine commands, the significance of tradition, etc. Most theories of this sort base political allegiance upon another obligation such as obedience to God, or at least upon very questionable assumptions such as the correctness of Hegel's metaphysics. The second type bases allegiance upon some act of the person, a contract or consent. According to social contract theorists, one has an obligation to political authority only if one contracted or consented to comply with the ultimate power-conferring rule. This approach is open to a devastating criticism, first formulated by David Hume.[7] To claim that one is obligated because one has consented to such a rule presupposes that one ought to comply with that to which one has consented. But one has this obligation whether or not one consents to it. If one's obligation to comply rested on a prior consent, there would be either an infinite regress of consents to comply with consents or no ultimate basis for the obligation. Thus, the obligation to comply with a power-conferring rule constituting a position of authority may itself be one which does not depend on consent.

Hence, contemporary writers in the social contract or consent tradition have substituted hypothetical consent for actual consent. One's actual consent to a rule is irrelevant. What matters is whether a rational and informed person would consent to the rule.[8] The answer depends upon what the rule is. All of the features indicated by the general form of such a rule—qualifications for holding the position, substantive and procedural limits, purposes, etc.—are relevant. However, the purposes for which norms are to be made are most important. Positions of authority exist because of the interest of those establishing them in achieving some purposes but not at the expense of other purposes and values. The most reasonable way of evaluating different qualifications for occupying positions of authority, the topics of norms, etc., is on the basis of their effectiveness in assuring that the purposes of the position are pursued without detriment to other purposes and values. Thus, before one determines what political system (democratic, authoritarian, etc.) is best, one needs to determine the basic purposes which political authority is to pursue. The more precisely one wants to determine the best system of political authority, the more precisely one needs to determine its purposes.

(Since the best systems of political authority depend upon purposes and values to be promoted and respected, a general argument for political allegiance is for having some system of political authority. Such allegiance will not by itself entail commitment to any given form or system. Consequently, it will not suffice to answer questions about when revolutions or coups d'état may be justifiable. These issues are not addressed in this book, although a few guiding remarks about the structure of allegiance are made at the beginning of Chapter IX.)

One is thus led to the third type of theory, which justifies political authority by its uses or functions. The most prevalent version of this type of theory is utilitarianism. However, utilitarianism also grounds political allegiance upon moral obligation, the moral principle of utility. However, it may be possible to develop a theory of this sort which does not base political allegiance on another obligation.

First, one must see that posing the issue as one of political obligation presents an insoluble problem. One can derive obligations only from other obligations or from principles which specify one's obligations. Hence, if one attempts to establish a political obligation, one must assume some pre-existing obligation or principle. But the issue concerns one's allegiance to, or commitment to, a power-conferring rule constituting positions of basic political authority. One need not have an obligation to commit oneself to such a rule.

Second, the reasons for commiting oneself to a rule constituting a position of authority need not be moral ones. Why should one commit oneself to abide by or follow the constitution of a scholarly society such as a philosophical association? Presumably, the answer is that it enables the group to arrange efficiently activities in which individual scholars may want to participate. In short, it is a good rule to follow in performing the functions of the society. The power-conferring rules constituting positions of basic political authority may be justified in just such a way. The crucial issue concerns the functions or purposes of political authority.

The most important norms issued by political authority are those adopted by legislatures. If political authority is to do the job for which it is constituted, these norms must be designed to pursue the appropriate purposes. The goodness or badness of the legislation passed is to be evaluated in terms of the purposes of political authority, which may be formulated as principles of legislation or legislative principles. The fundamental question about the use of political authority may be formulated thus: "What are the acceptable principles of legislation?"

LEGISLATIVE PRINCIPLES

Philosophers have distinguished between two different types of evaluation.[9] Some evaluations can be used to establish rankings. These evaluations are typically expressed by the terms good or bad. Objects can fulfill these norms in different degrees. Other evaluations are typically expressed by the terms right or wrong, correct or incorrect. An object meets the criteria of evaluation or it does not; it is not a matter of degree. Norms of evaluation of the "good-or-bad" kind may be called standards, and those for the "right-or-wrong" or "correct-or-incorrect" kind may be called rules.

Principles state the good- and bad-making characteristics or criteria used to evaluate objects by standards. Principles may be contrasted with rules in two interconnected ways.[10] (1) Rules apply in an all-or-none fashion; that is, if they apply to a case, they determine the evaluation without any room for a contrary one. There may, of course, be exceptions to rules, but they can in principle be stated as part of the rules. Principles, however, do not necessarily determine evaluations even in cases to which they apply. For example, the fact that a tomato has a worm in it does not determine the evaluation. A tomato with a worm may still be a pretty good one provided it is big, ripe, flavorful, and juicy. This point may be put another way: a principle provides only part of the basis for an evaluation, whereas an applicable rule provides the complete basis.

(2) Principles may be more or less important; they have "weight." Since each principle presents only one of several good- or bad-making characteristics, principles can be "added" together to give an overall evaluation by the standard. If several principles lead to one evaluation and one or two suggest the opposite, one may "add up" the force or weight of the principles on each side to reach an evaluation. But if a particular rule applies, it determines the evaluation. Other rules must be judged to be inapplicable to the case.

That some rules contain standards should not lead one to deny the distinction between rules and principles. For example, rules may require that a person exercise due care, bargain in good faith, or charge a fair rate. Due care, good faith, and a fair rate are standards and admit of degrees of fulfillment; i.e., there may be more or less care, etc. Thus, one might think that rules containing these standards permit the evaluation of conduct as better or worse. But when applied in a particular case, a rule requiring that one exercise due care will result in a judgment that the person did or did not do so. While there are degrees of care there is a point above which a person has met the requirement of due care and below which he has failed to do so. In a court case, whether or not a person has exercised proper care will be decisive. In short, rules containing standards require a certain degree of fulfillment of that standard, and the only significant issue is whether it is met. How little one missed doing so or exceeded it is irrelevant. These rules apply in an all-or-none way, since they merely divide the degrees of fulfillment into two classes— those which are and those which are not sufficient for compliance with the rule.

That rules incorporating standards do not become principles is related to a fundamental difference between standards (including principles) and rules. Standards and principles do not themselves create obligations.[11] Obligations are either fulfilled or not; hence, they must be based on rules. Standards, and the principles stating their criteria, may be more or less fulfilled. Moral virtues such as courage, honesty, and loyalty are standards. They guide human conduct by presenting character traits to be strived for. One ought to be honest, but one does not have an obligation to be so. Yet one does have an obligation to tell the truth because of a rule specifying the occasions on which truth-telling is obligatory. Compliance with that rule is one of the criteria of honesty. This last fact has led some philosophers to claim that the difference between rules and principles is simply the specificity of the conduct required.[12] However, while there usually is a difference in the specificity of the conduct involved, this difference is primarily due to the logical difference in the type of evaluation involved.

Three questions about the use of rules may be logically distinguished, although their separation in practice is not so clear. First, one may ask whether or not a rule pertains to a case. This question may be broken into two: is this rule relevant? Is this the rule which applies to or governs the case? In conflicts of rules, two rules may be relevant, but only one applies.[13] Second, one may ask for the meaning or interpretation of a rule. Third, one may ask what a rule requires in the light of the facts of a case. Questions two and three become quite mixed in making evaluations by rules, but this mixture is not a defect of reasoning. Also, the interpretation of a rule has an obvious bearing on whether or not it applies. But if a rule does apply, is properly interpreted, and the facts for its use are clearly presented, then no other evaluation can be correct.

Besides these questions about the use of rules, there is another distinct question, namely, is a rule a good one? Whether or not a rule is a good one depends in part upon how it is interpreted and applied. But there are many other features which are equally important in deciding whether it is a good one. For example, does it require conduct which is possible? If people conform to it, will the consequences be beneficial or harmful? If the rule is to be enforced by punishment, is the evil of the punishment likely to be greater than the value gained?

Legislative principles present the good- and bad-making characteristics of legislation. Since the goodness or badness of legislation depends upon its effectiveness in pursuing purposes of political authority without undermining the realization of other purposes and values, legislative principles formulate the purposes of political authority. Principles indicating purposes which political authority should pursue may be called positive principles of legislation. Principles indicating that legislation will have adverse effects may be called negative principles of legislation. For example, it may be thought that political authority should pursue the education of citizens and that it should not interfere with religious liberty. Thus, providing opportunities for education would be a good-making characteristic, while infringing upon religious liberty would be a bad-making characteristic.

Another point must be noted about a good- or bad-making characteristic of legislation. Such characteristics may not pertain to a particular piece of legislation. If an increase in welfare payments is proposed, it may not affect religious liberty. Thus, the negative principle of religious liberty would be irrelevant to the goodness or badness of the legislation. But if one were to hold that not increasing welfare is a bad-making characteristic of legislation, then any legislation which did not increase welfare, even if it were addressed to some other topic, e.g., protecting privacy, would have a bad-making characteristic. A characteristic may not be present in legislation at all, but if it is, then it must be taken into account. Of course, the fact that legislation has a bad-making characteristic does not imply that it is bad, for it may have enough good-making characteristics to outweigh the bad ones.

Since good legislation ought to be adopted and bad legislation ought to be defeated, principles of legislation state reasons for and against legislation. Characteristics may be more or less general. Providing free lunches, giving clothing allowances, and subsidizing low-income housing are all instances of providing welfare. If one established separate principles for each of these methods for providing welfare, one would have to establish a very large set of principles of legislation. Instead, principles of legislation present only very general characteristics which indicate the *kinds* of reasons for and against legislation.

To sum up, an acceptable principle of legislation states that a characteristic constitutes a good reason, but not a necessary or sufficient one, for or against legislation. The characteristic that a piece of legislation promotes welfare is not necessary because the characteristic in another principle, harm to others, may by itself justify legislation. It is not sufficient because it might not, in a particular instance, outweigh the reasons against such legislation. The same argument applies, *mutatis mutandis*, to principles against legislation. When principles for and against legislation are applied to a proposed law, they must be weighed against one another.

Collectively, all the acceptable principles for and against legislation present the standard of good legislation. Disputes as to which principles are acceptable are disputes as to good reasons for or against legislation. They are disputes as to what purposes and values political authority ought tó pursue and respect.

Principles of legislation should meet certain formal conditions. First, they must be general. There are difficult logical issues in determining whether or not an utterance has any particular referent. These issues do not make any practical difference in considering questions about principles of legislation. Essentially, the requirement that principles be general is met if they do not contain proper names or definite descriptions. This requirement excludes as a principle of legislation increasing the wealth of the king. It does not exclude any of the principles most frequently mentioned.

Second, legislative principles must be public. They must be known to all citizens or must be such that they may be proclaimed to all citizens. This requirement essentially prohibits secret principles of legislation. Legislation is in fact sometimes passed because legislators were paid to vote for it. But legislators cannot proclaim to their constituents that being paid for voting aye or nay is a good reason for doing so. In short, esoteric principles of legislation are no better than esoteric principles of morality.[14]

Third, principles are final. There is no higher appeal for evaluating legislation. Once the various acceptable principles of legislation have been determined, they provide the only good reasons for supporting or opposing it. Of course, there are arguments for and against the acceptability of a given principle, but these considerations are irrelevant to the direct evaluation of proposed legislation.[15]

At this point it may be objected that while the previous section argued that justifications of political allegiance should be independent of morality and based upon the functions or purposes of political authority, in considering legislative principles one has sneaked morality in the back door. However, legislative principles are not moral ones. They do not have the same role as moral principles. They do not specify good or bad features of persons or their conduct, but rules—legislation. Hence, they are not like moral rules or principles specifying good-making characteristics of persons, for example, that one ought to be honest. Nor do they have the same role as the positive principles on which moral rules are based, such as a principle of rule utilitarianism. Nonetheless, principles of legislation guide human conduct indirectly, by presenting criteria which political authorities ought to use. They state the purposes which political authority should pursue and respect. They are thus of great importance and affect the well-being of most people, but that is not sufficient to make them moral principles. They are like the criteria for determining whether a college course is a good or bad one; they serve to guide the activities of political authorities, just as the criteria for a good course guide the activities of teachers. Politicians may have a moral duty to pursue and respect the purposes relevant to the exercise of political authority, but persons in other positions of authority, such as teachers, may have a similar duty with respect to the purposes relevant to their positions. Since such a duty does not make the criteria of a good college course moral criteria, the criteria of good legislation are not moral ones. Thus, basing legislation upon such principles does not involve the enforcement of morals.[16]

Second, morality could be brought in the back door if the reasons for accepting legislative principles were based upon morality. Utilitarian arguments for legislative principles would do so. And, of course, such principles must be supported by values. But not all references to values involve morality: prudential arguments are based upon values, but not moral ones. Hence, while one must be careful not to assume moral values as the basis for accepting legislative principles, it is possible to present arguments for them which do not presuppose a specific morality or moral values.

OBJECTIVITY

Political allegiance must rest upon the justifiability of the ultimate power-conferring rule constituting positions of basic political authority. It needs to be shown that one ought to comply with it, that one "owes allegiance" to it. Moreover, the argument for the justifiability of this rule must be independent of moral assumptions. Such an argument, it has been claimed, can be made on the grounds of the functions of political authority, which primarily rest upon the purposes for which norms are established. Such purposes may be formulated as legislative principles. Hence, the crucial question is what are the acceptable legislative principles?

Many philosophers use the method of establishing what Rawls terms a "reflective equilibrium" between principles and considered judgments about particular situations.[17] Essentially, this method consists of applying a proposed principle to a set of real or assumed facts about particular cases to determine whether the results accord with one's judgment about such cases. If they do accord, everything is fine. If they do not, then the principle may be rejected. Usually, the results accord with one's judgments in some cases and not in others. If one is very confident of one's judgments, then the principle is rejected. If the principle gives results in accord with one's judgments in most cases, then in the few cases in which it does not, one may change one's judgments. If the results of the principle accord with one's judgments in most cases but not in a few cases in which one is confident of the accuracy of the judgments, one may modify the principle to achieve accord. When one finds complete accord between judgments and the principle, this is the condition of "reflective equilibrium," and when it is reached, the principle is acceptable.

However, this method as the sole or main procedure for determining the acceptability of principles has serious defects.[18] First, as Kant noted, such a technique is circular.[19] One cannot make judgments about particular cases without calling upon principles (often subconsciously). This method essentially establishes that one's principles are consistent with one's judgments about particular cases. Second, establishing consistency is not enough to settle major political differences. A priori, there is no reason for believing that communists, socialists, liberals, and conservatives cannot all hold consistent views. Hence, when there are basic differences between people, this method cannot resolve them.

Consequently, another form of argument is needed which does not presuppose legislative or political principles. But at this point, the issue of the possibility of objective judgments about such matters arises. On what grounds can one objectively say that a person's ultimate political judgments or principles are correct or incorrect? Many people seem to think objectivity is not possible about such matters. Indeed, perhaps one reason for the popularity of the method of reflective equilibrium is that it need not assume such objectivity.

As a first step, it is important to dispel three common misconceptions which may lead one to deny the possibility of objectivity concerning legislative principles. First, people do not differ about normative questions as often as one might think. For an ultimate disagreement between two persons, both must view the situation in the same way. Many disagreements stem from different conceptions of the facts or the issue to be decided. Unless two people understand a question in the same way, their different answers do not indicate an ultimate disagreement. Further, even if both persons understand the question in the same way, they may still reach different conclusions if they disagree about the facts of the matter. Hence, the range of ultimate disagreement may be much less than one might expect. However, such disagreement is still possible, which is why the method of reflective equilibrium is not satisfactory.

Second, everyone's judgment about some matter is not equally competent. There are differences in people's knowledge about the facts of a matter. Even assuming equal information, however, people's judgments are not of equal worth. The judgments of people who suffer from severe forms of mental illness, who are grossly retarded, or who are patently prejudiced or biased are not accorded equal worth with those of people not so handicapped.

Third, and perhaps most important, the existence of an objective method does not require that it be impossible for people to disagree. In non-normative matters, philosophers and others have seen the inappropriateness of a search for Cartesian certitude. Scientific method does not cease to be objective because there is room for reasonable disagreement, yet in normative concerns, many people still search for the holy grail of infallibility. Even John Rawls, who allows that different but equally reasonable decisions concerning the goals of one's own life may be made, seeks a "strictly deductive" proof of principles of justice.[20] A strictly deductive moral geometry is not necessary for an objective method. A method which can show some views to be unacceptable, although several others are plausible or not unreasonable, is also objective.

Contemporary social contract theorists have attempted to obtain objectivity by means of a hypothetical contract. One ought to comply with an ultimate power-conferring rule constituting political authority if a rational, informed person would consent to it. Usually, the hypothetical person, as in Rawls' theory, is assumed to be in a situation quite different from that of actual persons.[21] Hence, even if such hypothetical persons would consent, actual people may ask why they should conform in their real lives to principles which hypothetical people would adopt in quite different and hypothetical circumstances.[22] A satisfactory answer to this challenge is essential.

One answer to it is to claim that the differences are irrelevant. For example, the answer to the question of whether eighteen and seventeen equals thirty-five and of whether the earth is round does not depend upon the situation or psychological condition of the person being queried. However, the answer to a question like "should Professor Jones accept the research fellowship or the visiting professorship which has been offered to him?" does depend upon Jones' situation and desires. Nonetheless, the answer does not depend upon the situation and desires of the person answering the question. Similarly, it may be claimed, the answer to "is P an acceptable legislative principle for society S?" may depend upon the situation and desires of the members of S, but not upon those of the person answering the question. Consequently, if a rational, fully informed person answers "yes," it is because that principle is appropriate for that society.

However, this form of the question about the acceptability of legislative principles is not appropriate. It assumes an impersonal, external point of view such that one is concerned with what is best for all the members of the society. Thus, it appears to assume some form of utilitarianism or other moral principle and would deny the autonomy of political allegiance. Even if it does not assume a moral principle, it does assume that the person answering the question is completely benevolent. Most political disputes arise because policies are beneficial to some persons and detrimental to others. Moreover, many persons do not care as much about other members of society as they do about themselves. Consequently, in order to bring these issues to light, a different question must be asked: "Should X accept P as a legislative principle for his society?" Whether or not P is an acceptable principle for X is still objective, in that one who is fully informed about X's situation and desires may answer it. That X is factually ignorant or irrational is not relevant to a decision on whether he should accept P. In short, there are features of a person which are discounted. It is this element which makes justification objective.

There are also many differences between persons and their situations which are not discounted by the requirements for objectivity. For example, the amount of money a person has is relevant to his buying a new car; his physical condition is relevant to his engaging in strenuous exercise. These features of persons and their situations cannot be discounted in the way that irrationality and ignorance can be.

For current purposes, many differences between persons and their situations are not relevant. There are some features which are common to many people and situations and which are also usually the more important ones for deciding general issues. For example, if one is deciding whether to live in Albania or the United States, general facts about one's desires and the conditions in the two countries are apt to be of most importance. If one is deciding whether to live in this house or that, details about the plumbing and one's particular tastes are relevant. Consequently, since the issues being considered here are very general ones about the acceptability of the purposes of political authority and about power-conferring rules, small differences between people and their situations are not relevant.

Nonetheless, differences between people and their situations may still be relevant to the justifiability of power-conferring rules and the acceptability of legislative principles for them. At this point, all one can do is to note the assumptions being made about persons and their situations. For the most part, the following discussions rest upon minimal assumptions. However, at one or two points these assumptions have to be expanded if certain legislative principles are to be acceptable.

ACCEPTANCE CONDITIONS

One can assess the acceptability of legislative principles and the justifiability of power-conferring rules by considering what a 'reasonable person' would accept. A 'reasonable person' is simply one who meets the acceptance conditions presented below. These conditions are designed to provide minimum conditions for reasonable decisions concerning the acceptability of legislative principles and the justifiability of power-conferring rules. They contain both conditions involved in the concept of objective justification and others; that is, some conditions are designed to eliminate factors which are grounds for discounting judgments, while others specify relevant general features of persons and their situation. If the latter features pertain to a person and the arguments are sound, then such a person ought to comply with power-conferring rules of political authority whether or not he in fact consents to such rules. All the conditions are presented under categories of persons and their situation.

The first set of conditions or assumptions are all intended to clarify the mental state of persons who are deciding upon the acceptability of legislative principles and the justifiability of power-conferring rules. The first three conditions are meant to exclude persons whose mental states discount their judgments. The first condition is that the person is not mentally ill. There are all sorts of mental illness, but this condition requires that a person not suffer from the more severe forms of mental illness or disease, such as paranoia or schizophrenia. An absent-minded person or one suffering from a mild neurosis would not be excluded by this requirement except when his difficulty would be relevant to a specific issue.

The second condition is that the person have a minimal amount of intelligence. He must be capable of understanding principles and the kinds of legislation they would support under various conditions. People who score in the upper 75 percent on intelligence tests would meet this condition. In view of the cultural bias of such tests, it is not possible to say that a person who does poorly does not have the requisite intelligence, but, at the very least, this condition excludes persons with certain genetic forms of mental impairment.

The third condition is much more controversial and difficult to elucidate. The person must be reasonable. Sometimes a person says that someone is being unreasonable when he disagrees with that person. For example, when Miss X's employer rejects her latest demand for a pay raise, he is obviously being unreasonable. He is unreasonable even if she already makes more than anyone else is willing to pay her. While 'unreasonable' is sometimes used as an pejorative term for those who disagree with one, there do seem to be some generally agreed upon definitions of a reasonable person, although it is not easy to formulate them precisely. They are summarized below.

Perhaps the least contestable criterion of reasonableness is a person's willingness to obtain the facts of a situation. If a person refuses to investigate the facts of a matter or to listen to testimony of experts about it, he is being unreasonable. Of course, one may still hold the same opinion after he has obtained information. Another aspect of this same criterion is a person's willingness to reconsider his opinion when new information is provided. Unwillingness to receive information or to reconsider one's opinion in the light of new information is sufficient to count a person's judgment unreasonable.

A second feature of being reasonable is the willingness to listen to arguments for and against a given position. A person who is unwilling to listen to arguments of those who disagree with him is unreasonable. There is a question as to what "listening to" or "considering" arguments actually means. Radicals sometimes claim that others have not listened to or considered what they say if their hearers have not been persuaded to the radical point of view. Obviously, that is too strong a condition. Yet many people, especially those in positions of authority, have a knack of listening attentively to complaints and arguments without ever being influenced to the slightest degree by any of them. A person who never changes his opinion as a result of listening to arguments for the opposite viewpoint is either omniscient or unreasonable.

A third characteristic of being reasonable is the willingness to support one's position by reasons. A person may obtain information and listen to arguments but may never advance any reasons for his view. He may have reasons but not be willing to discuss the matter, or he may not have reasons. Various philosophical doctrines seem to support the contention that one need not give reasons for normative judgments: for example, the intuitionist theory might imply that reasons need not be given, and existentialists seem to recommend doing whatever most expresses oneself. However, both intuitionists and existentialists have been at pains to explain why one need not give reasons for ultimate normative judgments. If a person is willing to provide this sort of general explanation for not giving reasons, he is not unreasonable. Only the person who refuses to give reasons or who claims (without further justification) that he does not need any reasons is unreasonable.

The fourth general condition pertains to the motivation of the person. This condition is crucial, for various assumptions about motivation result in radically different legislative principles. Frequently, philosophers allow people their usual motives but require them to be strictly impartial. Such a condition would have the same result as formulating the question "Is P an acceptable legislative principle for society S?" which was rejected in the previous section. Further, it makes an assumption about desires or motivations which does not hold for most people: while most people are impartial some of the time, much of the time they are not.

The assumption here is that people are not impartial but are selfish and have limited benevolence.[23] People are not wholly self-interested. They usually do care for friends and some relatives and, at least upon occasion, have a concern for the well-being of strangers. Despite this, most of the arguments for specific legislative principles will be addressed to self-interest. When benevolence must also be assumed, it will be specifically noted and it will not be complete benevolence or impartiality (a concern for others equal to the concern for oneself). Instead, it will simply be used to mean some degree of concern for others or concern for some others.

People's desires, whether focused upon themselves or others, are assumed to be primarily for wealth, power (control of others), prestige, and security (security includes both security of the person and the security of wealth, power, and prestige). These goods are not taken to be the basis of principles, i.e., that by which principles are defined, but represent a general classification of the motives assumed. Ultimately, the purposes of legislative principles are satisfaction of desires. However, others cannot immediately satisfy one's desires; that is, they cannot give one a satisfaction but only something which can be used to satisfy a desire. The goods listed are capable of being used, and are usually necessary, for satisfying most desires.[24] They are particularly crucial for satisfying desires of major importance in most people's lives. Moreover, by considering only these four goods rather than, say, a motor boat, differences between people's specific desires can generally be ignored.

Since no condition of impartiality is being assumed, it is logically possible for a person to accept a legislative principle which discriminates on biological (race, sex, etc.) grounds. However, such a principle is not as easy to support as one might think. Legislative principles state the kinds of considerations which are relevant in determining the goodness and badness of legislation. Hence, if one type of biological consideration is admitted as relevant, others may be relevant as well, unless one can give reasons for permitting only one such consideration. Moreover, the conditions about one's social situation specified below require that one assume that others occupy positions of authority to which one is subject. If one permits discrimination on biological grounds, one runs the risk that those in authority will be "corrupted" and will discriminate against the wrong biological class, one's own. However, this topic of discrimination is too complex to be pursued here. It is discussed further in specific contexts.

These motivational assumptions do not vitiate the autonomy of political allegiance, the objectivity of the method, or the relevance of the argument to actual persons. The autonomy of political allegiance is maintained because the motivations assumed do not include moral or political grounds; that is, it is not assumed that people will accept or reject legislative principles because they believe they are morally right or wrong, nor are political judgments or principles assumed. While this method does not establish an objective method for determining the appropriateness of the assumed motives, the arguments for legislative principles are still objective. Even if desires for wealth, etc., are ultimately subjective and incapable of objective assessment, the question of whether, given these desires, one ought to accept legislative principles may be one to which an objective answer may be found. Moreover, the motivational assumptions are realistic. Almost everyone has these desires. In short, the argument goes from actual, non-moral, and non-political desires to legislative principles which one ought to accept. A reasonable person with certain desires would accept a given legislative principle. Since one has those desires, one ought to accept that principle.

The last condition concerns a person's knowledge. Ordinarily one would assume that a person possessed all available information. However, since the issues to be considered are very general, not all available information is relevant. Moreover, in order to make reasonable decisions about legislative principles, a person need not know the details of all the cases which have arisen or might arise under legislation. All he needs is general knowledge about the types of cases and their probable frequency. Consequently, a general understanding of society and its operation, so far as it is known, should suffice.

In this connection elements of the method of reflective equilibrium are useful. It is difficult to understand legislative principles fully when they are stated abstractly. By considering the results of applying principles to real or hypothetical cases, one may better grasp them. Such a method may show defects in general arguments for them; for example, there may be contrary considerations whose importance is made clear in certain cases. One may see that

an argument holds only if a principle is qualified in some respect
or if certain conditions are assumed for its application. Thus, examining the application of principles to particular cases or types
of cases is a useful technique even though the method of reflective
equilibrium is not satisfactory.

One also needs some indication about what a person knows which
indicates his situation. Specifying such knowledge essentially clari-
fies the issue, which was partially clarified by delimiting the nature
of legislative principles. Here, certain general factual assumptions
are made about a person's position in society and about the nature
of that society. Further specification of these matters is given in
specific contexts.

First, people are to judge principles on the assumption that they
will be subjects in a state in which legislation is based on them.
Simply put, one has to live with the principles one accepts. This
condition excludes many sorts of principles, for example, the principle that the state should prevent people from having more food
than necessary for minimum daily requirements of minerals, vita-
mins, etc. While one might be willing to accept such a principle
for others, one is not apt to agree to be governed by that principle
oneself.

The second assumption is that while legislation will generally
be in accordance with acceptable principles, it will not always be
so; that is, legislators are not infallible. They will generally adopt
good legislation, though perhaps not the best proposed. Further,
sometimes they may pass legislation which is clearly bad. Legislators are not omniscient and therefore pass bad laws even though
their decision is made on the basis of acceptable principles. Further,
they sometimes ignore principles and vote on the basis of self-
interest. Even these assumptions about the activity of legislators
may seem utopian when compared with the actual activities of
many state legislatures. However, they do not appear to be impossible.

The third assumption is that citizens will generally, but not
universally, comply with legislation. There are two elements of non-
compliance which must be noted. First, some citizens will comply
with few laws, while others will be very law-abiding. Second,
some laws will be complied with more than others. Laws prohibiting
murder may be generally obeyed. Laws against marijuana use or
automobile theft may be very little obeyed. Of course, as legislators
act on the basis of principles which citizens recognize as acceptable,
the amount of non-compliance, will be minimized.

The fourth and last assumption concerns the social, cultural, and economic state of the society. Obviously, people in a primitive hunter-gatherer society will accept different legislative principles from people in an industrialized one. Hence, the direction of governmental activity will depend upon the economic and cultural condition of the society. Legislation is rarely based on the actual state of society at a moment; foreseeable changes are also taken into account. Since political systems are intended to endure for more than one person's lifetime, one must assume that economic and cultural conditions may vary considerably. Consequently, while most of the following discussion is based on the general economic and cultural conditions of contemporary developed countries, many principles will be relevant to developing countries as well.

As the main question concerns the acceptability of legislative principles, a brief account of what it is to accept such principles is necessary.[25] Acceptance of normative principles is often defined by saying that a person acts on them. However, the reasonable person who is to determine the acceptability of legislative principles is not to consider himself a legislator; hence, he cannot act upon them by voting for and against legislation. Nonetheless, he can use such principles. To accept legislative principles involves using them to determine whether legislation is good or bad. If a person thinks legislation is good, then he is generally willing to comply with it. Of course, allowance must be made for reluctance to do so because of conflicting desires and weakness of will. Moreover, if a person accepts legislative principles, he will tend to approve of legislation based on acceptable principles and of those legislators voting for such legislation; conversely, he will tend to disapprove of legislation based on unacceptable principles and of legislators voting for it. Also, he will believe that the arguments in favor of accepting certain principles outweigh those against accepting them. These reasons may be based upon either self-interest or limited benevolence. However, they may not be based on the fact that others think they are acceptable, that is, on authority.

One final point about the method of argument must be noted. As the method is primarily individualist—based on what an individual desires for himself—the general structure might be thought to be open to a criticism raised by Brian Barry. Barry notes that merely because a person would prefer to have more rather than less of some good, one cannot infer that he would prefer a society arranged so that each person has as much of that good as possible. For example, a person might prefer to have a car, but might also prefer a society with no cars to one in which everyone has a car with the consequent noise and pollution.[26]

This criticism, however, does not apply to the arguments here. First, the arguments are for legislative principles which provide a good but not sufficient reason for legislation. Since principles may conflict, one is not committed to providing as much of a good as possible: other conflicting considerations will limit the pursuit of any given purpose. Second, since the system of political authority is not assumed to be perfect, there may be purposes such as preventing competent adults from harming themselves which a reasonable person would prefer not to have pursued by it. In effect, one is asking whether one wants a society strongly devoted to that purpose. Third, Barry suggests that one can avoid the fallacy by considering the strength of desires, for example, the desire for a free society versus the desire for a conformist one.[27] The arguments presented for and against various principles do depend to a large extent, then, upon the priority of a persons' desires.

III
LAW

Many political theorists in both ancient and modern times have strongly recommended government of laws, not of men. Obviously, no political system can be based on laws without men doing anything. Hence, it is important to clarify what is meant by 'governance by law' or 'the rule of law'. Moreover, there are various types of laws. Purposes of political authority may be more appropriately pursued by the use of some types of laws or legal techniques than by others. Consequently, it would be useful to have a classification of types of laws or legal techniques so as to determine which are appropriate for different purposes.

The exercise of political authority does not usually involve the issuance of norms which are laws. There are orders by courts and police, administrative decisions and directives, etc. Some rules issued by administrative agencies, such as the Internal Revenue Service, are operative laws. The activities of most, if not all, of these authorities are organized and directed by laws and policies made by persons in positions of basic political authority. The purposes of political authority are most clear at that level. The root notion of governance by law is that the norms established by basic political authorities must be laws. Hence, governance by law restricts the type of norms which persons in positions of basic political authority may issue and thus constitutes a procedural limit on the exercise of political authority. Given that the fundamental norms issued are laws, governance by law implies that decisions and activities of other political authorities must conform to these laws. Of course, to the extent that persons in positions of delegated authority, such as state or federal regulatory commissions, perform a quasi-legislative function, governance by law implies that the norms they issue should also have the form of law.

GOVERNANCE BY LAW

The exercise of authority involves control over the conduct of others by issuing norms, which "tell" them to act in certain ways. Laws are one type of norm issued by political authorities. Hence, the general aim of laws is to get people to act in specified ways without resort to the exercise of power. Usually the aim of laws is to guide conduct without resorting to the courts.

Certain conditions are required for governance by law. Most of these conditions specify characteristics of the norms issued. Each and every norm issued need not have every characteristic in order to be a law, but most laws will have all of them. A norm which lacks one of these characteristics may therefore be a doubtful instance of law; that is, if one of these characteristics is missing, that fact may be a good reason for claiming that a norm is not a law. What is more important, if one of these characteristics was missing from all the norms issued by a system of political authority, that system would probably not be considered a system of law. At the very least, the system would not be called one based on the rule of law even if the norms were still properly called laws.

Professor Lon L. Fuller has noted eight characteristics for governance by law.[1] They may be put into three groups: those ensuring the exercise of authority by rules, those ensuring the communication of rules, and those ensuring that citizens can conform to the rules. Two characteristics are required for the exercise of authority by rules. First, for a norm to be a rule, it must be general. That Harry Smith should appear in court at 10:00 A.M. on Wednesday, 13 April, is not a rule. It is an order or command. Rules may be only for individuals; a person can adopt a rule of never working on Sunday. Since political authority controls the conduct of many citizens, laws are usually general in two senses: they refer to classes of actions and to classes of persons.

The second characteristic for the exercise of authority by rules is that particular cases be treated in accordance with the rules issued. If authorities announce a set of rules but ignore them in particular cases, then the announced rules are not the operative norms and it is impossible for citizens to guide their conduct by them.

The next two characteristics pertain to the communication of rules to persons expected to guide their conduct by them. People obviously cannot guide their conduct by rules unless they know what they are, so the rules must be promulgated. A story is told of a king who had rules printed in very small letters on a plaque placed high upon the wall of the throne room. When he wished to get rid of someone, he would imprison them for violating one of those rules. Of course, the rules prohibited rather ordinary conduct, but even had they not, few people could have willingly complied with them since they had no practical way of finding out what they were. One may object that promulgation of rules is not a feature of most modern legal systems, for hundreds or even thousands of laws are passed each year which are not made known to the average citizen. But they are available in statute books, records of legislative proceedings, etc. Further, many laws do not pertain to any activity in which an average citizen is apt to engage. Only those who are apt to engage in an activity need find out the rules relevant to it. Businessmen usually know the laws relating to their business or have lawyers who advise them about the law. The average citizen knows most traffic and criminal laws and has some idea of the tax laws; few other laws pertain to everyday conduct.

The fourth characteristic of laws is that they be intelligible. Almost everyone has had the experience of trying to fill out a questionnaire or to follow directions and being completely unable to make sense out of them. If a person cannot understand rules, he cannot guide his conduct by them. One might object that the legal language of most modern laws renders them unintelligible to the average citizen. While to some extent this is true, there are lawyers to explain the rules—for a fee. Because average citizens have been unable to understand federal income tax forms, the government has offered free assistance in completing them.

Even if a rule is communicated, a person may find he cannot conform to it. If rules are not relatively stable but change frequently, a person will not be able to guide his conduct by them. The rules regulating some industries change with such bewildering rapidity that it is well-nigh impossible to know what they will be six months in the future. Almost everyone has had some unpleasant experience with changing rules. It is not infrequent for a motorist to go through a new stop sign or to discover that a street has become one way in the direction opposite to that in which he is traveling.

The sixth characteristic is that the rules be consistent. As a new resident of New York, I attempted to obtain license plates for my automobile. The handbook distributed by the state motor vehicle department stated that before one could obtain plates one had to have a certificate that the car had passed a safety inspection.

Upon going to a garage to have a safety inspection, I was informed that no inspection could be performed unless the car had current New York State license plates. This dilemma was finally resolved when I discovered that cars currently registered in another state were exempted from the safety inspection requirement for obtaining plates. Sometimes there is no such unannounced exemption.[2] In those situations, a citizen simply cannot conform to both rules. Apparent conflicts are often resolved by one rule taking precedence over another—federal law supplants state law—but sometimes the laws are on the same level and are simply inconsistent. It is then up to the courts to resolve the inconsistency.

There are two final characteristics which laws must have if a person can obey them. The first is that they must not be retroactive. In practice many retroactive laws are approved: for example, Congress retroactively decreased 1974 income taxes, and no taxpayer protested. Tax overpayments can be corrected, so conformity to such a rule can be achieved retroactively, but it is impossible to correct other past conduct in order to comply with retroactive rules. If an ordinance is passed prohibiting the burning of trash, and the ordinance is to be effective for the past year, anyone who burned trash during the past year has violated the rule, and there is no way in which he can bring his conduct into conformity with that ordinance. It is this aspect of much retroactive legislation which prevents it from guiding people's conduct. Moreover, even if one's previous conduct could be brought into conformity with a retroactive rule, most people would consider it unfair if the rule imposed a burden, since they could not have avoided it had they wanted to do so.

The last characteristic of law is that it must require conduct which a person is able to perform. This characteristic primarily applies to rules involving regulation and penalties, i.e., laws requiring that one not engage in certain forms of conduct or engage in them only under certain conditions. For example, this characteristic underlies many of the excuses in criminal law. A person who accidentally causes harm is understood to have been unable to avoid doing so. Usually, laws do not specify that the person violating a given law must have been able to avoid doing so, only that the average person must have been able to avoid doing so. Thus a person may be penalized for doing something which he could not have avoided, although the average person could have avoided it. This feature of laws does not prevent them from being guides to conduct for most people. The defect here is not a general one but a particular one about the law's application in specific cases. This eighth condition is only meant to exclude rules requiring actions which an average person subject to them could not usually perform. Some rules may be designed for special classes of persons who may be expected to have unusual skills, e.g., physicians.

Fuller calls these eight characteristics "the internal morality of law." He believes that they indicate a necessary connection between law and morals. If so, then there would be a moral reason for preferring systems of political authority involving governance by law to those which do not. A legal system would have certain morally good characteristics. Fuller suggests that certain grossly immoral norms cannot be law. Hence governance by law would guarantee the absence of certain types of iniquitous use of authority.

However, H. L. A. Hart objects to Fuller's calling these characteristics "the internal morality of law." Hart prefers the expression "the principles of legality." He does not believe that the characteristics are essentially connected with morality, but believes that they apply to making norms for any rule-guided conduct.[3] Principles requiring these characteristics are only prescriptions for efficiently accomplishing a purpose. These characteristics are compatible with the pursuit of immoral as well as moral goals, evil as well as good ones. In claiming that these characteristics are compatible with great iniquity, Hart does not mean they are compatible with any evil aim, clear or vague. However, there can be clear laws furthering evil ends. Clear laws are also incompatible with vaguely defined but good ends.

In reply to these criticisms, Fuller presents two general arguments to show that the characteristics he mentions do constitute an inner morality of law. The first argument is that a legal system is essential for people to establish moral relations among themselves.[4] For example, without laws defining property it is impossible to apply the moral principle "Do not take what belongs to another." The second argument is that these principles represent a commitment by lawmakers to regulate citizens in accordance with general rules previously declared.[5]

Neither of Fuller's arguments is satisfactory. The first argument at best shows that moral relations are more easily established in an orderly society. The argument does not show the principles to be internal moral ones; it only shows that a legal system conforming to them is instrumental in establishing moral relations among people. But principles for a condition instrumental to the establishment of moral relations are not necessarily themselves moral principles. Besides, these moral relations may exist independent of a legal system. To take Fuller's example, it is certainly possible for a moral code to spell out what belongs to others. Indeed, even when a society has a legal system, there is frequently a difference between the legal and moral codes concerning the ownership of "property." Thus, moral conceptions of ownership exist independent of, and along with, legal ones. Fuller's argument does not establish that these characteristics of legal systems are themselves moral ones or that a system of laws is necessary or on the whole instrumental in establishing moral relations between persons. Thus, it does not show that systems of political authority involving governance by law are preferable to others because of an internal morality of law.

Fuller's second argument, in effect, is a modern version of the social contract theory. He makes the characteristics, or principles requiring them, moral ones because legislators commit themselves to govern in accordance with them. But their moral status must be independent of any commitment or contract, for the important claim is that lawgivers *should* commit themselves to rule by law. The characteristics must have moral status prior to any social contract. To put the matter another way, the question is: what are the conditions of an acceptable social contract, or, what type of social contract would a reasonable man accept? Hence, it needs to be shown that any acceptable social contract would require governance by law, not that an existing contract does require it. In effect, the question is: what is the argument for preferring governance by law?

Nonetheless, Fuller is correct in asserting that the eight characteristics constitute basic normative requirements of good law, and Hart is also correct in claiming they are compatible with evil ends. Due to the autonomy of political allegiance and political principles, Fuller's eight characteristics are not strictly moral ones and must be justified by appeals to the limited self-interest of reasonable persons. The goodness of the exercise of political authority concerns means as well as ends. These characteristics apply to means. They might most aptly be called "the formal characteristics of governance by law." They are formal in that they do not directly prohibit evil ends or purposes. Although they might also pertain to making rules for games, there are significant differences between games and law.[6] Law controls much more important matters in life than games do. Unless the eight characteristics of law pertain, a person does not have the opportunity and capacity to comply with norms.

A reasonable person would not accept political authorities depriving him of life, liberty, or property for violating rules if he does not have the capacity and opportunity to comply with them. Hence, these characteristics present formal conditions for regulation of human conduct on pain of loss of life, liberty, or property.

One can see the significance of governance by law by considering two different societies governed by evil rulers. In one, announced rules are often not followed in particular decisions, retroactive rules are frequently adopted, and many rules are often changed. Life in it is miserable, for one does not know from day to day what is illegal or when one will be imprisoned for past conduct. In another society there are laws discriminating against various groups and prohibiting innocuous conduct. Although these laws are strictly enforced, one knows what they require.

A reasonable person would prefer life in the second society, in which one knows what the penalties are for various forms of conduct, to life in the first, in which the ruler varies the rules arbitrarily. Thus, one can consider whether or not the risk of penalty is worth the possible gain. In the first society, reliable judgments of this sort are not possible. To the extent that one is incapable of predicting the results of various actions, one is less likely to satisfy one's desires. Hence, a reasonable person would be less likely in the first society to achieve the forms of wealth and power he desires.

In the second society life is less unjust and evil than in the first. Although adherence to the formal characteristics of governance by law will not prevent a grossly unjust and evil system, it does prevent some forms of injustice and evil. A rule prohibiting murder does not cease to be a moral rule because it does not prohibit all evils. Likewise, Fuller's eight formal characteristics of governance by law do not cease to be important normative features of legal systems simply because they do not prevent all evils.

Unlike most principles of legislation, the principles of governance by law do not state the purposes of a given piece of legislation. Further, not all of the eight characteristics are features of the particular norms being legislated. Three of them pertain to what political authorities do with the rules, rather than to the character of the rules themselves. The characteristics of promulgation (being made known), operativeness (treating particular cases in accordance with the rules), and relative stability (absence of too frequent change) pertain directly to the actions of political authorities and only indirectly to the character of the legislation itself. However, the characteristic of stability, unlike the other two, also has a relationship to legislative action and may be formulated as a negative legislative principle: there is a reason against legislation which makes the law unstable (repeatedly and rapidly alters it). The other characteristics—generality, clarity, consistency, nonretroactivity, and the possibility of compliance—do pertain directly to the character of the legislation rather than to the actions of political authorities. Hence, they may each be the basis of a negative principle of legislation. These principles may be formulated as follows: there is a reason against legislation that (1) is not general, (2) is not intelligible, (3) is inconsistent (with itself or other legislation), (4) is retroactive and imposes harms, or (5) requires conduct which the normal person to whom it is intended to apply cannot perform. In the discussion which follows it will be assumed that legislation does not violate any of these principles.

LEGAL TECHNIQUES

The usual classifications of laws are as public or private; penal or civil; and concerned with contracts, torts, property, etc. Laws are instruments for carrying out legislative purposes. The crucial basis of classification is how laws operate to guide conduct. Thus, the following classification is of different techniques used to carry out various purposes which legislators may have.[7]

When ordinary citizens think of law, they are most apt to think of penal law. This first technique, the penal one, prohibits conduct which the political authorities deem undesirable and specifies punishment for doing so. Since other techniques may also prohibit certain types of action or actions done in certain ways, the threat and use of punishment to obtain compliance is an essential characteristic of the penal technique. Thus, punishment must be distinguished from other legal consequences.

Philosophers have generally agreed upon five characteristics of the standard instances of legal punishment.[8] There are, of course, instances of punishment in which one or more of these characteristics may be absent. First, punishment involves the infliction of an evil or an undesired state upon a person. Since corporal and capital punishment have been generally abandoned, the evil is usually deprivation of liberty (incarceration) or of wealth (fine). Second, punishment is levied for an offense against legal rules. Sometimes this characteristic is classified as an application of the principle of legality, *nulla poena sine lege*. Third, punishment is of an actual or supposed offender for his offense. Usually the person punished performed an action which is prohibited, i.e., he is not being held accountable for what someone else did. Fourth, punishment is intentionally administered by a human being: nausea resulting from public drunkenness is not punishment in the usual meaning of the term, but thirty days in jail is. Fifth, it is imposed by persons occupying positions of authority, as established by the rules of the system against which the offense was committed: French authorities do not punish people for crimes against English law.

The second legal technique for controlling or guiding conduct is the grievance-remedial. This technique is reparative, to right a wrong, and requires a person to "make good" the damage he has done. While compensation is the usual remedy, it is not the only one. Remedies may take the form of injunctions to cease and desist from an action. This technique usually does not prevent conduct from occurring but does repair the disruption caused by it. Thus, laws of this sort define justifiable grievances, the remedies for them, and the methods by which they may be invoked. Further, whereas in punishment the offender is normally the one who is punished, under the grievance-remedial technique someone other than the person who caused the grievance may be held accountable for it; e.g., parents may be liable for damage caused by their children and insurance companies may have to pay for damage caused by those whom they insure. This technique predominates in tort law, but it is not completely absent in other areas.

A third technique is the administrative-regulatory one. Like the penal and unlike the grievance-remedial technique, the administrative-regulatory technique seeks to prevent certain types of conduct or consequences from occurring. Whereas the penal technique waits for the undesired conduct or consequence to occur before taking action, with the administrative-regulatory technique preventive action is usually taken before the conduct or consequences occur. Warnings may be issued, licenses revoked, injunctions issued, etc. Further, whereas the penal technique prohibits a large category of conduct considered undesirable, the administrative-regulatory technique is usually concerned merely to prevent undesired consequences of conduct which is itself permissible. To take a trivial example, it is not thought undesirable to build a house, but regulations require that one provide adequate plumbing and electrical wiring. The main emphasis in this technique is upon the way in which things are done, i.e., who does it, when, where, and how.

A fourth technique is the public benefit-conferral technique, which affects conduct by distributing benefits. One is apt to overlook the element of law involved in this governmental activity. Laws determine who is to receive benefits and specify each person's share of them. Besides determining who gets what, and when, laws also determine the process by which the benefits are distributed through establishment of agencies charged with distributing them, such as the Social Security Administration and the Department of Health, Education, and Welfare.

A fifth technique is the public burden-imposing technique. It is similar to the benefit-conferral technique except that it imposes burdens or harms and involves some considerations which are not relevant to benefit conferral. Moreover, lawmakers usually consider the two separately. While many reasons may be advanced for requiring all benefit-conferring laws to impose the burdens necessary for providing such benefits, lawmakers do not normally operate in this way.

A sixth and widespread technique is the private-arranging one. This technique facilitates the carrying out of persons' desires. Laws of marriage, contract, and wills are examples of this technique. It grants legal powers to private citizens to make certain arrangements, it specifies procedures for legal recognition of these arrangements, e.g., licenses for marriage and witnesses for wills; and it accords legal significance to these arrangements. It may establish rights and duties of persons, as in contracts, it may provide for remedies, or it may confer a status such as that of a spouse or standing to sue. Other forms of legal significance are also possible.

The final technique is compulsory treatment. The use of this technique has greatly increased in the twentieth century, as exemplified in nonvoluntary commitment of the mentally ill and required vaccinations. Its primary aim is to correct or prevent an undesirable status by treatment. Although people sometimes object that compulsory treatment is a form of punishment, the two are distinct. Punishment must be for an offense against stated rules, and the offense must usually be a discrete item of behavior. Treatment, however, is usually for a state or condition of the person (a status). The immediate aim of punishment is to prevent specified sorts of conduct, whereas the aim of treatment is to alter or change a state or condition. Punishment imposes an evil, something the person does not desire. In treatment, although undesired means may be used, the person treated is to be benefited, at least in the opinion of the person providing the treatment. Thus, one may seek to remove all evils from treatment (painless dentistry), but it does not make sense to remove all evils from punishment. Punishment usually requires that the person be responsible for his offense, but in treatment it is irrelevant whether or not a person is responsible for his status. A person's responsibility for his mental illness is not pertinent to the issue of whether or not he should be treated.[9]

The compulsory treatment technique also differs significantly from the benefit-conferral and administrative-regulatory techniques. While both the benefit-conferral and compulsory treatment techniques may aim to promote the well-being of persons, there is a significant difference. Public benefits are not usually forced upon people—indeed, people usually try diligently to obtain them—while compulsory treatment is frequently avoided by persons. Moreover, while both the compulsory treatment and administrative-regulatory techniques may seek to avoid certain undesirable conduct or consequences by taking preventive measures, treatment is only incidentally a form of regulation. Regulation restricts the manner, time, or place in which conduct occurs, but treatment involves such restrictions only if, as a matter of contingent fact, such measures prove beneficial, e.g., dietary restrictions for persons with ulcers. Again, the primary aim is not to affect conduct but to change a person's status, although that change will result in altered behavior.

Besides the seven distinct legal techniques, there may be mixed cases, and in order to achieve a given legislative purpose, several techniques may be used in tandem. For example, to eliminate the unwarranted use of dangerous drugs the legislature may use the penal technique to prohibit illegal sales, the compulsory treatment technique to deal with drug addicts, and the administrative-regulatory technique to control drug production by pharmaceutical companies and prescription by physicians. However, in the following chapters legislation will frequently be described as penal (or criminal), benefit-conferring, etc. While many items of legislation combine several techniques, usually one predominates. Thus, even though a law establishing a form of contract may provide for certain remedies for grievances arising from the contract, it would be considered predominately private-arranging legislation.

It is important to note that the use of almost any of these techniques may be backed up by the penal technique. Thus, while the administrative-regulatory technique is apt to rely on warnings and injunctions, continued failure to conform to regulations may result in punishment, but there is a significant difference between using punishment in the first instance and using it as a last resort. The penal technique is only being used as a backstop for the other techniques.

There is no reason to expect a priori that every legal technique will lend itself equally well to each purpose which political authority may have. Some techniques may be ineffective for some purposes. Moreover, some purposes may not be of sufficient importance to justify all the different legal techniques. So after considering the various acceptable purposes which political authority may have, it is important to consider the acceptability of using various legal techniques to pursue them. Such an analysis permits considerable subtlety and variation in the principles of legislation. Permitting some principles of legislation to justify only some legal techniques is likely to result in a more plausible account of them. The acceptable combinations of purposes and legal techniques constitute the acceptable uses of political authority.

IV
LIBERTY

The principles of governance by law prevent some abuses of political authority and so make it more acceptable, but they concern how, not why, political authority is exercised. Perhaps the most frequent and important abuse of authority is denial of liberty. A main theme of modern history is the struggle of peoples against tyranny and for liberty or freedom, but political philosophers have disagreed about what freedom is, what kinds of it there are, and what freedoms are desirable. A reading of the classical writers on this topic leaves one in a confused state. Thus, before one can articulate legislative principles about liberty, one must clarify the concept of freedom. Several contemporary philosophers have taken significant steps toward this goal.

FREEDOM

If a person is free, he is free from something to do something. The basic condition for the intelligibility of statements about a person's freedom is thus a triadic relationship: X is free from L to do A.[1] In discourse about freedom one or more of the terms of this relation (X, L, or A) may not be explicitly mentioned and may have to be derived from the context. For example, suppose Professor Busby is having a conversation in his office with a student, and his colleague Gabbard sticks his head in the door asking to have a word with him. Busby may reply, "I won't be free until noon." Busby does not explicitly mention what he may be free from or what he will be free to do. In the situation these elements are fairly clear. He will not be free to talk to Gabbard. It is less definite what he will be free from, but it undoubtedly includes some or all of the following: counseling students, teaching classes, and attending committee meetings. Sometimes only one of the terms of the relation is left unspecified, e.g., freedom to worship as one pleases. However, whenever talk of freedom makes sense, X is always free from L to do A.

One must also specify the ranges of the terms of the relation— what kinds of things they may be. Indeed, most disputes about freedom can be viewed as disputes about such ranges.[2] Different kinds of freedom—political freedom, economic freedom, freedom of speech, freedom of religion—may be defined by the ranges of one or more of the terms. For present purposes, the easiest term to delimit is the subject of freedom, X. The subjects of freedom are taken to be persons in the ordinary sense, individual human beings to whom one may point. Thus, while for some purposes the law treats corporations as persons, they are not so considered here because corporations are incapable of accepting legislative principles. However, reasonable persons may desire to be free to form corporations, etc., and to do various things under those modes of organization. Some philosophers have taken as the subjects of freedom not persons in the ordinary sense but only their "real" selves. In some contexts, there may be a good reason for so doing, but much of the time such a view leads only to confusion.

One must also specify the range of A when persons are free to do A. In ordinary discourse, A may be any of a number of things: to perform an action, to omit an action, to be or become a certain type of person, or to have something. Nevertheless, there are reasons for reducing all these things to actions. The distinction between omissions and commissions is frequently difficult, if not impossible, to make. For example, is leaving one's shoes off a commission or an omission? Is not putting on one's shoes the same thing? Talk of omissions usually makes sense only against a background of required conduct. Since not all conduct is required, there is no way to completely classify all conduct as a commission or an omission. As omissions have traditionally been classified as actions, that tradition will be followed here: an action is either a doing or a forbearing to do.

It is less clear that being a certain type of person or having a certain thing may be reduced to actions.[3] Nonetheless, to be a person of a certain sort involves acting in some specifiable manner. If there is no difference between the actions of two different people, one cannot say that they are different kinds of people in the sense in which one might speak of being free to be a person of one sort or another. Being white or black is a difference between people which need not involve any difference in actions. When people speak of being free to be black, what they mean is that black people are free to do either the kinds of things white people are free to do or the kinds of things black people want to do but which white people do not. Demands to be free to be a homosexual or a drug addict are demands to be free to perform actions. Homosexuals engage in homosexual acts, and drug addicts take drugs. There are no laws in the United States against being a homosexual or a drug addict, only against performing homosexual acts and using or possessing drugs. Although a state of transcendental meditation may not involve any action or doing, not even thinking, to be free to be a transcendental meditator is to be free to enter such a state, and entering the state is an action.

Finally, having things usually involves some form of action, although it does not reduce to action as neatly as the other possibilities. In being free to have something, e.g., a car, one is free to acquire and use it. The minimal act of possession would be simply to put the object away in a box or drawer and leave it there. Usually, however, having something involves some minimal use of it, at least looking at it. (This discussion, it should be noted, concerns possession or having in a non-legal sense.) Ownership is quite different; it involves a set of rights and powers. If one does not agree that "having" may be reduced to actions, it will not make much difference to the rest of the discussion. Slight modifications may be required here and there, but they do not affect the main points.

The kinds of things which may be the third term (L) of the relation of freedom, the limits to freedom, are much more diverse than those for the other two terms. Limits to freedom either prevent or make it more difficult for a person to perform or choose to perform an action. Some limits completely prevent an action, while others only make it more difficult. Having two broken legs prevents one from jogging a mile. Sore leg muscles or a muddy track do not necessarily prevent one from jogging a mile, but they do make it more difficult. Limits of the first sort may be called 'preventing' limits, and those of the second sort 'difficulty-imposing' limits.

Some limits directly affect one's ability to perform an action, while others simply make it less attractive a choice. If one is bound hand and foot, one cannot chop down a cherry tree. If one is threatened with punishment or is ecology-minded, one is as physically capable of chopping it down as if one were not. However, it is more difficult to choose to do so; it is a less attractive course of action.[4] Many limits, of course, may directly affect one's ability to perform an action and so indirectly make it a less attractive choice: sore leg muscles make it both more difficult and less desirable to jog a mile.

Two other classifications of limits or constraints may be made. Some limits involve the absence of something—lack of money, or a skill—and others involve the presence of something—chains, guards, or laws.[5] Sometimes the former limits are called negative and the latter positive. In some cases the difference between these kinds of limits is clear, but in others it is not. The chief difficulty is that limits can frequently be stated as presences or absences. One may say that it is either the presence of a hangover or the absence of a clear head which keeps one from thinking well: in any event, one cannot say that only things which are present (absent) are limits to freedom.

Some limits may be internal and others external.[6] Internal limits are those in the subject of freedom, X. Whether or not a limit is internal depends upon how one restricts the range of the subjects of freedom. As persons in the ordinary sense are taken as that range, internal limits are physical or psychological states of the person. All other limits are external. Of course, external limits may operate by making certain actions less attractive choices. Thus, their function as limits may depend upon internal states of the person, but the factors are still external to him.

Not everything which prevents an action or makes it a less attractive choice is a limit to freedom. It would be odd to say that the fact that it is raining makes one not free to go on a picnic. Only those factors which human beings can change are limits to freedom.[7] It is not necessary that human beings intentionally bring about a condition for it to limit one's freedom. It need only be within their capacity to alter it.

This point is very important for understanding demands for new freedoms. In the past, many of the economic conditions which restricted people's conduct were thought to be natural laws of the marketplace, unalterable by human beings. When advances in economic theory suggested that many of these conditions could indeed be changed by using different economic policies, they came to be seen as limits to people's freedom. Hence, as people discover how to control various elements of nature, the elements may come to be seen as limits to freedom. A significant area for consideration in the future may well be the physical and mental capacities of individuals. By the end of the century, developments in genetics may well make it possible to control some inherited characteristics, and people may come to regard some inherited traits as limits to their freedom. However, since genetically inherited psychological traits are not now within people's ability to control, they do not count as limits to freedom. One's inherited lack of capacity for higher mathematics is not a limit on one's freedom to study the general theory of relativity. However, if one has the innate capacity, lack of knowledge and skills, perhaps the result of an inadequate educational system, may limit one's freedom.

A more difficult factor to classify is lack of desire. The desires one has, as modern advertising makes clear, depend to a large extent upon the social environment. For example, when the City University of New York adopted an "open enrollment" policy admitting all high school graduates, in some colleges the number of blacks did not significantly increase. Many blacks had previously failed to attend college because they had no desire to do so, not because they could not meet entrance requirements. Similarly, in the past many qualified women of working-class backgrounds did not attend college because they were raised to believe that women did not need a college education and should get married and become housewives. Are these people not free to attend college because they do not want to go?

So far the discussion has considered a person to be free or not free only when there is something he wants or desires to do. This restriction has strange consequences. Consider two people, Traveler and Rebel, living in a dictatorship and voting in an election in which only one candidate is on the ballot. Traveler is happy with the candidate and would vote for him even if there were other candidates, whereas Rebel disapproves of the candidate and would vote for any other candidate if he could. Obviously, Traveler can vote as he wants and Rebel cannot. Does this fact provide any basis for saying that Traveler is free and Rebel is not? It would seem strange to say that one is free and the other is not, yet many political philosophers have denied that laws which prohibit one doing something which one has no desire to do limit one's freedom.

A convenient distinction here is between actual and hypothetical or dispositional freedom.[8] A person is actually free if there are no limits to his doing what he wants to do, so Traveler is actually free, whereas Rebel is not. A person is dispositionally free if there are no limits to his doing something if he wants to. Neither Traveler nor Rebel is dispositionally free to vote for another candidate. Dispositional freedom is what is usually meant in ordinary discourse about freedom. Thus, freedom is perhaps best viewed as a state of having alternative choices. Lack of freedom results when alternative choices are made unavailable or less attractive.[9]

Lack of desire cannot limit one's freedom: hence, lack of desire to attend college does not deprive blacks and women of freedom to do so. Obviously, lack of desire cannot be a limit to actual freedom, for this concept applies only when a person desires to do something. Nor can lack of desire be a limit to dispositional freedom. A person is dispositionally free to do A if there are no limits to his doing A *if he wants to*. Limits must, therefore, exist independent of a person's desire to perform an action.

One must, however, distinguish between a person's desire in and of itself to do A and his desire, everything considered, to do A. Limits frequently operate by making an action a less attractive choice, that is, making it less desirable when all factors are considered. They do this by making relevant to one's choice desires other than the simple desire to perform an action. Jones may simply want to campaign for candidate Y. If Jones' boss threatens to fire him if he does, then Jones may not, considering everything, want to campaign for Y. He is not free to campaign because his boss has limited his freedom. But his boss would not be able to do so if Jones did not also want to keep his job. Jones' co-worker, Smyth, does not want to campaign for candidate Y, but if the boss similarly threatens him, he is not dispositionally free to do so, even had he a desire to do so. Only the absence of a desire to do A in itself is not a limit to freedom. Lack of desire to do A, everything considered, may be the result of one's freedom being limited.

Since the effectiveness of most limits depends upon the desires people have, most talk about freedom presupposes a model of a certain type of person choosing,[10] a person with normal desires who is making a rational choice to maximize his utility. Such persons are reasonable, mentally normal, at least minimally intelligent, and basically self-interested, with limited benevolence. They primarily desire wealth, power, prestige, and security.

Desires are relevant to discussions of freedom in yet another way. Gaining freedom to do one thing frequently eliminates one's freedom to do another. Removing a limitation on performance of one action may impose a limitation on performance of another. Suppose there is no law against mugging others. Then a person is not free to stroll through the park at night. However, he is free from legal restraints to mug others. Which condition one prefers, that with or that without a law against mugging, depends on one's desires.[11] Most people prefer freedom from being mugged to freedom to mug. However, a preference for one of the two must be the basis of choice: A simple appeal to freedom will not settle the matter.

Moreover, since people's desires may conflict, one person's exercise of freedom may limit another's. Suppose there are black-berries growing wild in a public park. Both Cobbler and Pye may be free from any legal limits to pick them, but if Pye picks all of them, Cobbler is no longer free to pick them. Gaining freedom to do one thing may limit one's freedom to do another, and the freedom of others may conflict with one's own. The problem is to determine what sorts of freedom are preferable to others. Ordinary discourse about freedom frequently presupposes judgments about the desirability or preferability of freedoms, but here the aim is to examine the grounds for such judgments.

However, most people seem to think that freedom in and of itself, independent of what one is free to do, has some value. To support such a belief one must show that there is value in having alternative choices, independent of what one may choose; that is, one must show that conditions of greater freedom are preferable to those of lesser freedom. To do so, one must be able to make comparative judgments as to which conditions have greater and which lesser freedom.

Such comparisons cannot always be made. First, as there are difficulty-imposing limits to freedom, there are degrees of freedom depending upon the amount of difficulty involved. One cannot always determine which of two limits imposes the greater difficulty. Is the red tape involved in adding a course to one's schedule more of a limit to taking chemistry than the boringness of the chemistry lecturer? Second, it is frequently impossible to compare the freedom to perform different actions.[12] Which condition involves the greater lack of freedom: not being permitted to criticize the government, or not being free to practice one's religion?

Hence, judgments about the desirability of freedom in itself must be based on simple cases in which the same actions are in question. For example, suppose one goes to a restaurant on two consecutive nights. The menu is the same on both nights. With any meal one has a choice of two of the following vegetables: baked potato, peas, carrots, and lima beans. On the second night one is told that the choices are the same with the exception of lima beans: they are out of lima beans. Obviously, one has less dispositional freedom on the second night than on the first. What reasons may be given for preferring the greater freedom of choice on the first night?

One reason is the greater possibility of satisfaction. If one wants lima beans the second night, one will be dissatisfied. The greater the number of alternatives, the less are the chances of one's being dissatisfied. However, one may not like lima beans and so may not be dissatisfied. Nevertheless, it is prudent to allow for a change in one's desires. A reasonable person would prefer to have all the choices available just in case he should want lima beans. Even if he is fairly sure that his desires will not change, he is less apt to be dissatisfied in the event that they do.

The second reason for preferring greater to lesser freedom is really a development of this possibility. Greater freedom means a greater choice as to what one will do. Thus, one's actions become expressive of one's self as constituted by one's character and desires. A reasonable person is apt to prefer to live his own life, making of it what he can, even if the results involve less total want satisfaction than if he were less free. In short, most people have a strong desire to decide themselves how they shall live. Of course, there are times and circumstances in which it is reasonable to give up some control over one's life. Indeed, acceptable purposes for the exercise of political authority specify purposes for which a reasonable person is willing to surrender some control over his life. But—and this is the point—he is giving up something, a certain kind of freedom. Of course, he may be gaining the freedom to do other things (e.g., freedom to walk in the park without being mugged). He is still giving up something which has some value even if he gains something of greater value.

LIBERTY-REGARDING PRINCIPLES

Liberty or freedom has been among the avowed purposes of many political activities—revolutions, reforms, and even wars. The terms 'liberty' and 'freedom' carry a favorable connotation. No one is likely to take a public stand against freedom. But, as the analysis in the previous section showed, the important questions are who is to be free, from what, to do what.

'Political freedom' has been used in many different senses by political philosophers. A very broad sense, the one used here, is freedom from norms issued by persons in positions of political authority and from the power used to obtain compliance with them. Thus, it is defined by the types of limits, and for present purposes the emphasis is upon legal limits. Frequently, political freedom is defined by the types of actions one is free to perform—criticize the government, participate in it, etc. These freedoms may be more conveniently considered to be civil liberties. The point of defining political freedom by the types of limits is to develop liberty-regarding principles for all legislation independent of its topic.

The question to be considered, then, is whether there is a reason for or against legislation because it increases or decreases one's freedom. If legislation does limit freedom, there is a reason against it. To the extent that legislation increases freedom, there is a reason for it. Since different types of legislation affect one's freedom in different ways and to different degrees, it is best to consider the different types of legislation or legal techniques separately. It must be remembered that the question concerns only the constrictions on freedom inherent in various types of legislation. The issue is not whether a penal law against mugging is on the whole desirable, merely a question of the limit to freedom involved in the penal technique.

It is sometimes said that a presupposition in favor of freedom places the burden of proof on those seeking to limit it.[13] But if a legal technique involves an inherent limit to freedom, anyone advocating its use must do more than merely shoulder the burden of proof; he must show that a substantial benefit will result from limiting freedom. The burden of proof is merely an evidential requirement, not a substantive one, while the presupposition in favor of freedom is substantive. There are two types of burden of proof—the burden of production or going forward with the evidence, and the burden of persuasion or the weight of the evidence. The burden of production merely relates to who must present his case first. The burden of persuasion refers to the strength of the evidence. If a presupposition in favor of freedom were merely a matter of the burden of proof, then presenting strong evidence that a small benefit would result from legislation limiting liberty would justify it. However, defenders of freedom are not satisfied with such a result. One must not only present strong evidence that a benefit will result from limiting liberty; one must show that the benefit is more desirable than the freedom lost.

The penal technique involves a greater inherent limit to freedom than any other in the law. First, it does not merely restrict when or how one might perform certain types of actions; it prohibits them. Second, if one does perform the actions, the steps taken against one greatly limit freedom. As the two main forms of punishment are deprivation of liberty and wealth, it obviously limits one's liberty. Except for death, incarceration is the greatest possible limit to one's liberty. One might claim that thought control or mind alteration is as bad as incarceration, since it may prevent one expressing oneself. However, if it is successful, one's former desires will be eliminated, so that the victim will not be dissatisfied. With incarceration, however, one is both unable to express oneself and dissatisfied. Thus, the first negative liberty-regarding principle is that there is a strong reason against any penal legislation. There is a sufficient reason against penal legislation if another technique will achieve the same purpose.

There are moderate negative liberty-regarding principles against the administrative-regulatory and grievance-remedial techniques. The administrative-regulatory technique does not prohibit actions, so it involves less of a limit to freedom than the penal technique. Nonetheless, it does limit the manner (time, place, etc.) of actions. Attempts are made to prevent untoward actions before they occur, but sanctions are usually minor, although seemingly minor sanctions can actually be severe. The loss of a broadcast license may bring financial ruin to the owner of a radio or television station. The Federal Communications Commission almost never revokes a license; the penalty is deemed too extreme. The strength of the reason against specific administrative-regulatory legislation depends

upon how much it restricts the conduct and the severity of the penalties proposed.

The effect of grievance-remedial legislation upon one's freedom
may be slightly less than that of the administrative-regulatory technique. The grievance-remedial technique often does not prohibit or
prevent one from performing actions of any type or under any conditions. Instead, it makes it more difficult to choose to perform actions of a certain kind or under certain conditions. One knows that
one will have to compensate anyone injured by one's actions. If,
however, the remedy is an injunction, then one is not free to perform
an action even if one is willing to pay for damages. Not all injunctions, however, are permanent. Some only prevent one's performing
an action for a period of time or until a stipulated condition is met.

If one views this technique from the point of view of the plaintiff,
there is no limitation on one's freedom. In considering the effect of
legal techniques upon freedom, one must assume the perspective of
a person whose conduct is being controlled or guided. While penal
laws against, say, assault, do give citizens freedom from assault, they
do not do so by controlling the conduct of law-abiding citizens but by
controlling that of others. In the case of the grievance-remedial
technique, it is by one's own actions of suing or filing complaints
that one will receive a benefit, a remedy. Thus the grievance-
remedial technique also facilitates recovering losses and therefore
increases one's freedom to use what one has. Unlike the administrative-regulatory technique, the grievance-remedial one does not directly prevent injuries or losses from occurring: it only makes good the
loss.

In view of the different ways in which the grievance-remedial and
administrative-regulatory techniques affect one's freedom, there does
not appear to be any basis for a general claim that one technique
involves a greater limit to freedom than the other. Thus, there is a
moderately strong reason against the use of either technique. Part
of what is meant in asserting that there is a moderate negative
liberty-regarding principle against such legislation is that less of a
limit to freedom is involved than with the penal technique. To make
what is meant completely clear, one must indicate what kinds of considerations might outweigh the reasons provided by the principles.

There is also a liberty-regarding reason against using the burden-
imposing technique. However, the effect on freedom of the burden-

imposing technique varies much more than do the two previous ones. The burdens imposed may vary from military conscription to a tax of one-half of one percent on purchases of a certain type of good. Such burdens limit one's choices of actions, since they make them less attractive.

The burden-imposing technique rarely limits freedom as much as does the penal technique. It does not prevent an activity. For example, tax laws are designed to provide revenues; their purpose would be defeated if they were so severe as to discourage everyone from engaging in the activity being taxed. Of course, upon occasion taxes are used to discourage people from some form of activity. In that case, they are more appropriately viewed as regulative or penal.[14] One test as to whether a tax law is being so used is to determine whether more revenue would be gained from a somewhat lower tax. Consequently, the negative liberty-regarding principle against the burden-imposing technique provides a moderate reason against it, and the strength of the reason against given legislation is proportionate to the burden imposed.

The benefit-conferral and private-arranging techniques do not limit one's freedom. Citizens are not forced to take advantage of benefits offered. One is not required to use parks or to claim Social Security or Workmen's Compensation benefits. The private-arranging technique uses political authority to help one carry out one's wishes. Laws do not require one to marry or to make contracts. Thus, there are no negative liberty-regarding principles involved.

Indeed, there are positive liberty-regarding principles for legislation using the benefit-conferral and private-arranging techniques. Benefit-conferring legislation enables one to do things one could not have otherwise done, e.g., live in decent housing. Similarly, private-arranging legislation enables one to do things one could not have otherwise done, e.g., make wills. Of course, both types of legislation may restrict what one can do with the benefits conferred or may restrict the types of arrangements one can make. These restrictions do not necessarily limit antecedent freedom; instead, they keep the legislation from increasing one's freedom as much as it might otherwise have done. For example, the fact that the law does not permit people to make polygamous or homosexual marriages does not deprive them of a freedom which they would have had without marriage laws, for before such laws they could not legally marry at all. Further, many of the associated laws which prevent people from acting as they desire involve the penal technique: it is penal laws which prohibit homosexual relations. And in most states there are no laws prohibiting a man and woman or several women or men living together; such arrangements merely do not have the legal standing which a marriage provides. (Restrictions or limits added to previous legislation do limit antecedent freedoms.)

Finally, the compulsory treatment technique does limit freedom. Frequently, this limitation is as severe as that of the most harsh penal legislation, i.e., confinement. It may also include thought control or mind alteration. While the aim of such legislation is to provide a benefit as judged by others, the direct effect is to limit the freedom of those affected. The alleged benefits may or may not justify the limitation on freedom, but the limitation is still there. Hence, there is a strong negative liberty-regarding principle against such legislation.

In conclusion, then, there are five negative liberty-regarding principles and two positive ones. Three of the negative liberty-regarding principles state that there is a moderate reason against legislation if it uses the (1) administrative-regulatory, (2) grievance-remedial, or (3) burden-imposing techniques. Two other negative liberty-regarding principles state that if legislation uses the penal technique, there is a strong reason against it, and that there is a strong reason against legislation using the compulsory treatment technique. Compulsory treatment legislation can, and frequently does, limit one's freedom to perform many actions. Finally, the two positive liberty-regarding principles state that there is a reason for legislation if it primarily uses the (1) private-arranging or (2) benefit-conferring techniques.

COMMUNICATION

Besides the liberty-regarding principles discussed so far, the Western political tradition places great emphasis upon freedom of speech. Thus, the question of whether there is a special liberty-regarding principle for speech should be considered. In the United States, much of the discussion of this issue has centered around the provisions of the First Amendment to the Constitution. This amendment prohibits Congress and, by the Fourteenth Amendment, the several states from prohibiting the free exercise of religion, abridging freedom of speech or press, or preventing persons from assembling peaceably and petitioning the government for a redress of their grievances. The grouping of these different freedoms—religion, speech, press, assembly, and petition for redress of grievances—suggests that there is some general principle underlying all of them, although there may not, in fact, have been any reason for putting them together except ease of expression or political considerations.

One basic principle common to all five is freedom of communication.[15] The notion of communication will not cover all of the specific instances of freedom protected by the First Amendment. It certainly will not cover all the protected activity resulting from the Supreme Court's interpretation of it. But communication is an essential part of each freedom. Freedom of speech and press are clearly concerned with communication. The purpose of peaceable assembly is usually to discuss matters, although it may be simply to engage in joint activities. However, freedom of assembly is closely tied to petitioning for redress of grievances, which is a form of communication (it seems likely that the Founding Fathers had uppermost in their minds assembling to discuss political matters). Finally, the exercise of religion involves the expression of an attitude. Most religious services involve communication and public expression of belief; one might even emphasize the notion of religious services as communication with God.

The meaning of 'communication' is here taken in a fairly broad sense. The core of the concept is an act in which one person attempts to make another person aware of a proposition or attitude.[16] The primary reference is to linguistic acts—speaking, writing, etc. Communication need not be successful; that is, the intended recipient need not become aware of the proposition or attitude. Also, the communicator normally intends that the recipient will believe that the proposition or attitude is justified or appropriate.

All defenses of freedom of communication (or free speech) resting upon a particular form of government are inadequate to support a negative legislative principle for communication.[17] For example, Alexander Meiklejohn's argument will not do.[18] He supports absolute freedom of speech with respect to public affairs on the ground that open discussion is necessary for self-government. Such an argument carries no weight for a system of political authority which is not intended to be a self-governing one. Yet most advocates of freedom of speech believe that it should exist under all forms of government. Moreover, the form of a system of political authority should at least partially depend upon the purposes which it should pursue or respect. No type of political system can be assumed.

Another type of argument which will not support a legislative principle of the sort sought here is Thomas Scanlon's. He primarily classifies unacceptable kinds of reasons for restricting communication. In his principle, he lists harms resulting from speech which do not provide good reasons for limiting it.[19] This method, illuminating as it is, does not provide a negative liberty-regarding principle. Instead, it supports limiting a positive legislative principle to prevent harms; that is, it provides grounds for restrictions upon the private harm principle (see Chapter V for discussion of this principle).

While Scanlon calls his principle the "Millian principle," John Stuart Mill's method of argument is significantly different from his. In Mill's famous defense of free speech, he considers the utility of allowing freedom of communication.[20] In so doing, he focuses on the reasons why persons other than the speaker may benefit from freedom of speech. Although Mill never explicitly states that truth is more likely to be discovered in a free market of ideas, many commentators attribute this claim to him. It is not at all clear that truth is more likely to be discovered in a free competition, however, and it could have disastrous consequences.

The following defense of freedom of communication involves a blend of the views of Mill and Meiklejohn. The approach is to consider the purposes a reasonable person might have in communication from two viewpoints. One is the point of view of a potential member of an audience; the other is the point of view of a possible communicator. Each point of view provides an argument for the desirability of freedom of communication. Both arguments connect, though not directly, with the general arguments previously advanced for the desirability of freedom.

First, from the point of view of a member of the audience, freedom of communication increases one's sources of information. A reasonable person gathers available information (or at least does not refuse to listen to potential sources of information) and considers arguments for and against matters and so wants them available. Further, provision of more information and discussion of the considerations for and against a given decision generally increase the probability of having true beliefs and correct attitudes, which are more likely to lead to judicious actions and want satisfaction than are false beliefs and unjustified attitudes. Moreover, if one is permitted to hear all arguments and claims, one is being treated as a reasonable, responsible person capable of making intelligent decisions and judgments. Restrictions on freedom of communication imply that one is not such a person. While this may in fact be true in specific situations, the general assumption is not one which a reasonable person can accept.

Second, from the point of view of a communicator, limitations upon the freedom to communicate decrease one's opportunities for self-expression. Limiting one's freedom to express oneself to others is apt to frustrate a basic desire of most persons. Further, such limitations appear to imply that one is neither intelligent nor reasonable enough to communicate anything of value. Thus, from both the point of view of a potential communicator and that of a potential listener, limits on the freedom to communicate deny one's status as an intelligent, reasonable, responsible human being.

A member of an audience is not accorded that status if he is not free to receive communications of any opinion on any topic or receives deliberately false and misleading communications. Thus, while a communicator may wish to give deliberately false information, an audience has little interest in receiving such a communication. Moreover, a potential communicator cannot claim that deliberately false communications promote self-expression (except as a liar), since they do not indicate his beliefs or attitudes.

Another point is crucial here. If a reasonable person is responsible for his judgments and actions, and if a member of an audience of such people causes harm as a result of a communication, he is responsible for it. As a general principle, responsibility halts when the causal chain reaches the voluntary act of another.[21] If X, a speaker, presents reasons for a building being bombed and Y, a member of the audience, judges these to be good ones and voluntarily does so, then Y is responsible for the harm, and X is not responsible. It follows that a speaker should normally be free to advocate any conduct he sincerely thinks is justified. If a member of the audience then performs an unlawful act, that person alone is responsible.

However, one must be careful to distinguish between advocacy and incitement and provocation. Incitement differs from advocacy in that it does not involve an appeal to reason. The attempt is to short-circuit the deliberative process and get people to act on the basis of unconsidered emotional reactions. Advocacy, in contrast, involves presenting arguments to convince others that a proposition is true, an attitude or action justifiable. Provocation is like incitement. The attempt is to make the listener angry or excited so that he cannot reason about the matters in question or exercise ordinary control over his behavior.

There is another context in which communication by one person usually makes him responsible for the voluntary conduct of another, namely, when one becomes a party to a subsequent crime. Being a co-conspirator or accomplice before the fact are the chief examples. In these cases, unlike those of incitement and provocation, the deliberative process of the second person is not short-circuited. However, they both differ from the usual forms of advocacy, such as that of draft resistance, in that specific criminal acts are involved. Furthermore, the speaker either intentionally agrees to or encourages the crime, and in that sense he makes it his own.[22]

Thus, a reasonable person has good reasons for accepting a special negative liberty-regarding principle for freedom of communication. However, it is very difficult to formulate such a principle. One difficulty stems from the types of limits which may be imposed. The penal technique is inherently the most freedom-limiting one. However, with respect to freedom of communication, prior restraint by the administrative-regulatory technique may be worse, for people may be completely prevented from communicating, not just penalized for it. In one small area, that of government secrets, prior restraint seems justified. Governments undoubtedly classify much more material as secret than need be, but the justification for official secrets seems clear. Yet official secrets do involve prior restraint upon communication. Consequently, no absolute principle of freedom of communication, not even against prior restraint, appears acceptable.

The strongest acceptable principle of freedom of communication may be the following: there is a reason against legislation which would limit freedom of communication with deceit as a criterion of application. Criteria of application state conditions for the use of principles in various contexts. The deceit criterion is that the communication is not deceitful. When a communication is deceitful, the principle in favor of freedom of communication does not apply because of the absence of reasons in favor of it. Since this principle is separate from the other liberty-regarding ones, it must be added to them where both apply. Thus, besides the basic liberty-regarding reason against penal legislation, there is an additional reason against penal legislation prohibiting communication. The same holds for the other legal techniques limiting liberty. Thus, there is always a stronger liberty-regarding case against legislation limiting communication than any other type of action.

Since the principle of freedom of communication is not absolute, however, laws limiting communication may be justified. The principle simply makes them more difficult to justify. The principle of freedom of communication applies to advocacy, incitement, conspiracy, and being an accomplice before the fact (at least by counseling). Laws against conspiracy and being an accomplice before the fact (based on counseling, etc.) become especially difficult to justify only if the freedom of communication principle is applicable to them. However, positive principles in favor of legislation may justify narrowly drawn laws concerning them.[23] In incitement, for example, the fact that the second person does not act completely voluntarily makes the reasons for restricting communication stronger.

PRIVACY

In addition to freedom of communication, the Western political tradition has also emphasized a closely related matter—privacy. One might think that privacy is a peculiar concern of the Western tradition. With respect to privacy from government, this claim may be correct; indeed, it is of particular concern in English-speaking countries.[24] However, the evidence is that some form of privacy is an element of all societies.[25] Precisely what is deemed private and the means by which it is protected vary greatly between societies, but certain forms of privacy are almost invariably present.

Privacy is not simply freedom, but it is closely connected to freedom. A voyeur at one's bedroom window does not make one unfree to do what one desires, yet he invades one's privacy. Nonetheless, freedom is an important aspect of privacy. The knowledge or belief that one's actions are not private may limit one's choices of conduct. The belief that an acquaintance can overhear a conversation may prevent one from telling the other conversant what one really believes about the acquaintance. More generally, widespread awareness of what one is planning to do may prevent one's doing it.

There is, however, a more important relation between freedom and privacy. The demand for privacy is a demand to limit or control others, to limit their freedom, e.g., to prevent the voyeur from looking in one's window. The control over others involved in privacy is not control over anything they might do. It is only control over some of their actions with respect to oneself. However, privacy does not involve control over the conduct of others in all respects which affect one. It is only control over the information which they have about one. Thus, Alan Westin writes, "Privacy is the claim of individuals, groups, or institutions to determine for themselves when, how, and to what extent information about them is communicated to others."[26] Privacy thus involves a limitation on freedom of communication. It limits freedom of communication about oneself by others without one's consent. Privacy also concerns access to information whether or not communicated by another. The voyeur, for example, is not the recipient of information from another person; he obtains his information directly.

This sense of privacy does not cover all the senses of 'private'. For example, Ernest Van Den Haag construes a right to privacy as entitling one to exclude all invasions of one's private realm by others. He thus takes noises and odors produced by others as invasions of one's privacy.[27] Such a conception goes beyond control of information to control of one's environment. In tort law, offensive odors and noises, whether public or private, have been treated as nuisances, not invasions of privacy, and there is no good reason to blur this distinction.

A better grasp of privacy requires consideration of the various forms it may take. The clearest form of privacy is solitude. In solitude no other person is present to observe one. Walking alone on a forest trail or sitting in one's room with the door shut provides solitude. Closely connected to solitude is intimacy. Intimacy involves the presence of another person or persons, but the number of other people is small. Both solitude and intimacy involving seclusion pertain to being or doing things in private—where others cannot observe. Hence, others cannot obtain information about one. Intimacy involves another aspect—the sharing of information with a certain person or persons which is not shared with others. The emphasis here is not upon what information is communicated, but to whom it is communicated.

This feature of intimacy, limitation of access to information to certain people, is also involved in another form of privacy—one's personal or private affairs. Communication of information about oneself to others, usually others with whom one is not intimate, is restricted to those who are involved and is of a limited nature. Thus, while one's banker knows how much money is in one's account, one's next-door neighbor does not know. It is private business, and the neighbor is not entitled to know unless one wants him to. Yet that neighbor may know other things about one, e.g., that one exercises in the back yard, which are unknown to the banker and of no concern to him.

The distinction between one's private and public affairs depends upon accepted norms. In this sense 'private' depends upon norms which determine the boundary between private and public.[28] 'Private' and 'public' are contrasting terms. The public is a wider community,[29] and, although it seems slightly odd, one's family may be the public; in this context, what is 'private' is what is not open to the other members of the family. However, the family may be a private realm with respect to the neighborhood. In all these forms, privacy is control by persons, couples, families, etc., of the information about them in the wider community, the public.

The desirability of privacy may best be considered by dividing it into three forms: solitude, intimacy, and personal (private) affairs. A reasonable person has several reasons for considering solitude desirable. Solitude affords a release from the psychological stresses of daily life.[30] One can simply relax without worrying about how others will be affected or will perceive one. Such relaxation is probably essential for one to keep calm and to be able to function in daily life. Solitude also provides an opportunity to analyze and assimilate information, to try out various ideas before committing oneself. Thus, solitude is essential to retaining one's status as a reasonable and informed person.

Privacy as intimacy is necessary for the sorts of personal relations with which it is inherently involved. Charles Fried has ably argued that the relations of love, friendship, and trust are not possible without privacy.[31] These relations are usually based upon or involve intimacy. Love and friendship always do; trust frequently does. One may, of course, trust one presidential candidate more than another, but there is a more basic trust which rests upon a deep understanding and respect for another person. The Nazi encouragement of children's informing authorities of unpatriotic comments and activities by their parents had a devastating effect upon parent-child relationships. To the extent that a reasonable person desires personal relations of love, friendship, and trust, he has reasons for the desirability of privacy as intimacy.

Finally, there is privacy as personal affairs. Like privacy as intimacy, this form closely relates to one's relationships with others. The differences between the information one's banker and one's neighbor have partially define the type of relationship one has with them. If one's banker has access to the same information as one's neighbor, the relationship with him changes. He ceases to be merely one's banker and becomes a friend or neighbor. As James Rachels has written, "because our ability to control who has access to us, and who knows what about us, allows us to maintain the variety of relationships with other people that we want to have, it is . . . one of the most important reasons why we value privacy."[32]

There are other reasons why privacy as personal affairs is desirable. It is instrumental to prestige and wealth. Everyone has engaged in conduct which, if widely known, would damage him in the eyes of others. The ability to control the information which others have about one is essential to one's prestige. Privacy in personal affairs may also be needed for wealth: some activities and plans would be ruined were they known in advance by others. Plans to open a business or to have a special sale might be disrupted if known in advance by competitors. Beyond the considerations of prestige and wealth, however, there is also that of not being intruded upon, of being free to go about one's business without interruption. Being allowed to conduct one's business on one's own signifies that one is being treated as a reasonable, responsible person.

Since privacy in its forms of solitude, intimacy, and personal affairs is desirable, a reasonable person would accept two principles of privacy. The negative principle is that there is a reason against legislation which requires invasion of privacy. It provides a reason against various sorts of legislation enabling government and citizens to have access to information about oneself. The prohibition of unreasonable searches and seizures is a constitutional embodiment of this principle: government may not invade privacy without good reason. Wiretapping and electronic bugging have been brought under such protection. Any form of governmental activity which involves amassing data about a person, e.g., the files of the Federal Bureau of Investigation or the Internal Revenue Service, invades his privacy. This principle also underlies legislation preventing the government from access to information exchanged between husband and wife, priest and penitent, lawyer and client. However, it does not provide an absolute bar to invading privacy when there is sufficient reason.

There is also a positive privacy principle: if legislation will protect privacy, that is a reason for it. This positive privacy principle is a strong one. To protect some forms of privacy, a reasonable person would be willing to risk the loss of freedom involved in some penal legislation. The positive principle supports penal laws against voyeurism, electronic surveilance, etc. Likewise, it supports legislation to remedy grievances, for example, unauthorized use of one's name or image for profit, as in advertising a product. Of course, a person must expect that much of his conduct will not be private, and he tacitly agrees to allow certain information about him to be public when he enters public places. The positive privacy principle also supports legislation designed to regulate information to ensure anonymity, e.g., institutional review committees which attempt to ensure the anonymity and privacy of human subjects of various experiments. It also supports limits on private arrangements to protect the privacy of personal affairs, e.g., to prevent banks from making known the financial transactions of their customers. However, burden-imposing, benefit-conferring, and compulsory treatment legislation are not relevant to the positive privacy principle.

It may be objected that privacy principles are unnecessary because other principles would cover everything they provide. For example, Judith Jarvis Thomson has argued that the right to privacy is redundant, in the sense that each right in the cluster denominated privacy may be explained on other grounds, such as the right to property and the right over the person. Thus, she claims, rights to prohibit others from seeing one's possessions or parts of one's body may be so grounded. In particular, she denies that one may violate a person's right to privacy by simply knowing something about him.[33]

However, there are several difficulties with Thomson's argument. She thinks that the possession of information about another person is of little or no importance. It is *how* the information is obtained which is important, and that involves the violation of other rights. This argument overlooks a crucial point. Mere knowledge about another person does not invade his privacy because privacy is defined as control over access to information about oneself. It is only violation of that control—another person's having the information without one's consent—which invades privacy.[34] Thomson essentially places such control over information in the right over one's person, which includes, among other things, the specific rights not to be listened to, not to be looked at, etc. Thus she makes it appear that the right over one's person may be a foundation for a right to privacy. But one may as easily contend that a right over one's person is composed of, among other things, rights to autonomy and to property (the right not to have one's image used for profit). In short, reducing a right to privacy to other rights merely shifts the issues to their incidents; and if one does not so reduce it, one may be able to better explain incidents of these other rights, since privacy, as Thomson acknowledges, does relate to many of these other areas of concern.

Moreover, Thomson argues in terms of rights, while legislative principles do not specify rights but the reasons for and against legislation. Consequently, she assumes rights, such as the right to property, whose existence depends on legislation. In the present context, such rights cannot be assumed. Specifically, she assumes that it is one of the incidents of ownership that one can prevent others from seeing one's property. But, one may ask, why should this condition be an incident of ownership? One good reason might be that it protects one's privacy. A similar argument could be made with respect to a right over one's person. While her argument may be plausible when made within the context of a system of legal rights, it is much less so when the question is one of creating one system of legal rights rather than another.

Consequently, there are three acceptable legislative principles concerned, directly or indirectly, with communication. A negative principle provides a reason against limiting freedom of communication. The positive privacy principle, however, provides a reason for legislation protecting people's control of information about themselves, including the communication of such information. Likewise, the negative privacy principle provides a reason against legislation which would limit citizens' control of information about themselves. Thus, there are principles concerned with communication which may have to be balanced against one another.

An example of this sort of conflict is provided by the legal case of *Time, Inc.* v. *Hill*.[35] In this case, *Time* magazine had run an article with pictures about the play "The Desperate Hours" indicating that the story was based on events a number of years earlier in the life of the James Hill family. In the play, convicts enter a house, hold the family prisoner, and mistreat them. While convicts had held the Hill family prisoner, they were treated courteously. James Hill sued for damages under a New York statute for invasion of privacy by knowingly and falsely reporting that the play portrayed an experience of the family.

Cases of this sort illustrate a conflict between the positive principle to protect privacy and the negative principle against limiting freedom of communication. Supposed "information" about the Hill family was widely disseminated. The Hills had not consented to this distribution of information; in their earlier ordeal, they had involuntarily come before the public eye; they had not sought the publicity nor given tacit consent to it as one may do when appearing on public streets. Moreover, the events took place several years earlier. Hence, it seems clear that privacy provides a reason for a law preventing the distribution of the information.

On the other hand, *Time* was communicating information about a new play. While some of the statements it made were false, it is unclear whether they were deceitful, i.e., made when known to be false. If they were not, the principle of freedom of communication provides a reason against laws restricting *Time*'s liberty to communicate. Moreover, the liberty-regarding principle against grievance-remedial legislation provides another reason against a law rendering *Time* liable for damages.

The Supreme Court held that *Time* was not liable unless the Hills could show that the magazine had knowingly or recklessly made the false statements. In terms of the principles of this chapter, the negative liberty-regarding principle of grievance-remedial laws plus the negative principle of freedom of communication would outweigh the positive privacy principle. However, if *Time* knowingly or recklessly made false statements, then the negative principle of freedom of communication would not apply and the positive principle of privacy would outweigh the negative liberty-regarding grievance-remedial principle. One may thus see how different principles must be weighed against one another, how criteria of application may determine the relevance of principles, and how laws may be formulated to take account of the various relevant principles.

V
HARM

The last two chapters have emphasized traditional negative principles for limiting political authority. Only three positive principles were advanced, two of which were of minor importance. This chapter, in contrast, considers the two purposes of political authority which have usually been considered the most basic, if not the only, ones. Thomas Hobbes and J. S. Mill believed that the main purpose of political authority is to protect men from each other. Some of Mill's writings suggest that protection from harm by others is the only acceptable purpose for political authority. Nonetheless, both Hobbes and Mill believed that a system of political authority is also justified in seeking to ensure its own continued existence.

These two purposes of political authority—that of protecting people from harm by others and that of ensuring its own existence— are accepted by practically all writers on the subject. Only anarchists, who deny that there are any acceptable purposes for political authority, reject them. Thus, little attention has been given to clearly and precisely formulating these purposes, nor has much attention been paid to their justification: it has seemed obvious. However, although their justification is relatively straightforward and simple, formulating these purposes is not easy. There are various problems of statement and interpretation. The bulk of this chapter is concerned with such matters.

INTERESTS

Various authors have discussed the use of political authority to prevent citizens from harming one another. John Stuart Mill's discussion is the most famous. He formulated the private harm principle in several ways, which are not strictly equivalent. Perhaps his best formulation is the following: "the only purpose for which power can be rightfully exercised over any member of a civilized community, against his will, is to prevent harm to others."[1] Two points should be noted here. First, Mill is concerned only with the exercise of power. Precisely how broadly one should interpret 'power' is unclear. However, it does not include legislation which does not limit liberty, i.e., legislation of the benefit-conferring and private-arranging types, although limits upon the types of private arrangements which can be made are included. Second, Mill does not restrict his principle to political authority. He was as much concerned with the exercise of unofficial social pressure as he was with political authority.

Mill's principle involves two claims: first, that power can be exercised over a person to prevent him from harming others; second, that this purpose is the only acceptable one for exercising power over others. This chapter is concerned only with Mill's first claim. The second one is a denial of the acceptability of any other purpose. Since a positive privacy principle has already been shown to be acceptable, Mill's second claim appears to be false. However, he might have included protection of privacy as protection from harm by others. Hence, the correctness of his second claim—that no other principles are acceptable—depends upon the soundness of the arguments for other principles presented in subsequent chapters.

Taken literally, Mill's principle provides a reason for limiting all sorts of actions which most people do not think should be controlled. For example, suppose X opens a clothing store in competition with Y. Since X is a more shrewd and economical businessman, he undercuts Y's prices and Y goes out of business. Y might well claim that he has been harmed, that "there oughta be a law" prohibiting such strong competition. Although most people believe competition should be regulated to ensure that it is fair, they do not think it should be prohibited altogether. Thus Mill's principle appears to be too strong in this case.

Mill himself recognized that such activities are often desirable; indeed, he was generally an advocate of free trade.[2] The conduct of citizens which Mill thought could be limited is conduct damaging "the interests of one another, or rather certain interests which, either by express legal provision or by tacit understanding, ought to be considered as rights."[3] However, Mill's description of the types of harm which may be prevented is not satisfactory. He essentially asserted that power may be exercised to prevent persons damaging the interests of others which legally or morally ought to be protected. But the question is, what are these interests? Hence, his account is circular. Power ought to be used to prevent damage to those interests which ought to be protected by the exercise of power.

Despite their inadequacy, Mill's formulations of the principle and what constitutes harm do indicate the general direction in which to look for more adequate formulations. What is needed is a specification of the kinds of harm which count for the application of the principle. Since only some types of harm count, an easy way to indicate this point is to introduce a technical term, 'injury', which will be used to indicate those harms which count for the private harm principle. Moreover, Mill's formulation suggests that injury relates to a person's interests. Accepting this suggestion, it is necessary to explicate the concept of interest for use in the private harm principle. It is also important for the principles considered in Chapter VII.

'Interest' has many uses. One may speak of what a person's interests are in the sense of what he is interested in, what he likes to do or investigate. One may also speak about what is in a person's interest. Usually, but not always, a person is interested in things which are in his interest. However, even though something may be in a person's interest he may be uninterested in it. Finally, one may speak about what a person has an interest in. Some theorists take this last usage as basic for defining injury, but that blurs the distinction between what a person is interested in and what is in his interest. Thus, the expression 'L is in X's interest' appears more appropriate. Unfortunately, however, philosophers have proposed many different definitions for the expression. One proposed is that it is equivalent to 'X wants L'. However, there are crucial objections to this definition. As noted above, something may be in a person's interest but he may not want it. He may not realize that it is in his interest. Indeed, the fact that L is in X's interest is a good reason for his wanting it. Thus, one cannot define its being in his interest in terms of his wanting it. Moreover, even if X wants L, it makes sense to say that it may not be in his interest:

parents frequently do not let children have certain things which they want because they do not think it is in their interest to have them.

A second proposed definition equates 'L is in X's interest' with 'L will give X more pleasure than any alternative open to him'. Since this definition basically rests upon hedonism, it is open to most of the objections to that view. There are more purposes and motives for human behavior than gaining pleasure. Also, a lawyer may be given power of attorney and told to look after one's interests while one is away. He can do so without knowing in any detail what gives one pleasure. Thus, this proposal is also unsatisfactory.

A third definition equates 'L is in X's interest' with 'L would be a justifiable claim on the part of X'. To this definition Brian Barry objects that it makes perfectly good sense to say, "L is in X's interest, but would it be justifiable for him to claim it?"[4] However, Barry's objection rests on an ambiguity as to what is justifiable. One must distinguish between 'L would be a justifiable claim by X' and 'it would be justifiable for X to claim L'. The second expression is concerned with when a person may appropriately make a claim, while the first is concerned with when the claim itself would be appropriate. It may be justifiable for X to claim L without the claim itself being justifiable. Conversely, a person may have a justifiable claim but may not be justified in making it. For example, one may have a justifiable claim that an old, impoverished person pay one a thousand dollars, but if one is very rich and does not need the money, one may not be justified in making the claim. Precisely this point was made when banks foreclosed on home mortgages during the Great Depression of the 1930s. Barry's objection is thus inappropriate, for X may have a justifiable claim to L, but it may not be justifiable for him to claim it.

Nonetheless, while Barry's objection is not satisfactory, there is a crucial objection to the third definition. L may be in X's interest, but his claim to it may not be justifiable. In deciding whether or not claims are justifiable, more may be involved than a person's interests. The interests of others may also have to be considered. Thus, it may well be in X's interest to have Y's television set, but it does not follow that X's claim to the television set is justifiable.

Virginia Held offers what she takes to be a modified version of this third definition. She contends that 'L is in the interest of X' is equivalent to 'a claim by or in behalf of X for L is asserted as justifiable'.[5] As stated, that is certainly untrue. The expression 'L is in the interest of X' is not about anyone's asserting anything, yet Held's proposed equivalence states that a claim is asserted as justifiable. Put another way, L may be in the interest of X without anyone's ever asserting his claim. Put still another way, Held is offering an equivalence in terms of someone's *making* a claim, but surely the best one can say for 'L is in the interest of X' is that X *has* a claim (of some sort) to L.

One might try to modify Held's definition in at least two ways. First, one might contend that it is not that the claim *is* asserted, but that someone *could* assert it. Then 'L is in the interest of X' would be equivalent to 'a claim by or in behalf of X for L is assertible as justifiable'. That equivalence is surely too weak. A claim by X for L is assertible as justifiable even if L is not in X's interest; that is, on this construction, 'L is in the interest of X' would be true no matter what L happened to be. Almost any claim, no matter how far-fetched, is assertible as justifiable.

Second, one may say that the point is not what people can assert, but what there is a good reason to assert. There should be some good reason why X should have L, even though, everything considered, perhaps he ought not to have L. Thus, one might reformulate the definition as follows: 'L is in X's interest' is equivalent to 'a claim by or in behalf of X for L is prima facie justifiable (there is a good reason to support it)'. This reformulation also avoids the objection to the original equivalence, that L would be a justifiable claim by X. The reformulation does not imply that, everything considered, X ought to have L, only that there is a good reason for his having L.

However, even this reformulation is open to a decisive objection. It has reversed the relationship between interests and reasons for claims. L is not in X's interest because there is a reason for his claim to it; instead, the fact that L is in his interest is a reason for his claim to it. Put another way, it makes perfectly good sense to say, "a claim by or in behalf of X for L is prima facie justifiable because L is in X's interest." On the proposed definition, however, this statement would be equivalent to saying "L is in X's interest because L is in X's interest." In short, the fact that something is in a person's interest is a reason in favor of his claim to it, not vice versa.

Despite the inadequacy of all these proposed definitions, they do contain elements of an adequate one. Interests, as the first definition suggests, are related to a person's wants. What is in a person's interest must somehow affect the fulfillment of his wants. And the discussion of the third proposed definition suggests that there is a difference between something being in a person's interest and its being justifiable for him to have it. Moreover, although something may be in a person's interest, it may be that, everything considered, he should choose something else more in his interest. Thus, the fact that something is in a person's interest is not a sufficient reason, even on self-interested considerations alone, for him to choose it.

While what is in a person's interest must be related to his desires and wants, it cannot simply be what he wants. Held recognizes that a normative aspect is involved in judgments of interests, but she misidentifies it. To speak of something being in a person's interest means that it is, in some sense, "good for him." Thus, an evaluation is made of the effect of L upon the person, and this evaluation pertains to L's fulfilling his desires or wants. If one assumes that people have a prima facie claim to that which is good for them, then the fact that L is in X's interest implies that X has a prima facie claim to L. But the basic evaluation rests upon L's fulfilling X's wants.

For L to be good for X, its overall effect on X must be beneficial. L might, for example, lead to the fulfillment of one of X's desires but frustrate several others. If these desires are of roughly equal weight, then L would not be good but bad for X. In determining that L is good for X, one must compare or evaluate its total effect on the fulfillment of X's wants. Thus, 'L is in X's interest' is equivalent to 'L would make X more able to fulfill his self-regarding wants (everything considered)'.[6] Similarly, 'L is contrary to X's interest' is equivalent to 'L would make X less able to fulfill his self-regarding wants (everything considered)'.

Several elements of these definitions require explication. First, the term 'ability': a person is able to do something if there is nothing which prevents his doing it if he wants to do it. Thus, the concept of ability is closely related to the concept of freedom. However, only things which human beings can alter are limits to freedom. Conditions which prevent a person from being able to do something are not so restricted. A genetic defect may make a person unable to do something. There can be degrees of ability, just as there are degrees of freedom. Even if a person can do something, it may be more or less easy for him to do it. A person may be able to paint a room with a one-inch paint brush, but it would be easier if he had a paint roller. Thus, providing him with a paint roller may be in his interest. To say that L makes X more able to fulfill his self-regarding wants means either that he can fulfill some wants which he could not fulfill without L or that it is easier for him to fulfill them than it would be without L.

Second, self-regarding wants are those which essentially refer to oneself. A desire for other people to have something for their own sake—for example, for one's children to receive a good education—is not self-regarding. Here one must distinguish between the fulfillment of the want and its satisfaction. The fulfillment of a want or desire consists in the desired state of affairs obtaining; its satisfaction consists in the affective state of a person who believes that the desired state of affairs obtains. A desire that one's children have a good education does not become self-regarding merely because their failure to receive it will cause one to be dissatisfied. A want is self-regarding if the description of the state of affairs which would fulfill it essentially refers to oneself. 'One's children having a good education' refers to oneself only in that the persons whose education is in question are described by reference to oneself, as 'one's children'. However, this reference is not essential, for they could be referred to by name. A desire is not self-regarding if there is a description of the desired state of affairs which does not refer to oneself, even if that is not the description under which the state of affairs is desired. However, one's existence may not be necessary for the existence of the state of affairs which would fulfill a self-regarding desire. A desire for a good posthumous reputation is self-regarding because there is no description of the desired state of affairs which does not refer to one.

Use of this concept of self-regarding wants in the definition of interests does not imply that a person cannot be mistaken about what is in his interest, nor that a person necessarily wants policies adopted which are in his interest. A person may not realize the effect a policy will have on fulfilling his desires and thus may support a policy which is not in fact in his interest and may oppose one which is. Moreover, even if he recognizes that a policy is in his interest he may still oppose it. He may think that it would be unfair.

Held has objected to definitions of 'L is in X's interest' on the basis of self-regarding desires. She contends that a person may have an interest in promoting the well-being of others, e.g., in promoting civil rights.[7] Her claim is true, but she is speaking of what one may be interested in, not what is in one's interest. One may promote a policy, yet recognize that it is contrary to one's interest: one may support some civil rights activity because it is just. Such policies cannot suddenly become in one's interest simply because one decides to promote justice. If that were the case, there would be no conflict between duty and interest so long as one was strongly interested in doing one's duty. Unfortunately, being moral is not that easy.

However, Held's objection does indicate a difficulty in restricting harm to interests which are defined by self-regarding desires. A policy is not in one's interest because it accords with a principle one has adopted. However, one may have desires which are not self-regarding and are not matters of principle, e.g., one's concern for one's children. And non-fulfillment or frustration of these desires might be said to constitute injury to oneself. Physical injury to one's children may also be considered as injury or harm to oneself.

However, there are good theoretical reasons for not including desires and interests regarding others as a basis for injury under the private harm principle (and, *mutatis mutandis*, other legislative principles developed in later chapters). First, as discussed in the section "Acceptance Conditions," arguments in favor of legislative principles should not assume a concern for others. However, in this case one is not assuming such a concern but only contending that if there is such a concern, then it should be considered to be in a person's interest. Second, it makes the calculation of the effects of policies preventing injury much more complicated, if not impossible. Suppose X and Y desire each other's well-being, and Z beats up X. Z has injured X, but because of Y's concern for X's well-being, he has also injured Y. But since X is concerned for Y's well-being and Y has been injured, X has suffered further injury. Obviously, one is here faced with a possibly infinite regress. Third, desires and wants regarding others need not be for the welfare of others; they may be desires to do them harm. Suppose X hates Y, and Z helps Y out of some difficulty. If one includes X's desires for others as interests included in injury to him, then Z has injured X in the process of helping Y.

Nevertheless, one may indirectly include adverse effects upon wants and desires regarding others as a basis for injury. If X has a concern for Y, and Z's conduct in injuring Y so disturbs X as to adversely affect the fulfillment of his self-regarding wants, Z has also injured X. However, Z has injured X only because he has prevented the fulfillment of X's self-regarding wants. For example, suppose Z negligently runs down X's child in his automobile, and X witnesses the accident. If X suffers severe shock and requires medical attention, Z has also injured X.[8] The precise conditions under which such injury may be said to occur need not be spelled out here.

The crucial point is that X's interests are involved only if there is a effect upon his self-regarding wants. Consequently, it suffices to define interests in terms of self-regarding wants.

So far nothing has been said about the range of L, about what kinds of things may be in a person's interest. It would appear that all kinds of things could be in a person's interest—actions, policies, situations, goods, etc. Barry contends that the range of L is limited to actions and policies.[9] This contention raises several problems. A farmer might assert that the current situation of no price controls on farm products is in his interest. However, there may not be any deliberate policy: the government may never have considered the question. Nonetheless, a farmer probably would not make the remark unless some alternative had been proposed, and Barry is willing to agree that the continuance of the status quo is itself a policy.

This last point raises the question of whether 'L is in X's interest' is always at least covertly comparative, as Barry also contends.[10] There is a sense in which this claim is true. L is in X's interest if it makes him more capable of fulfilling his self-regarding wants. To determine this, one must see what his situation is now and what it would be were policy L adopted. Thus, it only makes sense for the farmer to speak of the current situation as in his interest if he is comparing it with some other, i.e., one with price controls. If one counts the current situation as a policy, then all judgments about what is in a person's interest compare his ability to fulfill his self-regarding wants in two different sets of conditions. However, one does not have to compare two policies altering the present situation. Thus, to say that L is in X's interest means it will make him more capable than he is at present of fulfilling his self-regarding wants.

One might, then, define a person's interests as all those L's which are in his interest. However, the range of L has been limited to actions and policies in this discussion, and philosophers and legal scholars frequently speak of a person's interests in health, financial security, etc., which are not actions or policies. The expression 'X has an interest in G' can be explicated in terms of what is in X's interest. 'X has an interest in G' refers to those items or conditions—goods—which enable X to fulfill his self-regarding wants. The range of G, in effect, is those things which actions or policies in X's interest would provide. Hence, X has an interest in G if and only if, other things being equal, an action or policy providing X with G would be in his interest. For example, assuming everything else to be equal, a policy which gave X more money would be in his interest. Thus, X has an interest in having more money, and having more money is one of X's interests. The various things in which X has an interest are closely related to his self-regarding wants, e.g., physical health.

PRIVATE HARM

The point of explicating the concept of interest is to provide a more precise notion of injury. It is sometimes said that injury involves the invasion of an interest.[11] However, not all actions which adversely affect one interest of a person constitute injury. An action may adversely affect one interest of a person but may promote several others. Consequently, for X to be injured by an action or policy L, L must be contrary to X's interest. Of course, if it is, it must adversely affect his interest in some G. Usually injuries primarily affect one interest of a person; for example, a robbery primarily affects a person's interest in having money.

For purposes of the private harm principle, however, an injury need not in fact make one less able to fulfill wants. If Flick throws a knife at Fred and misses, Fred will hardly agree that Flick's liberty should not be limited since he was not injured. Instead, he will believe that Flick's freedom creates a danger to him. So one is concerned not only to prevent others from actually damaging one's interests but also to prevent their putting one's interests at risk. However, almost all actions risk the interests of others; it is only unreasonable risks which constitute injury.

Legislators have to determine whether certain types of actions create unreasonable risks to the interests of others. There are some kinds of considerations to be taken into account in deciding whether or not A, an action of Y, creates an unreasonable risk to X's interests: (1) the probability that A would decrease X's ability to fulfill his self-regarding wants; (2) the seriousness of the harm to X, i.e., how contrary to his interest these results would be; (3) the probability that A would achieve Y's goal; (4) the importance of the goal Y is seeking, i.e., how much it is in his interest; (5) the possibility of other actions Y could perform to achieve his goal.[12]

Even if Y's action creates an unreasonable risk of decreasing X's ability to fulfill his self-regarding wants, Y may still not have injured X in the technical sense. Suppose X and Y are playing football and Y tackles X, causing him a shoulder separation. Few people would say that political authority should limit Y's freedom to do so, provided X is playing voluntarily. This point rests upon an old maxim: *Volenti non fit injuria*. The underlying principle is that if someone voluntarily participates in an activity involving a risk to him, any harm which results is not injury for which others are responsible. Mill was aware of this maxim but rejected it because, taken literally, it implies that no one is injured if he consents to an action.[13] Mill correctly believed that more than mere consent is needed to prevent the harm being injury. If the consent was the result of fraud, as the courts recognized, the person has been injured. Thus, Mill suggested that harm does not constitute injury if people are affected "only with their free, voluntary, and undeceived consent and participation."[14]

Thus, a criterion of application for the harm principle which may be incorporated in the concept of injury is as follows: a person is not injured by actions contrary to his interest if he voluntarily participates in the activity of which they are a part. By 'voluntarily participates' is meant participates under no compulsion, no psychological disturbance such as that caused by anger or alcohol, no misrepresentation, and no easily avoidable ignorance.[15] In part, these conditions help ensure that a person is reasonable when he consents. If these conditions are not met, a person will not be able to make reasonable choices. Further, that a person so participates does not merely create a presumption that he is not injured; it establishes it conclusively.[16] Thus, no matter how battered a prize-fighter may be, if he voluntarily participated, he was not injured in the technical sense. This voluntary participation criterion explains why a clothing merchant driven out of business by his competitor is not injured—he voluntarily participated in a competitive activity. However, he would have been injured had the competition been unfair. Fairness is usually based upon rules set up to regulate a competitive activity, and the businessman only consented to participate in the competition as regulated by these rules.

Injury must be distinguished from non-benefit. If X stands on the end of a pier and watches Y, a perfect stranger, drown when he could easily have thrown him a lifeline, then most people would say X has injured Y. However, if X refuses to give Y five thousand dollars, few people would say he has injured Y. Yet both of X's actions would have been in Y's interest. Some basis seems to be needed to distinguish those cases in which failure to help constitutes injury from those in which it merely constitutes non-benefit.

Joel Feinberg suggests that injury and non-benefit may be partially distinguished on the basis of needs. X injures Y if he fails to give Y something Y needs. X merely fails to benefit Y, if he fails to give Y something which Y does not need. Yet elsewhere Feinberg defines needs as things the lack of which will injure a person.[17] Thus, X injures Y when he fails to give Y something Y needs, but Y needs something only if his failure to have it injures him. Feinberg's analysis is unsatisfactory since it is circular. The crucial question thus appears to be how one determines what Y does and does not need.

No approach based on needs will do. The point is to distinguish those things which Y is entitled to have from those which he is not entitled to have, in such a way that failure to provide what he is entitled to have constitutes injury. The concept of need is brought in because presumably Y is entitled to what he needs. For intelligibility, the concept of need presupposes a triadic relation: Y needs G for A. These conditions must be spelled out. If Y says, "I need a screwdriver," it always makes sense for X to ask, "What for?" If Y is not entitled to the A for which he needs G, then the fact that Y needs G for A will not support his claim that he is entitled to have G. For example, if Y wants the screwdriver in order to break into a house, the fact that he needs it does not support the claim that he is entitled to it or ought to have it. Thus, needs claims alone do not provide reasons for a person having something: they presuppose that the person is entitled to A for which he needs G. Yet the point of considering needs was to determine what people are entitled to have, so that failure to provide it constitutes injury.

Another approach to distinguishing injury from non-benefit is a modification of Feinberg's approach.[18] It defines injury as impairment of a person's welfare interests. Roughly, welfare interests are interests the fulfillment of which is indispensable to the fulfillment of most other interests and goals; they include interest in life, in physical health, etc. On this view, failure to throw a lifeline to a drowning person prolongs the non-fulfillment of such interests and at least exacerbates harm or injury, while failure to give a person five thousand dollars does not usually affect the fulfillment of his welfare interests and so is non-benefit.

However, this analysis is ambiguous. It may mean that a person is injured only by conduct which affects his having G when he has a welfare interest in G. On this interpretation, if one steals two hundred dollars from a very rich person who does not need it to fulfill his welfare interests, one has not injured him. Thus, the private harm principle would not provide a reason for legislation to prevent theft from the rich. The analysis may mean, however, that a person is injured by conduct which impairs interests which are included in a person's welfare. On this interpretation, wealth would be an interest included in a person's welfare, so conduct impairing it would be injury. But, as failure to provide a person five thousand dollars would adversely affect his interest in wealth, it too would be injury.

Neither of X's actions—his failing to throw a lifeline or to give the five thousand dollars—involve his injuring Y. X's failure to give the money to Y is not contrary to Y's interest: it does not make Y less able to fulfill his self-regarding wants. Nor does X's failure to throw Y a lifeline injure him: the drowning Y is not able to fulfill any of his self-regarding wants, so X does not make him less able to do so. Of course, this contention does not imply that X has no duty to throw the lifeline to Y, but that duty, like many others, is a duty to benefit others. One can see this point if one compares the example of the drowning man with the parable of the Good Samaritan (Luke 10 : 33). Neither the Good Samaritan nor the Levite injured the man by the road, but the Samaritan, unlike the Levite, aided him. Likewise, X is not drowning Y—he is not forcing his head under—so he is not injuring Y any more than the Levite injured the man by the road. In failing to throw Y a lifeline, X is acting like the Levite who passed by the injured man without aiding him. Thus, injury involves actions contrary to another's interest, while non-benefit is failure to perform actions in another's interest.

The analysis of injury is not yet complete. The concept of L being in X's interest was defined by its increasing his ability to fulfill his self-regarding wants. A policy may increase one's ability to fulfill one want while decreasing one's ability to fulfill another want. To decide whether or not the policy is in one's interest, one must be able to decide which want is more important, i.e., to rank one's wants. Such a ranking is also needed to decide which of two incompatible freedoms is preferable. Similarly, in considering whether Y's action creates an unreasonable risk to X's interests, one must consider the importance of the interests in question. Thus, some priority of self-regarding wants is needed in order to specify injury; some self-regarding wants may be too trivial to be included in a legislative principle.

Richard Taylor suggests that there are only three ways in which men can injure one another—by assault, by theft, or by fraud.[19]

While he defines each of these terms fairly broadly, he primarily restricts them to physical damage and loss of wealth. He claims that each of these types of harm or injury is natural and that all others are conventional, i.e., dependent upon what a person has learned or upon his society's culture. Thus Taylor would restrict the private harm principle to natural injury or harm.

The distinction between natural and conventional harm or injury is inadequate for the use Taylor makes of it. Property, as Taylor recognizes, depends upon cultural conventions specifying what properly belongs to people. But, he claims, the resentment that one feels in being deprived of property is not culturally conditioned.[20] Unfortunately for Taylor's thesis, neither is the resentment one feels towards conventional harms or injuries. For example, Taylor wishes to exclude whatever offends one's fundamental moral or religious beliefs from the category of natural harm or injury. However, the resentment one feels toward the desecration of sacred religious objects or toward gross immorality is also natural. Classifications of sacred objects and immoral conduct may, like property, depend upon conventions, but the resentment does not. Hence, if one needs only the feeling of resentment to be natural, then almost all harms or injuries are natural. If the loss which causes resentment must be specifiable independent of conventions, then there are very few, if any, natural harms or injuries.

A better method for determining injury is simply to classify and rank, so far as possible, different interests. When a person has an interest in something, that interest is usually based on one or two fundamental wants or desires. Since interests are defined in terms of self-regarding wants, a classification and ranking of wants will provide the same for interests. Such a ranking is based upon the notion of a reasonable person. In a way, however, it further specifies the psychology of such a person, for it ranks his desires or wants.

The most important want is for continued life. Without continued life, few of one's other self-regarding wants can be fulfilled or exist. While it is a necessary condition for the fulfillment of other self-regarding wants, mere life itself may not be of much value. For example, there would be little reason to continue existing were one to be continually unconscious. Thus, continued life is primarily an instrumental good. Bodily integrity and capacity appear to be the object of the second most important want. This ranking may be partially justified by the greater pain and chance of loss of life more often involved in bodily injury than in other types of injury. Gunshot wounds, knife cuts, and beatings, for example, involve significant pain and risk to life. But even if the pain and risk of loss of life are rather small, people still have a strong desire for physical integrity. If one were compelled to undergo the amputation of a finger in a hospital, the chances of one's dying would be small, and anesthesia would prevent most pain. Yet most people would believe they had been grievously injured were nothing wrong with the finger. However, the strength of the want for bodily integrity obviously depends on the extent to which violation of bodily integrity may result in incapacity and pain.

One also has desires for psychological states. One may not want to be emotionally upset or unhappy. A reasonable person, as defined earlier, is not mentally abnormal, unreasonable, or unintelligent, and presumably such a person will not want to become so; that is, people desire a "normal" mental capacity. Hence, the main forms of psychological injury may be restricted to those which make one unintelligent, unreasonable, or mentally abnormal. If X does something which makes his wife angry but does not affect her in any other way, he has not caused her psychological injury. If, however, he systematically undertakes to drive her insane, then he has caused her psychological injury, according to the private harm principle, for a person who suffers psychological injury is almost certainly less able to fulfill his other self-regarding wants.

A desire for wealth, especially in the form of personal property, may be next in importance. While people's desires for wealth vary, almost everyone has a desire for personal property, i.e., possessions such as clothing, a place to live, a car, etc. A minimal amount of personal wealth is necessary for fulfilling other wants such as those for food. Other forms of wealth are also desired, but not as much. All major economic systems recognize personal property: one owns one's toothbrush and clothes even in communist countries.[21] The difference between capitalist and communist or socialist systems is the extent of private ownership or private property permitted.

Finally, most people also have a desire for prestige or reputation. Such a desire is frequently very important to them. However, a decrease in a person's reputation usually stems from communication by others. Protecting a person's prestige by political authority may conflict with the principle of freedom of communication. Nonetheless, a person has an interest in his reputation. The conflict with freedom of communication must be settled by balancing freedom of communication against the injury which it may cause others. However, by the criterion of deceit, the principle of freedom of communication does not apply to false statements about one. And the personal injury in loss of reputation may also affect one's other interests, e.g., in wealth.

It is obvious why a reasonable person would wish to avoid being injured. Injury makes one less able to fulfill basic self-regarding wants. A reasonable person wants the ability to fulfill his self-regarding wants. If a person wants something, then he wants the conditions which will enable him to have it (at least if he knows that such conditions are necessary to fulfill his desire). Hence, since people do not want to be injured, they will desire to have others prevented from injuring them. Since the wants involved in injury are basic ones, the desire to have others prevented from injuring one will be strong. The private harm principle may be formulated as follows: there is a reason for legislation that protects individual persons from injury by others. This legislative principle is a strong one.

There is another way of looking at the justification of the private harm principle, namely, as providing for peaceable settlement of conflicts of interest. Given any item of property, say, a sofa, it would frequently be in the interest of both X and Y to have it. Suppose Y has it. If X took it from Y, this would be in X's interest but contrary to Y's interest. Thus there is a conflict of interest. If political authority does not determine to whom the sofa belongs and does not ensure that the owner retains it, X and Y are apt to resort to coercive power to determine who gets it. The result is likely to be injury to both of them. Political authority determining and protecting ownership prevents conflicts of interest which may erupt into fights. Thus, by acting to prevent one person from injuring another, political authority brings about the peaceable settlement of conflicts of interest.[22] Indeed, the threat to punish X for attempting to take the sofa from Y may remove the conflict of interest. With the prospect of punishment, it may no longer be in X's interest to try to take it.

Without having a full set of acceptable legislative principles, it is impossible to make conclusive judgments about what legislation is justifiable. However, certain general points may be made about the application of the private harm principle. First, it may be thought that a negative private harm principle is also needed.[23] Sometimes laws are objected to as creating private injury. A dramatic example occurred when pickpocketing was a capital crime in England. The public executions drew large crowds, with the result that during executions more pockets were picked. Such a law against pickpocketing appears to create private harm, and a negative private harm principle appears to be needed to argue against it. However, this contention is not correct. Legislation is to be evaluated by its efficacy or probable efficacy in preventing injury by others. As the law against pickpocketing simply failed to prevent people from injuring others, the private harm principle did not provide a reason for it. In the absence of any other good reason for it, there was no reason for its existence, and there was a strong liberty-regarding reason against it.

Second, one must balance principles for and against legislation in evaluating it. Some positive principles may not be able to out-weigh the negative principles against certain types of legislation. Hence, it is useful to consider whether there is any type of legislation which a principle alone may not justify. It might never be capable of outweighing the principle against some type of liberty-limiting legislation, or it might simply be inappropriate for some type of legislation. If a principle by itself can justify a type of legislation, then whenever it is relevant it can support such legislation even if it is not sufficient by itself to justify the particular legislation in question. However, if a principle by itself cannot justify legislation of a certain type, then it will not here be taken to support such legislation. (One could develop a theory without this last assumption, but it would have to be much more complicated than the one developed here.) The private harm principle, however, is not re-stricted in this sense; that is, by itself it can justify any type of legislation. The easiest way to show that it is not so restricted is to consider the types of legislation against which there are the strongest negative principles, i.e., penal and compulsory treatment legislation.

The private harm principle may support both penal and com-pulsory treatment legislation; that is, by itself it may provide a sufficient reason for such legislation. For a reasonable person, avoidance of some injuries is worth the loss of some freedom. For example, protection from murder is worth having one's freedom to murder others limited by the threat of a ten-year prison sentence. It might not, however, be worth the loss of freedom which is in-volved in capital punishment for murderers. One must balance the chance for the individual's greater loss of freedom against his increased protection. If capital punishment is no more of a deterrent to murder than a life sentence, then there is no reason to favor the loss of freedom in capital punishment over the lesser loss in life imprisonment. Similarly, the private harm principle might justify compulsory treatment. One might be willing to trade the loss of freedom involved in treatment of pyromania for protection from pyromaniacs. One might become a pyromaniac, but protection from fires set by pyromaniacs is worth the risk of loss of freedom in compulsory treatment of pyromania.

Since the private harm principle supports penal and compulsory treatment legislation, it also supports grievance-remedial, burden-imposing, and administrative-regulatory legislation, as the negative principles against them are not as strong. It further supports benefit-conferring and private-arranging legislation, since there is no negative liberty-regarding principle against them. However, the private harm principle is rarely relevant to private-arranging, benefit-conferring, and burden-imposing legislation. It is very difficult to see how legislation of these types can prevent private harm. Nonetheless, restrictions upon the types of private arrangements which can be made may prevent private harm. Some restrictions can prevent fraud. Likewise, some people contend that the most effective way to minimize crime is not by the use of penal legislation but by removing the causes of crime—poverty, racism, and sexual discrimination. To the extent that providing people with certain benefits does indeed reduce the chances that they will injure others by murder, theft, etc., the private harm principle gives a reason for legislation which will do so.

PUBLIC HARM

In the two previous sections, Mill's harm principle was developed into an acceptable private harm principle. Mill thought the harm principle supported the limitation of liberty to do more than merely prevent one citizen from injuring another. He thought it also provided a good reason for requiring each person to bear "his share (to be fixed on some equitable principle) of the labors and sacrifices incurred for defending the society or its members from injury and molestation."[24] Mill had in mind some form of burden-imposing legislation. However, to require one to bear a share of labor and sacrifice for the protection of society does not directly prevent one from harming others. Thus, a principle other than the private harm one is needed to support such legislation.

Feinberg has formulated a public harm principle to prevent "impairment of institutional practices that are in the public interest." He applies this principle to a broad range of legislation including taxation to support the Social Security fund, parks, libraries, museums, etc.[25] The lack of such things may injure people by depriving them of what they need. However, there are difficulties with Feinberg's principle. First, one cannot "impair" an institutional practice which does not exist. Thus, taken literally, his principle does not support the introduction of compulsory Social Security taxes, for there is no institutional practice of 'social security' which may be impaired. Such legislation, rather than preventing impairment of an existing practice, institutes a practice in the public interest. Second, the classification of libraries, national parks, and museums as needs is very questionable. Moreover, in the previous section his analysis of needs was shown to be unsatisfactory. Third, such a principle, as used by Feinberg, places considerations of quite different weight under one heading. A better understanding of the strengths of these considerations can be achieved by dividing his one principle into several different ones. Most of these are discussed in Chapter VII, "Common Good," below. Only one very strong principle will be developed here.

The proposed public harm principle is as follows: there is a reason for legislation that prevents impairment of the operation of public institutions. Before considering reasons for accepting it, two phrases must be clarified—'public institutions' and 'impairment of the operation'. Institutions are complex human activities governed by rules. Thus, the government, in the broad sense of the people in positions of authority, is an institution. Likewise, banks, colleges, and businesses are institutions. A small business such as a corner grocery is not usually thought of as an institution. However, it is not odd to speak of the institution of corner groceries, meaning the general pattern and activity of corner groceries.

The difficult task is to separate public institutions from private ones. As noted in Chapter IV, 'public' and 'private' are contrasting terms. One way of defining public institutions would be as those providing goods and services essential to society. Yet while General Motors and IBM provide goods essential to society, they are not usually thought of as public institutions. A variation would be to classify as public institutions those providing goods and services of such importance to society that if they were not privately provided the government would be justified in doing so. However, such a definition is also unsatisfactory. There are several private postal businesses in the United States. They are not considered public institutions simply because the government would be (and is) justified in providing postal service.

Perhaps the best way to define public institutions, then, is with respect to their control by government. Government is the clearest example of a public institution. To the extent that it controls an institution, the latter is a public one. The difficulty is to specify the degree of governmental control necessary for an institution to be classified as a public one. For purposes of preventing racial discrimination, the Supreme Court has generally held that very little government control is necessary to make an institution public. All businesses providing goods and services are established under state or federal laws and so are deemed public. However, social clubs such as the Loyal Order of Moose, even though àlso subject to some state laws, e.g., liquor licenses, have been held not to be public and therefore to be entitled to exclude potential members on racial grounds.[26]

As the term is used here, a 'public institution' must be under substantial governmental control. The best way to indicate the amount of control required is to give examples. Besides the government itself, public institutions include agencies and institutions set up and funded by the government such as schools and universities. Further, if a government owns businesses, such as nationalized coal mines, then they are public institutions. In many instances the government may not own but may strongly regulate businesses, especially those which by their nature must be monopolies, e.g., electricity and telephone companies. Thus, such privately owned utilities are included.

There are also problems in interpreting 'impairment of the operation'. The clearest case of an action which would impair the operation of a public institution is treason. 'Treason' against the United States is defined in the Constitution as "levying War against them, or in adhering to their Enemies, giving them Aid and Comfort."[27] Thus, it consists in attempting, or helping those who are attempting, to destroy the government by force. Such activity is aimed at destroying the authority by which the government operates. If successful, it would prevent the government from doing anything, for the government would cease to exist.

Levying war against a government involves killing or injuring its personnel or citizens and destroying its facilities. Thus, blowing up a military supply dump is an act of war. More generally, destroying the facilities of a public institution impairs its operation. Prior to the 1968 Democratic National Convention, some officials were alarmed by rumors that LSD might be placed in the Chicago water system. Such an action is not clearly aimed at impairing the operation of a public institution, but if one takes the aim of the water system as provision of non-contaminated drinking water, then such an action would impair the operation of a public institution. A more diabolical plot might have been to blow up the Chicago sewer system.

Another way of impairing the operation of the government is to prevent government officials and employees from performing their duties. The most obvious instance of such activity is interference with a policeman in the performance of his duty. But one may also interfere with other officials. Sit-in demonstrations may prevent office employees from carrying out their tasks. Further, at public universities preventing classes from meeting also constitutes such impairment.

More difficult cases concern the refusal to give aid or support. Suppose a policeman chasing a suspect asks a passerby to telephone police headquarters to send him help. Would the passerby's refusal constitute impairment of the policeman's performance of his duties? One's first inclination is perhaps to assert that the person is not preventing the policeman from performing his duties. It is not as though he is standing in the policeman's way. However, in most jurisdictions one is required to aid a policeman. If a policeman is merely walking his beat and asks a passerby to make his hourly call for him, the passerby is not required to do so. The difference involved is that in the first case, but not the second, there is an emergency.

A similar situation may arise with respect to military conscription. Some people claim that military conscription is not justified unless a country is involved in a war which poses a clear threat to its continued existence. Thus, it is sometimes held that conscription for the Vietnam war was not justified, whereas it was for World

War II. In the latter case, there was a clear emergency and a threat that the United States government would not be able to fulfill its functions; this was not so in the former case.

Both the policeman and the conscription cases, like that of the drowning man in the previous section, appear to involve aiding or benefiting rather than impairing or injuring. One may slightly extend the public harm principle to cover them by asserting that non-aid or non-benefit constitutes impairment if, in an emergency situation, it is unlikely that the necessary function can be performed without the aid. A somewhat different approach is to specify that in emergency situations ordinary citizens become agents of the government. This approach has two advantages. First, if (as is argued in Chapter VII) one function of the government is to provide for the public welfare, and if drowning is contrary to a person's welfare, then one may assert that in an emergency an ordinary citizen, as an agent of the government, has a duty to aid a person whose welfare is threatened; that is, one can also provide a rationale for Good Samaritan situations. Second, one may also provide a rationale for a citizen who acts in an emergency having a limited tort immunity for injury caused in his good-faith attempts to aid. The citizen, as agent of the government, has governmental immunity. On either approach, the underlying concept is to perceive the citizen's conduct as necessary to the achievement of the purposes of political authority. Because of this element, the argument provided below for the public harm principle also applies to them.

There are good reasons for a reasonable person to accept the public harm principle. If there are acceptable purposes for political authority to pursue, then there are good reasons for its activities in furtherance of them. Thus, public institutions pursuing these activities are desirable and acceptable. Since the activities are desirable, impairment of them is undesirable. Not to permit political authority to protect its operation from impairment would be to deprive it of the means of pursuing its purposes. In short, if there are any other acceptable principles of legislation, then the public harm principle is acceptable. If the argument for the acceptability of the private harm principle is correct, then the public harm principle is also acceptable.

The strength of the reasons for legislation provided by the public harm principle depends upon the importance of the purpose being pursued by an institution and the risk that an impairment of its operation would cause that purpose not to be fulfilled. Since these purposes can be as important as any, the public harm principle can provide as strong a reason for legislation as any other principle. However, because of its nature, it is not usually appropriate for certain types of legislation.

The most obvious sorts of penal legislation which the public harm principle supports are those covering treason, sabotage, and assassination. However, it does include many other sorts of activity, such as bribery of public officials and perjury, which impair the operation of public institutions. The principle also supports penal legislation covering those who make secret documents public. However, the reason for such legislation must be balanced against the negative principle of freedom of communication as well as the principle against penal legislation. Thus, it must be clear that the information, if made public, would indeed seriously impair important operations. The development of special weapons systems, such as the atomic bomb in World War II, may be of such importance as to justify secrecy. But the secrecy of the myriad reports and papers currently classified in most countries cannot be justified. Frequently, such material is kept secret years after it has ceased to be relevant. Such restrictions on freedom of communication do not in fact protect any governmental operation from impairment. Moreover, much "secret" material concerns trivial matters knowledge of which could not have seriously impaired significant governmental operations even at the time of their classification, much less later.

Further, even if the purpose pursued by a public institution is important, short interruptions in its operations may not be sufficient to justify penal legislation. Consider legislation prohibiting strikes by public employees. Traditionally, all government employees have been prohibited from striking. However, there are good reasons for distinguishing among public employees in this respect. One may distinguish compensable and non-compensable impairment. A compensable injury is one for which a person is entitled to compensation. A compensable impairment is one which can be made up. If policemen go on strike, then political authority has lost the ability to prevent private injury. The purpose simply cannot be fulfilled. However, if teachers go on strike, it may still be possible to pursue the purpose of education to the same extent. The time lost from classes can be, and usually is, made up at the end of the school year. The impairment of activity can be compensated.

If the public harm principle can justify legislation over the negative principles of freedom of communication and penal legislation, then it can justify any other types of liberty-limiting legislation. It is difficult, however, to imagine practical situations in which it might support compulsory treatment legislation. A person in a high position of political authority might develop a condition, e.g., alcoholism, which would impair the operation of a public institution. However, the simplest remedy would be to remove him from office; compulsory treatment goes beyond removing the impairment. Administrative-regulatory legislation is quite frequent in this area. Many regulations require businesses to report all sorts of information such as employee earnings to the government. Grievance-remedial and private-arranging legislation do not appear very appropriate to the public harm principle. They are primarily compensatory and facilitative, while the public harm principle is basically preventive. However, some grievance-remedial legislation, especially that which provides an injunction as a remedy, may be of importance in preventing public harm.

Finally, benefit-conferring and burden-imposing legislation may be supported by the public harm principle. Benefit-conferring legislation may be needed to support activities the absence of which would impair government operations. Direct grants or subsidies may be made to businesses supplying essential materials for a government operation, e.g., war materials. In the same connection, burden-imposing conscription legislation may be supported by it. Likewise, commandeering private property may be justified if without it a governmental operation would be impaired. However, such legislation, like that requiring one to aid a policeman, should be restricted to emergencies.

Taxation is also generally thought to be supported by the public harm principle. However, it is not clear that the public harm principle is always the relevant one. It only supports taxation to maintain current operations. Taxation to support new governmental activities cannot be supported by it. Hence, the only increases in taxes which it supports are those necessary to keep the public institutions operating. Public interest and welfare principles (discussed in Chapter VII below) are probably more important than the public harm principle for supporting taxation. They are the only ones which support taxation for new governmental activities. Thus, while the public harm principle is a strong one, it does not support a broad range of legislation.

VI
PATERNALISM

The previous chapter considered preventing persons from harming others as a reason for legislation. A related reason for legislation is preventing persons from harming themselves. Such a basis for legislation is called paternalism because of its obvious similarity to the authority parents have always been thought to justifiably exercise over their children. Paternalism is an ancient legal doctrine, *parens patriae*, originally based on considering the king to be the kinsman of certain incompetent subjects.[1] Today, paternalist considerations are among the major ones offered to justify the legislative goals of the welfare state. However, the philosophical underpinnings of paternalism as a purpose for political authority have only recently been subjected to careful scrutiny, and most people are not as ready to accept paternalist principles as they are to accept the harm principles.

DEFINITION

The common premise of all paternalism is that something may be done to or for a person for his own good without his assent, or even despite his dissent. Some authors primarily define legislation or behavior as paternalistic.[2] However, since legislation may be supported by several principles, what one needs is a concept of paternalistic reasons for it. There are two key elements here. First, one must believe that it is for the good of the person to or for whom something is done. Thus, the reason does not relate to one's own good or to that of some other person (as with the private harm principle). Second, one is prepared to do it without the person's assent—even despite his denial—that it is for his own good. Thus, a parent may make a child take a bath or go to the dentist even though the child does not want to do so or think it necessary.

Ordinarily, a paternalistic reason is invoked for doing something which limits a person's liberty. However, there is a type of case in which liberty is not limited. Something may be done to a person which does not involve controlling his behavior. For example, an unconscious person might be subjected to medical treatment, e.g., a blood transfusion, which he would refuse were he conscious, and this fact might be known. Such a case might therefore involve the use of compulsory treatment legislation. Since the person is unconscious, his conduct is not controlled, nor is his liberty limited. However, since these cases are quite rare, the following discussion assumes that paternalistic reasons involve limiting liberty and uses such expressions as 'controlling a person's conduct' and 'making a person act'.

There are two main types of paternalism, "promotive" and "preservative." Promotive paternalism seeks to improve the well-being of a subject by requiring him to perform or omit actions. Preservative paternalism seeks to prevent a person from harming himself. The purpose is not to increase a person's well-being but to prevent his diminishing it. Most previous discussions have considered only preservative paternalism. While the two types are different, the justifications offered for them are frequently similar. Further, it seems that preservative paternalism is apt to be a stronger principle than promotive paternalism, for avoidance of harm is usually more strongly desired than achievement of benefits. Thus, if preservative paternalism is unacceptable, it seems likely that promotive paternalism is too. On the other hand, if promotive paternalism is acceptable, then preservative paternalism probably is too.

Paternalist principles are most apt to be confused with either the private harm or legal moralist principles. The private harm and paternalist principles are quite distinct. Although they both seek to prevent harm, they are seeking to prevent its occurring to different people. The harm principle requires that X's action cause injury to Y. Preservative paternalism requires that X's action or choice result in harm (injury) to himself. The private harm principle logically involves two distinct persons, one whose actions are controlled and another who is injured, while paternalism logically involves only one person.

Gerald Dworkin argues against this distinction, asserting that paternalism may involve controlling the actions of one person in order to protect the well-being of another. The manufacture of cigarettes might be banned in order to prevent people being harmed by smoking them. Such a restriction differs from prohibiting a person from polluting the atmosphere, he claims, because individuals can, if they choose, avoid the harm from cigarette smoking but not that from pollution. "It would be mistaken theoretically and hypocritical in practice," he writes, "to assert that our interference in such cases is just like our interference in standard cases of protecting others from harm."[3]

However, Dworkin's argument fails because he has not recognized the relevance of the private harm principle's voluntary act criterion. With the voluntary act criterion used, harm befalling a person in activities in which he voluntarily participates does not count as injury. One need not use the voluntary act criterion with the private harm principle: cigarette manufacturers then injure smokers even though the latter smoke voluntarily. With the voluntary act criterion, cigarette manufacturers do not injure voluntary smokers, but air polluters do injure others, since few people voluntarily breathe polluted air. Thus, a ban on cigarette manufacturing rests upon the private harm principle without the voluntary act criterion.

Consequently, Dworkin is correct that a ban on cigarette manufacturing differs from one on polluting the air. But the difference is not that in the former paternalism is the reason and in the latter the operative principle is that of private harm. Rather, the difference is that in the case of cigarette manufacturing the private harm principle cannot be used with the voluntary act criterion, but it may be in the case of air pollution. However, requiring warning labels on cigarette packages does not involve using the private harm principle without the voluntary act criterion; it simply ensures that people only smoke voluntarily, i.e., with full knowledge of the dangers.

The voluntary act criterion can also be used with respect to paternalism. For use with the private harm principle, the voluntary act criterion was defined as consent to, and participation in, activity by and with others. With paternalist principles, it means fully voluntarily choosing or performing acts. A man who voluntarily goes skiing and breaks a leg suffers damage or harm, but he is not injured. Of course, 'injury' is used here in a technical philosophical sense, not in a medical one. With respect to the private harm principle, the voluntary act criterion was taken as conclusively indicating that a person is not injured. At least for the present, it will not be taken as conclusive for paternalism.

Thus, there may be strong and weak versions of the paternalist principles. The weak preservative paternalist principle uses the voluntary act criterion, so actions cannot injure a man if he voluntarily chooses or performs them. The strong preservative paternalist principle does not use the voluntary act criterion, so a person's own actions may injure him even if he voluntarily chooses and performs them. As applied to promotive paternalism, the voluntary act criterion essentially implies that as far as political authority is concerned a man is the best judge of his own benefit as long as his judgment, choice, and actions are fully voluntary. Thus, a man who voluntarily fails to act in his best interest because he believes it is his duty to act otherwise acts for his own benefit so far as political authority is concerned. If the voluntary act criterion is not used, then a person is not necessarily the best judge of his own benefit even if his acts are fully voluntary. Hence, even his fully voluntary acts may not be for his own benefit. The effect in practice is that weak promotive paternalism provides a reason for controlling a person's conduct for his own benefit only if his conduct is not fully voluntary. Strong promotive paternalism provides a reason for controlling a person's conduct for his own benefit even if it is fully voluntary.

Donald H. Regan attempts to assimilate directly the paternalist principles and the private harm one.[4] He contends that for some purposes different time segments of what would ordinarily be regarded as one person may be taken as different people. Thus, X may not now be the person who occupied his body many years before. In particular, if a person's mental outlook alters drastically over a considerable period of time, then that person is not identical with the person of years ago. With respect to paternalism, then, what a person, X, voluntarily decides to do now may be construed as injuring another person, X', who many years later occupies the same body. X' may be classified as a different person from X if X' has a different attitude toward the consequences of the earlier conduct. Moreover, even if X does not change his attitude, his voluntary choice now creates a risk of injury to a possible other person, X'. For example, suppose that thirty years ago X voluntarily decided to smoke cigarettes; ten years ago he quit smoking; now he has developed cancer. Due to the change in attitude toward smoking, the person with cancer is X', a different person from the one who smoked.

There are various difficulties with this argument, particularly with respect to the concept of personal identity. Only a few brief comments may be made here. First, on only one view of identity do radical changes constitute two different individuals. On the genetic or causal view of identity, great dissimilarities do not imply nonidentity.[5] Second, one may admit that how a person should be treated depends partly on his character without claiming that if he had a different charcater he would be a different person. Third, the argument does not claim that the person suffering the consequences is in fact different from the person who made the voluntary choice, only that he might be. Thus, there are no voluntary choices which do not involve injury to others. Whatever consequences might result, one can always contend that some person might have been injured by them because the actor might develop an aversion to them. Hence, any voluntary choice may be said to risk injury to another person. Moreover, one can also always imagine a possible individual who would welcome the consequences and consider them a benefit. The distinction between injuring and benefiting others is then obliterated. While Regan's view might be revised so as to avoid this problem, it is best, as was done at the beginning of Chapter IV for the subjects of freedom, to take the people involved as persons in the ordinary sense.

Patrick Devlin has argued that paternalism leads to legal moralism.[6] Since his argument concerns only preservative paternalism, the promotive versions are not considered here. For present purposes, the legal moralist principle may be taken to state that there is a reason for legislation if its result is to decrease conduct contrary to popular morality.[7] Devlin claims that the injury which paternalism seeks to prevent must be moral as well as physical. Parents, for example, are not merely concerned with the physical well-being of their children; they also look out for their moral well-being. A reasonable paternalism would also be concerned with moral well-being. But if one seeks to prevent moral injury to people, then one must prevent them from acting contrary to strongly held rules of popular morality. So paternalism has the same practical results as legal moralism.

Devlin's arguments to the contrary notwithstanding, one does not, logically, have to move from physical to moral paternalism. First, the fact that parents are concerned with both the moral and the physical well-being of their children does not imply that the two considerations cannot be distinguished. Indeed, Devlin himself makes this distinction. Second, one may decide to protect only the physical well-being of persons because judgments of physical injury do not appear to involve controversial value judgments. For example, most people believe the loss of a limb to be injury, but there is little agreement as to whether being a homosexual is injurious. Third, an attitude which is proper toward children need not be proper toward adults. From a legal standpoint, very young children are incapable of consent and, thus, of fully voluntary actions, so that only weak paternalist principles are needed to support control of children, but that is not usually the case with adults.

Even if paternalism includes prevention of moral injury to a person, it remains logically distinct from legal moralism in two respects. First, the moral injury which paternalism seeks to prevent may be defined by either popular or rational critical morality. Thus, paternalism may have implications contrary to legal moralism if it defines moral injury by rational critical morality: for example, homosexual relations may be immoral by standards of popular morality but not by those of rational critical morality. Paternalism would not provide a reason for limiting homosexual relations, while legal moralism would. Likewise, paternalism may give a reason for limiting as morally injurious actions which are commonly thought to be permissible, e.g., drinking alcohol.

Second, even if moral injury is defined by popular morality, paternalism does not necessarily provide a reason for restricting all the actions which legal moralism does.[8] Legal moralism requires only that actions be contrary to popular morality, not that a person be morally injured by them. It follows that paternalism and legal moralism will not always provide a reason for limiting the same actions. Moral injury may take the form of corruption of a person's moral beliefs. If a man does not believe his actions are immoral, he cannot be morally injured by them. Moral paternalism does not provide a reason for limiting homosexual conduct by an adult who does not think it immoral. If it be objected that moral injury may also consist in the development of a disposition toward immoral conduct, then the argument moves back one step, for then paternalism will not give a reason for limiting homosexual conduct by practicing homosexuals. The basic point is this: someone can be so fixed in his conduct in a certain respect that conduct of the relevant sort cannot make him worse.

In the rest of this chapter, paternalism will not be taken to include a concern for a person's moral good because most discussions and uses of paternalism have not been concerned with it; because legal moralism covers the most important form of considerations of a person's moral good; and because in a society of moral pluralism, judgments of a person's moral good are extremely difficult to establish. But paternalism will not be restricted to a person's physical well-being if doing so restricts it to his physical integrity. It pertains to the basic interests of people with which the private harm principle is concerned: life, bodily integrity, psychological capacity, and personal property. Thus, the primary ingredients of a person's good are his interests.

In sum, paternalism gives a reason for legislation which promotes or preserves the well-being of the subject being controlled. All the paternalist principles are positive. Promotive paternalist principles give a reason for legislation which makes a person act to promote his well-being. The strong promotive paternalist principle does not use the voluntary act criterion, while the weak promotive paternalist principle does. Preservative paternalist principles give a reason for legislation to prevent a person from injuring himself. The strong preservative paternalist principle does not use the voluntary act criterion, while the weak preservative paternalist principle does. It is essential to note that paternalist principles apply only to liberty-limiting legislation. Since the aim is to get the controlled person to act in a way other than he would choose to do (voluntarily or not), only liberty-limiting legislation can achieve the purpose.

JUSTIFICATIONS

In order to adopt the strong paternalist principles, one must justify rejecting an adult's voluntary decision that on balance an action is not injurious to him or is for his own good. Some arguments presented for doing so only justify greater caution in deciding that a person chooses and acts voluntarily. In special situations, one can be justified in rejecting a person's voluntary decision, but one must still present arguments to justify liberty-limiting legislation in order to get people to omit or perform such actions. Since preservative paternalism is more likely to be acceptable than promotive paternalism, unless otherwise noted the discussion in this section concerns the preservative principles.

H. L. A. Hart argues against weak paternalism and for the strong version. The voluntary act criterion of weak paternalism, Hart claims, generally has been, and should be, abandoned. His reasons are that there has been a decline in the belief that a person knows his own interests best and that there is a greater awareness of factors which prevent actions from being fully voluntary. "Choices may be made or consent given," he writes, "without adequate reflection or appreciation of the consequences; or in pursuit of merely transitory desires; or in various predicaments when the judgment is likely to be clouded; or under inner psychological compulsion; or under pressure by others of a kind too subtle to be susceptible of proof in a court of law."[9] To these plain facts may be added the sheer complexity of the modern world, which makes it difficult for people to know all the circumstances and consequences of their choices and actions.

But the burden of this argument is not to ignore a voluntary choice but to observe that frequently people do not choose and act voluntarily. If someone's judgment is clouded or subject to subtle pressure or psychological compulsion, that person cannot choose or act fully voluntarily. The only conditions possibly compatible with voluntary choice and action in which Hart wishes to control a person for his own good are when that person does not adequately reflect or when he pursues transitory desires. Gerald Dworkin argues for the justifiability of paternalism in similar situations.

Dworkin attempts to support strong paternalism by invoking the future consent of fully rational persons. When children are made to do what they do not want to do, moral justification assumes that when they grow up they will come to see the correctness of parental decisions. Similarly, it is sometimes wise to agree to let others coerce one. For example, to avoid succumbing to the enchantment of the sirens, Odysseus ordered his men to lash him to the mast and ignore any future orders to release him. Likewise, Dworkin argues, a government has a good reason for limiting a person's liberty if the restrictions are such that fully rational persons would accept them as protections, much as Odysseus did.[10]

This argument would justify limiting or overriding voluntary choices at the moment of action but would insist on voluntary choice elsewhere. A person's voluntary actions may be limited whenever it can reasonably be claimed that fully rational persons would voluntarily choose the restrictions. This thesis with respect to preservative paternalism implies that fully rational persons would view the actions as injurious. Since actions may be deemed injurious to an actor despite the fact that he performed them voluntarily, this argument defends strong paternalism.

When it comes to particular situations, it is less clear that Dworkin would limit voluntary actions. He mentions as instances of such justifiable paternalism the prevention of taking drugs which are "physically or psychologically addictive" and will hinder reasoned choices, and attempting suicide "under extreme psychological and sociological pressures." Neither of these cases seems to involve limiting fully voluntary actions. Dworkin's main instances of paternalism involving anything approaching limitations on fully voluntary actions are the prevention of actions due to an incorrect weighting of values or to weakness of will.[11] These cases resemble Hart's cases of inadequate reflection and transitory desires.

These types of cases do involve limiting fully voluntary actions. A person may believe that he ought to stop smoking but may lack the willpower to do so; he pursues a transitory desire and sacrifices long-range to short-range interests. A person who values avoidance of injury may think that he would rather not suffer the inconvenience of fastening a seat belt and may thereby risk serious injury. His decision may involve either an incorrect weighting of values or inadequate reflection, both of which may fall under the general rubric of incorrect determination of interest. Both the cigarette and seat belt cases involve, in one way or another, an irrational choice. The voluntary act criterion does not guarantee that a person will choose rationally. It only sets necessary conditions for so doing. Hence it is possible for a choice to be fully voluntary and yet not rational. Thus, in the sorts of cases mentioned by Hart and Dworkin, one can assert that a person may be injured by his own voluntary actions, and thus, with respect to paternalism, the criterion is not necessarily conclusive.

Regan presents a somewhat different argument for strong paternalism in such cases as cigarette smoking and seat belts. Strong paternalism may be justified to maximize freedom.[12] By preventing people from smoking cigarettes and requiring them to use seat belts, one prevents them from destroying their freedom. Cancer or crippling injuries which may result from smoking or not using seat belts limit people's freedom to perform various actions. Hence, the restrictions in question increase freedom rather than decrease it.

There are two main difficulties with this argument. Regan emphasizes the loss of freedom if the untoward results occur. However, in maximizing freedom one must also consider people who do not suffer untoward consequences from similar conduct. Restrictions upon them decrease rather than increase freedom. Whether or not laws requiring seat belts and prohibiting smoking increase freedom over all is not clear. It depends upon how many such people are likely to develop cancer or to suffer crippling injuries. Then, there are problems in making comparative judgments about which of two actions maximizes freedom. Regan is aware of the difficulties in making such judgments and the relevance of value judgments about the importance of what one is free to do. However, he does not fully realize the significance of the fact that comparative judgments of freedom depend upon values. In particular, they depend upon the values people have with respect to such actions as fastening seat belts and smoking cigarettes. In this context Regan does not present any general argument for rejecting the voluntary judgments of individuals that their freedom is maximized by performing these actions. Insofar as he does present such an argument, in the context of the persons becoming different because of changes in attitudes, his view resembles Dworkin's contention about what a fully rational person would do or choose.

The difficulty with limiting voluntary actions in these situations, whether one takes Regan's view or that of Hart and Dworkin, is that it assumes that everyone has the same values. Both the seat belt and cigarette smoking cases assume that a person prefers a greater chance of a long life to the small inconvenience of fastening seat belts or the pleasures of smoking. In a pluralistic society with persons committed to various value systems, many such persons may not be choosing irrationally. They may simply have different values. Hence, limiting such actions may involve limiting the freedom of large numbers of persons who have not chosen irrationally; that is, fully rational persons with these different values would not think the consequences of the actions injurious, nor would they consent to the limitations.

Dworkin is aware of this difficulty but does not meet it. He does not solve the problem of the Christian Scientist who would rather die than have a blood transfusion. Instead, he shifts to the seat belt case and assumes that the person in the automobile has conventional life plans, and in the end he simply places on legislators the burden of proof for showing consequences of acts to be injurious.[13] The burden of proof, even the burden of persuasion, does not provide any substantive safeguard for liberty. It would permit, for example, in support of a smoking prohibition, strong evidence that one out of every one hundred smokers desires to quit but is too weak-willed to do so. Moreover, the values of legislators do not represent all those in society; they do not represent, say, the Moonie sub-culture. The problem which remains is simply this: limitations on the voluntary actions of rational, strong-willed people with uncommon values would be invoked in order to get people with ordinary values to do what they would do voluntarily if they were not weak-willed or irrational.

Two solutions to this dilemma are to deny that there are great differences in value systems or to claim that certain values are irrational. The first solution is simply false to the reality of modern pluralistic societies. The second faces many difficulties too complex to be adequately discussed here: it requires a generally acceptable method of determining which values are irrational. Needless to say, value theorists are divided as to whether or not there is such a method, let alone what it is. The method of judging principles of legislation adopted in this book is not strong enough to determine which values are irrational. At best, it only provides a method for excluding some as unreasonable.

Society can decide the rationality of personal values (i.e., goals pursued for oneself subject to the moral dictum to respect others) by a minority or a majority decision. If a minority is the arbiter of the rationality of values, then a moral dictatorship becomes a distinct possibility. A reasonable person would not be willing to accept this risk. Democratic theory generally assumes that a majority is more likely to be correct than a minority. Many different justifications of this assumption are possible. It appears most reasonable when each person is judging matters which affect him, that is, social policies which affect his personal values (interests) or social values pertaining to him as a member of the community. But on this ground, members of a minority are the best judges of their own personal values unless their choices are involuntary or are obviously not consistent with their values as exhibited in their conduct.

Further, majority decisions on personal values do not answer the appropriate question.[14] Each person decides which values are most rational for him, given his circumstances, background, dispositions, and abilities. But the crucial question is what values are most rational for the members of the minority, given their circumstances, backgrounds, dispositions, and abilities. Differences in these factors are most relevant to personal values and life styles. On the basis of this examination, there seems little reason to believe that majority opinions are more likely than minority ones to be correct concerning the rationality of personal values for the minority. As a reasonable person must consider the possibility that he will be in the minority, the benefits which one may expect do not outweigh the risk of loss of freedom.

A third way out of the problem of legislating personal values for a minority would be to accept as a criterion of application that the liberty of some should be sacrificed to prevent injury to others. Even weak preservative paternalism, together with this criterion, supports limiting some fully voluntary actions not injurious to others. For example, slavery is a condition a person would not normally enter voluntarily. It can be argued that in some circumstances a person might voluntarily enter a contract to be a slave for life, but political authorities may refuse to enforce such contracts. The difficulties of proof and consequent chance of mistake involved in ensuring that such a person has made this contract voluntarily are too great. Hence, to prevent injury to those who would not voluntarily contract to be slaves but might mistakenly be believed to have done so, one may accept legislation forbidding any such contracts.[15] A reasonable person would conclude that avoiding the risk of injury by involuntary slavery is worth his loss of the freedom to voluntarily enter it.

There is a crucial difference between strong and weak paternalism with respect to the criterion of sacrificing liberty to prevent injury. Under the weak version, the resulting injury occurs through no fault of the person injured. Since his choice is involuntary, the injury is not his fault. It may not be anyone's fault. Under strong preservative paternalism, the resulting injury is the person's own fault. It results from his weakness of will or irrational determination of interest. While it seems reasonable to risk liberty to prevent injury which would occur due to no fault of one's own, it does not seem reasonable to do so when the injury would be one's own fault. Hence, only weak preservative paternalism is an acceptable principle for liberty-limiting legislation, and the voluntary act criterion is also conclusive for paternalism. However, the criterion of sacrifice of the liberty of a few to protect many from involuntary self-injury must be allowed in a few cases.

Once the sacrifice criterion is accepted, another objection may arise. In the previous section it was claimed that a ban on cigarette manufacturing would involve the use of the private harm principle without the voluntary act criterion, rather than paternalism. But with the sacrifice criterion, one could contend that the freedom of cigarette manufacturers is sacrificed to prevent smokers from harming themselves. Hence, paternalism cannot be restricted to those situations where only one person is involved.

Two main points may be made in reply to this objection. First, one must distinguish paternalistic principles from paternalistic arguments. Paternalistic principles always refer to one person, e.g., preventing X from harming himself. However, a paternalistic argument may contain other premises which may extend the class of persons whose conduct is to be controlled beyond the group whose well-being is in question. The sacrifice criterion will so extend this class.

Second, whenever the sacrifice criterion with paternalism would support restrictions on second parties such as cigarette manufacturers, there is a more direct argument from the private harm principle. For paternalism and the sacrifice criterion to support prohibition of an activity, one must show that the injury to those who would not engage in it voluntarily which has been prevented is greater than is the freedom of those who would engage in it voluntarily. But the private harm principle applies directly to second parties with respect to those who do not voluntarily engage in the conduct, that is, cigarette manufacturers are injuring those who do not smoke voluntarily. And since, *ex hypothesi*, the injury they cause is greater than the benefit they supply, the private harm principle supports a restriction on their conduct.

Since the strong preservative paternalist principle is unacceptable, the strong promotive paternalist principle is as well. But the acceptability of the weak preservative paternalist principle does not imply the acceptability of the weak promotive one. A reasonable person may be willing to accept limits on his liberty to prevent involuntary injury but not to avoid involuntary failure to promote his good. However, there are some reasons for accepting the weak promotive principle. A reasonable person desires to be able to choose and act fully voluntarily. Thus, he desires that if he becomes incapable of fully voluntary choices, he may return to a condition in which he is capable of them. Thus, he could accept weak promotive paternalism when it is designed to further his good by making him capable of fully voluntary choices.[16] In this respect, weak promotive paternalism is somewhat different from weak preservative paternalism. The preservative principle supports preventing a person from making less than fully voluntary choices which result in injury. But promotive paternalism aims not to prevent one from making such choices, but to enable one to make fully voluntary choices. For example, compulsory education is designed to enable one to choose voluntarily (promotive paternalism), while limits upon maximum interest rates are to prevent injurious borrowing (preservative paternalism).

This argument still leaves open the question of whether weak promotive paternalism should be accepted for legislation which is not designed to enable one to choose voluntarily but is intended merely to limit one's liberty for one's own good. However, there does not appear to be any strong reason why a reasonable person could not accept it. When it pertains, one is not, *ex hypothesi*, able to decide voluntarily what will promote one's good. Thus, one may be willing to let others make that judgment for one. If, because of one's ignorance of the stock market, it is reasonable to allow an investment counselor to determine how one's money should be invested, it may also be reasonable to permit the legislature to determine what is good for one. However, while one is always free to reverse particular judgments of an investment counselor, one is not free to do so with a legislature. Hence, a reasonable person would require that it be clear that people's decisions are not voluntary and that the alleged benefit be widely recognized to be such.[17] If weak promotive paternalism is thus acceptable, so is weak preservative paternalism.

LIMITS

The argument in the previous section showed that the strong paternalist principles are not acceptable but that the weak ones are generally acceptable. However, the general acceptability of principles does not necessarily imply that they are acceptable for all types of legislation. The purpose of this section is to consider the acceptability of the weak paternalist principles for the different types of liberty-limiting legislation.

Not even the weak paternalist principles are acceptable for penal legislation. If the preservative principle is unacceptable for penal legislation, the promotive one is too, so the argument is presented in terms of the weak preservative principle. It provides a reason for legislation limiting less than fully voluntary actions which are injurious to the actor. It is not obvious that the use of criminal laws is an effective method for preventing such actions. Such actions will not be voluntary, so threats of punishment may not prevent them.[18] The effectiveness of criminal laws as a deterrent is a complex topic, but for purposes of argument, it may be assumed that they will deter. Even so, they will not always do so, and sanctions may have to be imposed on those who violate laws. Of course many offenders may escape punishment if *mens rea* is required, for they will be in excusing conditions. Still, if some offenders are not punished, the laws will cease to deter.

At this point paternalism as a reason for penal legislation becomes morally inconsistent. The reason for accepting paternalism is to avoid injury by one's involuntary (less than fully voluntary) choices and actions. If penal legislation justified by paternalism is to be enforced, offenders must be deprived of liberty or property, i.e., imprisoned or fined. The result is injury to those punished. In order to accept paternalism as a reason for penal legislation, one would have to be willing to accept the possibility of being injured in order to avoid injury. Kant would certainly reject this principle as involving a contradiction in the will. Of course, this application of paternalism is not logically inconsistent, but there is a moral inconsistency between motive and means—being injured in order to avoid injury.

However, it may be claimed that the point is to deter persons from injuring themselves, and that the risk of punishment is the lesser of two evils. Such a defense, based on choosing the lesser of two evils, is not feasible. First, it must be shown that the risk of punishment involved in penal legislation is a lesser evil than the injury to be avoided. If it is not, then a reasonable person would not accept paternalism as a principle for penal legislation. Second, the strong liberty-regarding principle against penal legislation implies that there must not be any legislation less limiting to liberty which is as effective,[19] but such legislation is almost always available. The government could undertake an advertising campaign to show the injury involved, as the American Cancer Society has done in its campaigns against cigarette smoking. A given conduct could be made less attractive by administrative-regulatory legislation limiting the times and places in which it may occur, or burden-imposing legislation could be used to tax the activity and make it less attractive, as with cigarette and alcoholic beverage taxes. Such legislation may be as effective as penal legislation, but even if it is not, since it involves less loss of liberty it may be preferable. Thus not even weak preservative paternalism is acceptable for penal legislation.

To some political philosophers, this conclusion may appear disastrous. They believe that some paternalist principle is necessary to support penal legislation which is obviously desirable. To counter such an objection, one needs to show either that paternalism is not needed to support the legislation or that the legislation is not in fact desirable. This cannot be demonstrated here for all penal legislation for which paternalist principles may be thought necessary, but to counter the objection it is necessary to consider at least some such legislation.

Paternalism has frequently been suggested as the basis for denying the consent of a victim of assault or homicide as a defense.[20] But if X assaults Y, denial of Y's consent to the attack as a defense for X does not invoke paternalism. X is punished for injuring Y; Y is not punished for injuring himself. At most, the private harm principle without the voluntary act criterion is involved. One need not even abandon the voluntary act criterion; one need only limit the freedom of those who would consent to protect those who would not. Protection rackets, for example, thrive on the threat of property damage and assault. If the law permitted consent as a defense, victims could be coerced, by threats of further assaults, into testifying that they consented to the original attack. Such statements of consent would frequently be false, but courts would have much trouble ascertaining that. A reasonable person may be willing to forgo the liberty of those instances in which he would consent to assault for the sake of being protected from those instances in which he would not, i.e., to accept the sacrifice criterion.

Paternalism fares little better as a reason for legislation against drug abuse. First, it is not always clear that a person takes drugs voluntarily. An addict is under psychological compulsion and, therefore, is not acting fully voluntarily. A novice may be ignorant of the known effects of drugs. Still, some persons may voluntarily choose to use addictive drugs. But to prevent their being sold to those who do not so choose the law may have to prohibit all sales. Again, liberty is sacrificed to prevent injury. While for nonaddictive drugs these considerations about voluntary choice are less clear, there may be subtle social pressures to use drugs among an "in group."

Second, one must distinguish between selling drugs and using them. Paternalism is not directly relevant to the sale of drugs. Again the seller, X, is being prevented from contributing to the injury of the buyer, Y. Paternalism only provides a reason for making drug use illegal, and it is becoming widely recognized that punishment of drug addicts is futile. It neither cures nor deters them. It may deter users of non-addictive drugs, but such people are more likely to have taken them voluntarily. Further, the claim that their use causes injury is highly controversial.

Paternalism has frequently been suggested as a reason for prohibiting suicide. The presumption against a person's voluntarily harming himself so seriously is great. Nonetheless, someone may rationally decide that suicide is the best course of action; to prevent it involves prohibiting his fully voluntary action. Thus, since it may be rational, Dworkin does not advocate absolute prohibition of suicide.[21] Further, since a person who commits suicide cannot be punished, the notion of punishment for it is absurd. Only people who attempt it and fail can be punished. Many persons who attempt suicide do not do so voluntarily. Often they are subject to none too subtle pressures or mental disturbances. There are methods more humane than punishment for dealing with such people, e.g., counseling, financial aid, and the help of social workers. However, the administrative-regulatory technique might be used to ensure that a person has indeed made a fully voluntary decision to take his life. Further, if the vast majority of persons attempting suicide do not do so voluntarily, and if it is too difficult for government to sort out those who do from those who do not, suicide might be prohibited. Again, one sacrifices the liberty of voluntary suicide to avoid involuntary suicide. But punishment is still unacceptable.

Perhaps in recognition of these points, the Model Penal Code does not make attempted suicide a crime,[22] but it does make causing, aiding, or soliciting suicide or attempted suicide a crime. Once again, however, one is beyond paternalism and is concerned with the private harm principle here, for one person is causing another to commit suicide. Nor does such a law necessarily involve rejecting the voluntary act criterion. One must cause the other to act by force, duress, or deception. Soliciting may involve psychological pressures, e.g., shouting "Jump!" to a person perched on a high ledge. Moreover, since there is a strong presumption that the person does not act voluntarily, it should be assumed that he will be injured until it is established that he has voluntarily chosen to kill himself. Hence, the private harm principle can account for these crimes.

Finally, jaywalking, motorcyclists' crash helmets, auto seat belts, cigarette smoking, and homosexual conduct do not involve any injury recognized by weak paternalism. Hence, it does not support limiting liberty in these cases. It cannot be plausibly claimed that people who jaywalk or fail to wear crash helmets or seat belts do not do so voluntarily. They may indeed consider the risk worth taking for some reason. At most, weakness of will is involved. Dworkin does not wish to make the failure to wear seat belts criminal: he wants only to assign all financial liability for their injuries to those who do not wear them.[23] This proposal does not involve paternalism. Rather, it uses the private harm principle with the voluntary act criterion. X is not liable to Y for harm which results to Y from his voluntary decision not to wear a seat belt. A similar policy might be used for jaywalking and crash helmets. An argument for such a policy is either that the people involved are weak-willed and so are partially at fault or that they assumed the risk. Similar considerations apply to cigarette smokers. Of course, paternalism would be involved only in prohibiting cigarette smoking, not cigarette manufacturing and sales. Lastly, there are no reasons for believing homosexual relations between consenting adults to be injurious.

The weak paternalist principles are not relevant to grievance-remedial legislation. The grievance-remedial technique provides X a remedy against actual or possible injury caused by Y. Since the injury is not self-inflicted, paternalism is not relevant.

Nor is it relevant to supporting private-arranging legislation as a whole; however, it may support limits upon the types of private arrangements which are allowed. As previously mentioned, weak preservative paternalism may support limits upon slavery contracts in order to protect people who do not enter them voluntarily. The same point applies to requirements of disclosure of information for contracts in general. But only the preservative principle is relevant, and it only ensures that one enters such arrangments voluntarily. Since one is not required to take advantage of the possible private arrangements afforded by legislation, the promotive paternalist principle cannot be relevant to it.

A similar rationale can be applied to accepting and using pater-

nalism for administrative-regulatory legislation. Since such legislation is primarily preventive, it cannot be used to promote well-being. However, it may be used to prevent people from less than fully
voluntary actions injurious to themselves. Nevertheless, most administrative-regulatory legislation is not supported by paternalist
principles because usually the restrictions are not placed upon the
person whose well-being is to be preserved. For example, while
regulations on food quality are designed to preserve the well-being
of the consumer, it is the producers' actions which are limited. Instead, the public welfare and interest principles (see Chapter VII)
are usually the most relevant ones for this type of legislation.

Burden-imposing legislation alone cannot often be supported by
paternalism, but it may be when combined with benefit-conferring
legislation. The mere imposition of a burden cannot promote a
person's well-being, but it may help to prevent him from injuring
himself by making a given activity less attractive. Usually, however, burden-benefit schemes are involved. The welfare state rests
upon compulsory burden-benefit schemes, e.g., a social security
and health insurance system. Perhaps the clearest example is social
security retirement annuities. The aim is to preserve or promote a
person's good by providing financial resources for his old age.
However, it is not clear that the compulsory feature of a social security system can rest upon acceptable paternalist principles.

The United States social security program combines death benefits to one's family with disability and retirement annuities. The
first element does not involve paternalism, for it concerns the well-
being of others. And a principle for it would not justify compulsory
insurance for unmarried persons unless it is assumed likely that a
person will get married. Nor can it plausibly be maintained that
only people incapable of fully voluntary choice would refuse to
enter a social security program for disability and retirement annuities. Thus, the basic element of compulsory social security appears
to rest upon strong rather than weak paternalism.

It might be contended that many persons are not capable of
fully voluntary decisions about social security, and so compulsory
enrollment in such a system sacrifices the liberty of those who *are*
able to make such decisions for the sake of the well-being of those
who are not. This argument is not satisfactory. Those who would
refuse to participate are probably either making a voluntary choice
or giving in to a desire for higher income now as against future income; that is, they are succumbing to transitory desires and are not

rationally calculating their long-range interest. But that does not mean that their choices are not fully voluntary, so strong paternalism is still the required principle. Hence, the rejection of strong paternalism as a basis for liberty-limiting legislation implies that paternalism does not support compulsory social security programs. This conclusion does not imply, however, that there is no support for them on the basis of other acceptable principles of legislation.

Finally, both preservative and promotive paternalism may be accepted as a basis for compulsory treatment legislation. A reasonable person desires to be and to remain capable of fully voluntary choices. Thus, such a person would accept weak preservative paternalism to support compulsory treatment should he become incapable of making reasonable, intelligent decisions and thus likely to injure himself. Compulsory treatment legislation for mentally abnormal persons who are a danger to others is supported by the private harm principle. Preservative paternalism supports compulsory treatment legislation only if a person is a danger to himself.

A more crucial issue concerns support by weak promotive paternalism of compulsory treatment legislation for those who are not a danger to themselves or others. A subject of treatment must still be incapable of fully voluntary choices. However, most forms of mental abnormality prevent one from making fully voluntary choices about some things. Phobias and neuroses can prevent fully voluntary choices about some things. However, a reasonable person would not accept compulsory treatment designed to make him capable of fully voluntary choices if the only choices which he could not make voluntarily were minor ones. The loss of freedom in compulsory treatment would not be worth the potential benefits.

The crucial question thus becomes whether promotive paternalism is an acceptable principle for compulsory treatment of conditions which render one incapable of fully voluntary choices about many matters even though one is not a danger to oneself or others. A reasonable person would, of course, prefer to be capable of fully voluntary choices. But is the desired goal worth the loss of liberty involved? It does not appear worth the loss of liberty involved in involuntary commitment to a mental institution.[24] The loss of liberty is great, as great as that involved in criminal legislation. Further, the current chance of being restored to a condition in which one is capable of voluntary choice is not great. Psychology and psychiatry, in their present stage of development, simply are not capable of guaranteeing a cure. Indeed, for some forms of

mental illness, the chances of failure are greater than those of success. Sometimes the chances of cure with treatment are not significantly greater than the chances of cure without treatment.
Finally, acceptance of such a principle is fraught with danger. In
many instances, persons who are capable of fully voluntary choices
but who disagree with governmental policies have been incarcer-
ated on this basis: in the Soviet Union agitators against the state
have often been eliminated in this way.

However, there is one class of persons for whom the principle
of promotive paternalism does support compulsory treatment—
children. Support for compulsory blood transfusions or other medical treatment for adult Christian Scientists and others who do not
choose it requires strong paternalism. Even if their decisions are
irrational, they are or may be fully voluntary. But the promotive
paternalist principle does support compulsory medical treatment
for children of Christian Scientists. Children are not capable of
fully voluntary choices. The issue, then, is whether their parents
or the political authorities should make such decisions for them.
Paternalism will be involved in either case. When parents make
choices based on peculiar values of their own, the government may
limit parental control for the good of the child. The point of such
limits will be to protect and promote the child's well-being until
he is capable of making voluntary choices for himself.

This use of promotive paternalism is more generally exemplified in compulsory education. As this legislation imposes a duty on
parents to see that their children attend school, parents are for
this purpose agents of the state; they have legal custody of their
children and so are directed to ensure that the children attend
school. If the parents do not have legal custody of their children,
then the duty falls upon whoever does have it. The underlying conception is that education will enable children to make fully voluntary choices; that is, one purpose of compulsory education is to
overcome the child's inability to make reasoned and informed
choices. Thus, weak promotive paternalism appears to be the appropriate principle. Of course, other principles may also apply,
such as the public interest in a skilled work force. But weak promotive paternalism is still one reason for such legislation and
would probably suffice even if a country did not need a highly
skilled work force. However, a point does arise in which conflict
between the claims of parents and those of the government to exercise paternalistic authority over the education of children must

be decided, but the resolution of this conflict cannot be based on paternalistic principles.[25]

One can also perceive limits to weak promotive paternalism in this case. Consider legislation requiring that all children between the ages of six and twelve learn how to swim. The children are not capable of fully voluntary choices as to whether or not to learn how to swim. Also, the legislation is apparently designed for their own good rather than, say, to save the lives of others who might be drowning. It might be justified by an appeal to preservative paternalism, to prevent the children from drowning in boating accidents. But it might be supported simply on the ground that the enjoyment and physical development involved in swimming is for their good. Similar arguments underlie college course requirements in literature, music, etc. In the case of required swimming, the good which will result is not obvious enough to support the legislation: the ability to swim is not of sufficient value to override the limits to liberty. However, compulsory physical education might be different, for such a broad requirement is more obviously directed toward improving the physical well-being of children.

In sum, the acceptable uses of paternalism are very limited. First, it is relevant only to liberty-limiting legislation. Second, the strong paternalist principles are not acceptable. Third, neither of the weak ones is acceptable for penal legislation, nor is either relevant to grievance-remedial legislation. Weak preservative paternalism is acceptable for limiting private-arranging legislation to ensure that arrangements are voluntarily entered, for administrative-regulatory legislation to ensure that actions are fully voluntary, for burden-imposing legislation to make not fully voluntary choices less likely, and for compulsory treatment when one is a danger to oneself. Either version of weak paternalism is acceptable for burden-benefit legislation when it is clear that a person's decision not to participate in such a system would not be fully voluntary; however, such cases are relatively rare. Weak promotive paternalism is also acceptable for compulsory treatment legislation for children and adults if incarceration is not involved. Since a reasonable person places a greater value on avoiding injury than on obtaining a good, the preservative paternalist principle is stronger than the promotive one. Indeed, the latter provides a weak reason for legislation. Being so limited, the paternalist principles do not provide a firm foundation for the legislative goals of the welfare state.

VII
COMMON GOOD

The private harm and paternalist principles concern the well-being of particular persons. Paternalism is for the good of the person whose conduct is being controlled. The private harm principle aims to prevent injury to particular persons; that is, if injury is not prevented, it will happen to identifiable persons. However, sometimes the effects of a given conduct upon the well-being of people cannot be traced to particular persons who are injured or benefited. For example, studies show that air pollution increases the incidence of specific diseases. However, one cannot say precisely whose health is thus endangered, for some people will not be injured. Furthermore, even those who do contract one of the diseases cannot show that pollution caused it in their particular case, let alone which polluting source was the cause. Thus, purposes pertaining not only to the well-being of individuals but also to that of a large, indeterminate group of people—the public—have also been thought appropriate for political authority.

This chapter concerns legislative principles dealing with harm and benefit to large, indeterminate groups of people. The terms used in discussions of such principles include 'the public good', 'the general welfare', 'the public interest', 'the public welfare', 'the general good', and 'the common good'. Amongst political philosophers there are no distinctions among these various terms which are generally agreed upon, nor does common usage provide any sharp distinctions. Hence, any distinctions made among them must be largely stipulative. The expressions used in this chapter are 'public welfare' and 'public interest'. While there is, perhaps, some foundation in common usage for the way they are here distinguished, the chief basis for the distinction is theoretical.

141

PUBLIC WELFARE

The concept of the public welfare may be analyzed in terms of the welfare of individuals. The welfare of individuals relates to the fulfillment or satisfaction of their self-regarding wants. In common usage, the expression 'X's welfare' seems to refer to the actual fulfillment of certain self-regarding wants. 'Interests', as defined at the beginning of Chapter V, do not refer to the actual fulfillment of self-regarding wants but to the ability to fulfill them. A person may possess a good and be able to fulfill a want but may not do so. If the want is not fulfilled even though a person has a good which enables him to do so, it would be a bit odd to say his welfare has been provided with respect to the want. However, usually political authorities cannot directly fulfill wants; they can only provide goods which may be used to fulfill wants. For example, political authorities cannot directly fulfill a person's desire to eat, but they can provide food or money to purchase food. Hence, for the present purposes there is no reason why 'X's welfare' cannot be analyzed in terms of X's interests. The crucial question concerns which interests are involved in the concept of welfare. And since most interests are primarily based upon particular self-regarding wants, this question may be answered by indicating which wants are included in a person's welfare.

Brian Barry gives a narrow definition of welfare. He believes that it is closely restricted to considerations of health—material, moral, or spiritual. Material welfare he restricts to fulfilling self-regarding wants for the minimum conditions of health. He even suggests that retirement pensions and sick pay go beyond the welfare state.[1] Such a definition is so narrow as to be misleading, for it rejects some of the cornerstones of the welfare state dating back to Bismarck's introduction of the concept in Germany.

David Braybrooke calls welfare a "convoy concept."[2] By that, he means that it refers to goods which fulfill an indefinite group of self-regarding wants the list of which varies with public opinion. Among the self-regarding wants currently a part of welfare in the United States, according to Braybrooke, are those for food, clothing, shelter, health, education, companionship, and congenial employment. The phenomenon of rising expectations involves adding new wants to those already included in the concept of welfare. Hence, the content of 'welfare' changes as the public comes to expect higher standards of living.

While Barry's definition is too narrow, Braybrooke's is too broad and relativistic. Television sets might now be included as part of welfare in the United States, since over 90 percent of the population has one. Further, the concept is relativistic: one cannot say that welfare pertains to fulfilling the same wants for a man in India as for one in Orange County, California. Yet many people wish to argue for, and the United Nations apparently encourages its member nations to achieve, a basic level of welfare for everyone everywhere. Braybrooke's concept might more properly be called that of a decent standard of living, as the word 'decent' brings in a reference to publicly accepted norms which may vary with the economic well-being of a given society.

Nicholas Rescher agrees that Barry's definition is too narrow, but it is not clear how much he differs from Braybrooke. Rescher does distinguish between what a person needs and what he expects or aspires to, and suggests that expectations and aspirations frequently go beyond welfare to a person's vision of the good life. Yet he also insists that welfare involves comparisons in the amounts of goods various people have, and he recognizes that advances in welfare or standards of living escalate expectations. If the advances occur more among the upper classes than among the lower classes, they will also increase welfare requirements so long as such requirements depend upon comparisons among people. Nevertheless, Rescher suggests that welfare improvements can be subject to saturation because of the inability of society to make further improvements. He also suggests that there are limits on the improvements in welfare which the state ought to make.[3]

Rescher's account of a person's welfare may seem to be relativistic and too broad, but it does indicate the chief elements of a more narrow and non-relative concept of a person's welfare. Welfare, he writes, "relates to the *basic requisites of a man's well-being in general.*" It especially concerns health, mental as well as physical, and at least a minimal level of economic well-being. Rescher also includes some factors which have already been considered under other headings, such as freedom from crime, and privacy. With respect to crime, the point here is not that bodily integrity is not part of welfare but that crimes of violence threaten it in a different way from the way in which industrial and automotive accidents do. Moreover, Rescher includes a person's second-order desires for the well-being of some others as part of his welfare.[4] However, it was argued at the beginning of Chapter V that for theoretical purposes one should not include a person's other-regarding wants as a basis for interests in analyzing the private harm principle. The same arguments apply to the inclusion of other-regarding wants in a person's welfare and need not be repeated here. Nevertheless, other-regarding wants (limited benevolence) may be necessary in order to justify welfare principles.

A person's welfare may be defined as his interests in goods needed to fulfill his self-regarding wants to the extent involved in maintaining a minimal (rather than a decent) standard of living.[5] The minimal standard of living does not refer to the economic well-being of a society but to those conditions necessary for normally good health, sufficient wealth to provide personal necessities, and security. Such a minimal standard of living certainly includes competent medical service, a nutritionally adequate diet (although it may not contain much meat), and sufficient clothing and shelter to keep one warm and protected from the elements. Life at the welfare level is not a bed of roses, but at least at that level body and soul can be kept together.

Whether or not these conditions can be provided and which goods are involved in doing so depends to some extent upon the economic development of a country, the state of its medical science, and cultural standards. For example, in the United States most persons need a supply of natural gas or electricity for heating, while that is not true in all other countries. Providing beef to Hindus would not enable them to fulfill their wants for food, since they are constrained from eating it. On the whole, however, there is not much variation from time to time and place to place, and the basic wants are always the same even though the goods needed to fulfill them vary.

The public welfare pertains to the welfare of all members of the public. It is the sum of the welfare of persons. The welfare of the public is composed of all of the subjects of a political system, including children and all other non-voting residents. When the public welfare is not achieved one can often say who lacks it, but the concept does not directly refer to particular individuals. Many measures for the public welfare provide benefits spread over a large, indeterminate number of persons, e.g., the prevention of dangerous levels of air pollution.

Levels of public welfare depend upon amount and extent. Since a person's welfare consists of his interests in goods which fulfill self-regarding wants, one may speak of the amount of his welfare as the number of these wants he is able to fulfill and the degree to which he is able to fulfill them.[6] For example, a person with adequate shelter but insufficient food has a smaller amount of welfare than one with both. However, there is an upper limit to a person's welfare—namely, the ability to fulfill easily all of the wants to the extent included. Levels of welfare also depend upon the extent to which it is provided—how many members of the public have a given amount of welfare. Public welfare is completely provided when everyone is able to fulfill easily all his relevant self-regarding wants.

Levels of public welfare may either be maintained at, or decreased or increased from, a given base. The base for this comparison is always the current level of public welfare. As judgments as to whether L is in X's interest depend upon X's being more capable than he is at present of fulfilling his self-regarding wants, judgments of public welfare should use the same base. A legislative bill will leave the public welfare unaffected, will increase it, or will decrease it. Two pieces of legislation can be compared in terms of how much each will increase or decrease public welfare. Thus, there are two plausible types of public welfare principles: preservation principles, designed to prevent decreases in current levels of public welfare, and a promotion principle, designed to increase the current level of public welfare.[7]

There are two public welfare preservation principles, a negative one and a positive one. The negative principle is that if legislation will decrease the level of public welfare, that is a reason against it. The positive preservation principle is that if legislation will prevent a decrease in the level of public welfare, that is a reason for it. This positive principle provides a reason for legislation which offsets or prevents conditions which will decrease the public welfare: for example, it supports legislation preventing the importation of contaminated food. The negative principle protects the public welfare from governmental action which would decrease it. There is only one public welfare promotion principle because the fact that legislation will not increase the public welfare is not a reason against it. Legislation may have some other purpose and may not affect welfare, in which case the fact that it would not increase welfare is not a reason against it. So the only promotion principle is the positive one that if legislation increases the level of public welfare, that is a reason for it.

Public welfare principles are widely accepted in some form or other throughout the world. Most persons in Western civilization probably think it wrong for some people to have more goods than necessary for a minimal standard of living when others do not have enough.[8] Indeed, a minimal standard of living is considered so fundamental that it is part of the United Nations' Universal Declaration of Human Rights: "Everyone has the right to a standard of living adequate for the health and well-being of himself and his family, including food, clothing, housing and medical care and necessary social services, and the right to security in the event of unemployment, sickness, disability, widowhood, old age or other lack of livelihood in circumstances beyond his control."[9] Thus, the United Nations has signified world-wide acceptance of public welfare as a proper goal of political authority.

These considerations appear to be based upon benevolence, but the question is whether a reasonable self-interested person would accept the welfare principles. Obviously, a reasonable person desires the goods necessary for his welfare. It has already been remarked that consideration for bodily integrity is, next to life, probably the most basic self-regarding want. A person's welfare includes that want plus those wants involved in normally good health and enough wealth to avoid misery. These are among a person's strongest self-regarding wants; they underlie the desire for most personal property. However, it may be objected that while one's welfare is very desirable, a reasonable person would not accept public welfare principles.

There are perhaps two major objections that might be made to the public welfare principles. First, it may be claimed that while each person obviously desires his own welfare, it is more likely to be achieved if each individual pursues it on his own rather than having political authority pursue it. This contention primarily rests upon a claim of fact, namely, that over the long run more people will be better off in terms of welfare if the provision of goods and services is left to a free economic market rather than the government. There has never been a good way to test this claim, but the limited evidence indicates that there is always a fairly large percentage of the population at a very low level of welfare unless political authority operates some system to provide for it. This is not to say that all welfare programs are effective; some may indeed be less effective than free market mechanisms. The contention is simply that there are some government programs which will increase the level of public welfare. Since life below the level of complete welfare is miserable, a reasonable person would prefer to minimize his chances of falling below that level and so would accept the welfare principles.

The other objection is that a reasonable person, being primarily self-interested, would not necessarily approve of the public welfare principles as formulated because he would not be concerned with the welfare of all subjects of a system of political authority. Instead, he would prefer a principle directed to a smaller group to which he belonged, for example, limiting the group to white people if the person is white. This objection essentially raises the issue of impartiality which was partly discussed under "Acceptance Conditions" in Chapter II and is discussed further early in the next chapter. With respect to some aspects of public welfare, there is a strong reason for impartiality. Some conditions for welfare involve public goods which cannot practicably be restricted to specific groups of the population. Since public goods also pertain to the public interest, discussion of them is deferred to the next section.

While self-interest by itself provides a rather strong reason for accepting the welfare principles, it may not support them to the full extent, and some appeal to limited benevolence may be needed. A benevolence which extends to only a few people—family and friends —will not suffice in light of the second objection. It must include all residents of a person's country. However, it need not extend to residents of other countries. Thus, a Canadian concerned for the well-being of Canadians but not for that of people of other countries could accept the welfare principles. Further, a person need not have as strong a concern for the well-being of others as he does for himself. He need only be concerned that they not be below the minimal standard of living. He need not wish them every success. Moreover, his benevolence need not be expressed directly, by personal action, but may be expressed vicariously, in that he is willing to make provision for others through the political system.[10]

Finally, it should be noted that the welfare preservation principles provide stronger reasons for and against legislation than the promotion principle. The preservation principles prevent decreases in the level of welfare, while the promotion principle supports increases. Decreases in one's amount of welfare are harms (but not necessarily injuries in the technical sense used in Chapters V and VI), while failures to receive increases are non-benefits. A reasonable person is more concerned to avoid harms than non-benefits. Hence, assuming equal changes in goods, the welfare preservation principles have more weight—provide stronger reasons—than the promotion principle.

While the negative welfare preservation principle, like all negative principles, provides a reason against any type of legislation to which it pertains, it is not clear that the positive welfare principles will support all types of legislation to which they pertain. At first glance the public welfare principles appear to be irrelevant to criminal legislation; however, one can imagine situations in which the positive preservation principle might support it: given the current sophistication of biological warfare research, one might well think that the public welfare preservation principle could justify making it illegal to possess or use some of the more virulent germs and viruses which have been developed. There are also various situations concerning public goods in which either positive public welfare principle would support criminal legislation. These sorts of public good cases are discussed below.

Administrative-regulatory legislation, which is sometimes quite similar to criminal legislation, may be supported by either positive public welfare principle. The preservation principle supports all sorts of legislation to prevent pollution, impure foods, etc. Instances of the use of the public welfare promotion principle are harder to imagine, but auto safety legislation might be one. Environmental Protection Agency regulations on automobile emissions of pollutants are basically designed to increase the public welfare. If one views such legislation as designed to prevent increased pollution, then it falls under the preservation principle. However, the basis of comparison is the level of public welfare at the time the legislation is considered. To the extent that legislation is designed to decrease air pollution, it comes under the promotion principle.

One might object that one should not take the comparison base to be the time at which the legislation is considered, but some other time: the goal of pollution control might be to go back to the pollution levels of 1940. However, once one moves from the time of enactment as the basis for comparison, there is no adequate procedure for determining what the comparison base should be. For example, one might argue that the base for air pollution should be 1890. In England at that date, the air pollution of many cities was worse than it is now, and not even the preservation principle would support legislation to decrease air pollution levels. Further, since one has available both the preservation and promotion principles, there is little reason to focus on bringing certain types of legislation under one rather than another of them.

Grievance-remedial legislation is not especially relevant to public welfare. Traditionally, it has been primarily confined to harm to particular individuals. However, the newly developed class action suits permit using this legal technique to obtain injunctions on behalf of an indeterminate group of persons. Further, there is a strong argument for using this technique as the main legal weapon to protect the environment.[11] So far Michigan seems to be the only state to have enacted legislation providing a broad basis for use of the grievance-remedial technique in this way. One must also keep in mind that much environmental deterioration is not directly threatening to public welfare; what it threatens is a standard of living higher than the minimal. Thus, considerations of public welfare are not always the main ones. Moreover, the promotion principle is not relevant to grievance-remedial legislation, since a grievance requires a harm or the danger of one.

Benefit-conferring and burden-imposing legislation are perhaps the most relevant techniques for public welfare principles. Many attempts to promote the public welfare involve benefit-conferring legislation such as provision of public sanitation, health services, food stamps, and welfare payments. Burden-imposing legislation is exemplified in public insurance schemes such as workmen's compensation and disability insurance. In these sorts of programs, burdens are directly associated with benefits; that is, unlike sales, property, and income taxes, the revenues collected are channeled into specific uses. Public welfare principles support such legislation and the imposition of whatever burdens are necessary to finance the projects. They are thus acceptable for this type of legislation so long as the benefits are not above the minimal standard of living nor the burdens excessive, i.e., greater than the expected benefits.

Both the public welfare preservation and the promotion principles support private-arranging legislation. The promotion principle primarily supports legislation to facilitate private arrangements for the public welfare, such as medical groups, health insurance, and private pension plans. The preservation principle primarily supports limiting the permissible types of private arrangements. Many landlord-tenant laws provide for private arrangements (leases) with certain restrictions and may be supported by the public welfare principles. Of course, one important element of many of these laws is provision for the right of a tenant to sue a landlord if his housing is below minimum standards (grievance-remedial technique), but that feature is characteristic of all private arrangements with implied warranties, and should not be taken as determinative of the type of legislation involved. Since private-arranging legislation does not limit one's liberty, and the public welfare principles are acceptable for legislation that does, there cannot be any objection to their supporting this type of legislation.

The final type of legislation is compulsory treatment. Much of the compulsory treatment which the public welfare principles might support would not involve incarceration. For example, people are required to be inoculated with vaccine against diptheria, tetanus, and whooping cough in many states and against smallpox and other diseases in many nations. Part of the justification for such treatment has, in fact, been in terms of paternalism, and the weak preservative paternalist principle supports legislation requiring minors to be vaccinated. Only strong paternalism supports compulsory inoculation of adults. However, the public welfare principles support it for adults. The point, then, is not to protect the individual from disease but to preserve and promote the public welfare by eradicating contagious diseases. Since the limit on freedom in such legislation is minor, it may be based on the public welfare principles.

More liberty-limiting compulsory treatment involves quarantine of persons with severe and highly contagious diseases. The public welfare principles must be applied with caution in these cases. There are people who wish to be protected from any possible disease, even the common cold, and might be inclined to quarantine anyone with a communicable disease. The use of the public welfare principles to support quarantine in such cases appears extreme. The loss of liberty in being quarantined does not seem worth the decreased risk of catching the disease. Thus, a reasonable person would probably find the positive public welfare principles acceptable for compulsory quarantine and treatment only if the disease involves a high rate of death or permanent disability.

The public welfare principles are thus acceptable for all types of legislation except for the promotion principle, which cannot be used as a basis for grievance-remedial legislation. Further, they provide quite strong reasons, but this is because the standard of living which they ensure is minimal. Most people believe political authority should also pursue a higher standard of living for those subject to it. Principles for such purposes are considered in the next section.

PUBLIC INTEREST

Perhaps the most widely used expression concerning the common good is 'public interest', but that expression has been variously defined. One writer has been driven to despair that it will ever have any clear meaning and has suggested that it simply be dropped from political vocabulary.[12] One of the admitted difficulties with 'public interest' is that it tends to expand and include within its meaning all things which people believe are good for the population.[13] If the concept of the public interest is so all-inclusive, then each of the different principles considered in this book merely provides one element of it. However, courts and administrative agencies, as well as some legislators, appear to be capable of making fairly reasonable decisions which they support by appeals to a narrower concept of public interest.

Two steps are involved in making the public interest a more useful guide for policy decisions. The first step is to provide a precise explication of the concept. The second step is to provide empirical tests for determining what is in the public interest. The concern here is with the first step. Even when the concept is rather precisely explicated, it may be difficult to determine which of two policies is most in the public interest. This fact does not imply that the concept cannot be applied or that one cannot decide between two such policies. Atmospheric testing of nuclear weapons over major cities is patently contrary to the public interest. If one cannot decide which of two policies is most in the public interest, one may be able to decide between them on the basis of other principles.

After a long and intensive examination of different analyses of the public interest, Virginia Held provides a definition similar to her definition of something being in a person's interest. She defines 'L is in the public interest' as equivalent to 'a claim by or in behalf of the political system for L is asserted as justifiable'.[14] This definition is subject to the same sorts of objections raised in Chapter V against her definition of something being in a person's interest: it is not necessary that anyone make an assertion for L to be in the public interest. Again, her definition may be modified to avoid some of these problems. So modified, 'L is in the public interest' is equivalent to 'a claim by or in behalf of the political system for L is

prima facie justifiable'. Nonetheless, that L is in the public interest
is a reason for a claim to it being prima facie justifiable rather
than vice versa.

Any version of Held's definition of public interest is open to
another and more fundamental objection. Restricting the public
interest to what affects the political system makes it too narrow a
concept. It becomes restricted to topics already considered under
the public harm principle, for the political system is the system of
political authority. Only policies which strengthen or protect the
system of political authority would be in the public interest. People speak, however, of tariffs, railroad strikes, wildlife refuges,
transit systems, monopolies, etc., being for or against the public
interest without having any opinion as to their effect on the political
system.

Brian Barry believes that the individual interests included in the
public interest are only those which all members of the public have
in common. In his view, two people have a common interest when
there are two policies, L_1 and L_2, such that L_1 is more in the interest of each of them than L_2. The obvious objection is that there are
no policies which are common interests of all members of the public. When almost any policy is compared to another one, at least
some members of the public will find one more in their interest
than the other. In order to avoid this problem, Barry restricts the
interests in question to those which people have as members of the
public.[15] However, being a member of the public is hardly a role
sufficiently well-defined to be compared with the role of businessman or union member.[16] Thus, Barry's definition does not seem
workable.

While Barry primarily restricts the public interest to what is in
the interest of each person as member of the public, Theodore Benditt attempts to avoid Barry's restriction by dropping the requirement that policies be in people's interests. Instead, he takes common
interests to be interests which each person has. His example is
that everyone has an interest in having enough food.[17] There are,
however, two difficulties with this approach. First, as Benditt recognizes, the interests must be fairly abstract or must be relative to
people for everyone to have the same interest. For example, having
enough food to eat is both abstract (type of food) and relative
(what is enough for a given person). One difficulty is that the description of the interests may be so abstract as to be of little
use; another is that there are very few interests which all people
have. Hence the notion of public interest may be trivialized. Second,

when politicians claim that bills are in the public interest, they do not imply that all persons have some interest in common:[18] for example, a bill to preserve wild rivers may reasonably be claimed to be in the public interest even though ghetto dwellers have no demonstrable interest in wild rivers.

Benditt does not even include in the public interest all interests which everyone has. He requires that a public interest be one "the satisfaction of which is out of most individuals' hands, such that the interest is not likely to be protected or advanced unless it is furthered by the state." He then takes a policy to be in the public interest if implementing it "would result in protecting or promoting an interest of the public more than it disserves other equally important interests of the public." Thus, a policy is in the public interest if it improves the chance that all (most) members of the public will be able to satisfy some want which all have.[19] Instead of determining a policy to be in the public interest because it has a favorable effect on the interests of individual members of the public, he determines it to be in the public interest because it has a favorable effect on the interests of the public collectively.

Benditt's analysis is open to strong objections. First, as has already been noted, there are few precisely definable interests which all members of the public have. Second, to be in the public interest, legislation need not be in the interest of any one person. It is possible for legislation to be in the public interest yet be contrary to the private interest of every individual member of the public. Third, a policy may promote a public interest even though it affects very few persons.[20] Giving some persons a benefit may be in the public interest even though it does not help many other persons because it increases the chance that all (most) persons will be able to satisfy some common want. Consequently, a loan to Lockheed Aircraft Corporation could be in the public interest merely because it enables the stockholders and employees to satisfy a common want for continued income or employment. But in cases of this sort, appeals to the public interest must be supported by considerations of the effect of policies upon people other than the stockholders and employees of Lockheed. Indeed, the interest of the stockholders and employees of Lockheed would usually be taken to be a special interest, not part of the public interest.

The analysis of public interest proposed here differs from those of Barry and Benditt. The individual interests involved in the public interest are not restricted to interests which all members of the public have or to the interests which they all have as members of the public. Most of these interests have already been accounted for by the public welfare principles.[21] The individual interests involved are any which individual members of the public have except to the extent that they are included in a person's welfare.

Since the interests involved do not include those involved in welfare, legislation might be in the public interest but still be contrary to the public welfare.[22] While this possibility may be somewhat confusing, it seems preferable to keep considerations of public welfare and interest mutually exclusive. An alternative would be to require that legislation in the public interest shall not affect welfare. However, legislation might slightly diminish welfare interests but might greatly promote others. Hence, it seems best to allow for possible differences in legislation with respect to public welfare and interest.

Next, the public need not always include virtually the entire population of a country, as it must for public welfare. However, it always refers to an indeterminate group of persons.[23] It consists of all those residents not associated in an activity whose non-welfare interests may be affected by the legislation. For·example, 'the public' of a hospital consists of all those people who are not employees. In the Lockheed loan example, the public does not include the stockholders and employees of Lockheed. To show that the loan is in the public interest, one must show that it has a favorable effect on the non-welfare interests of other people: an example from the Lockheed case would be preventing an economic depression in the Seattle area and maintaining military defenses. And the public need not include all those who are not associated with an activity: some in that group may not have any non-welfare interests which would be affected. For example, in considering telephone rate increases, the public includes all those not associated with the telephone company who are potential users of telephones. It does not include, for example, deaf-mutes.[24]

To determine whether a policy is contrary to or in the public interest, then, one must consider its effects upon the non-welfare interests of the members of the public. It makes no difference whether the public interest is determined by the sum of the effects on each individual member of the public or by the sum of the effects on individual wants or interests. Like public welfare, public interest is also an aggregative concept, essentially a utility function.

However, there is an important difference between the public interest and the public welfare. Because there is an upper limit to a person's welfare, a point is reached at which further benefits to a particular individual do not increase the public welfare. To promote the public welfare, the benefits must be provided to another person who does not have a full amount of welfare. This feature of the concept of welfare introduces an element of equality into public welfare considerations. At least for practical purposes, there is no upper limit to providing for a person's non-welfare interests, so that the public interest can be promoted by indefinitely providing benefits to a particular person.

Since the public interest is only one consideration among many, the severe disadvantages of simple net utility considerations with respect to distribution are avoided. The public welfare principles must also be considered. If a bill promoted non-welfare interests of some people at the expense of the welfare interests of others, the negative welfare preservation principle would provide a reason, although not necessarily a conclusive one, against it. Moreover, distributive considerations with respect to equality of opportunity must be considered (see Chapter VIII). Finally, one of the chief areas of the use of political authority with respect to the public interest concerns public goods. In providing public goods, the issue of distribution is moot.

'L is in the public interest' means that L's effect upon the non-welfare interests of the members of the public is more favorable than unfavorable. Since non-welfare interests enable people to fulfill self-regarding wants not pertaining to welfare, the public interest may be specified in terms of them. L is in the public interest if it makes the members of the public more able to fulfill non-welfare self-regarding wants. Similarly, 'L is contrary to the public interest' means that L's effect upon the non-welfare interests of the members of the public is more unfavorable than favorable.

As with public welfare, there are three public interest principles—two preservation principles and one promotion principle. Preservation principles aim at safeguarding the public interest. The negative public interest preservation principle is that if legislation is contrary to the public interest, that is a reason against it. The positive public interest preservation principle is that if legislation will preserve the public interest (prevent conditions contrary to the public interest), that is a reason for it. The public interest promotion principle is a positive one: if legislation will promote the public interest, that is a reason for it.

Considerations of the public interest, like those of public welfare, require some basis of comparison, which is the situation when the legislation is proposed. Two proposals may be compared with this base and thus with one another. If it is clear that both proposals are in the public interest, the easiest method of evaluation may be to compare the two policies directly. Obviously, the more a policy is in the public interest, the stronger the reason for it provided by the promotion principle. Similarly, the more the conditions legislation will create or prevent are contrary to the public interest, the stronger are the reasons against or for it provided by the preservation principles.

The reasons for the desirability of the public interest principles are similar to those for the public welfare ones: people necessarily desire to fulfill their self-regarding wants. However, the reasons in favor of the public interest principles are not as strong as those in favor of the public welfare principles because public welfare pertains to more basic or important self-regarding wants than does public interest. By definition, welfare wants are those involved in a minimal standard of living. Public interest wants are therefore those involved in a more than minimal standard of living, and their fulfillment often requires that welfare wants be fulfilled. By and large, people attend to their welfare before other things, although they may occasionally skip a meal in order to see a good movie. Thus, much of the political argument in underdeveloped countries which have yet to provide a minimal standard of living for all subjects is, or should be, based upon public welfare considerations. In affluent, developed countries where a minimal standard of living has essentially been achieved for all persons, public interest is apt to be a more frequent consideration. Apart from some serious gaps, the United States has achieved a minimal standard of living for all. Thus, arguments about the elimination of poverty—based on, for example, a guaranteed income of $8,500 a year for a family of four—are not based upon considerations of public welfare but on those of public interest or equality of opportunity.[25]

Since the public interest refers to the interests of a large, indeterminate number of members of the public, each person has a good chance of being included in it. What is contrary to the public interest is likely to decrease one's ability to fulfill non-welfare self-regarding wants. Thus, one has a good reason for seeking to prevent that which is contrary to the public interest. Of course, an individual member of the public may be a net loser; that is, a policy may protect the public interest but may be contrary to the interest of a specific member of the public. In the most obvious cases of this sort, the person will not be a member of the public but of a special interest group. For example, a policy placing limits on the profits of oil companies in order to protect the public interest is most likely to be contrary to an individual's interest only if he is connected with the oil industry. Political authority is an efficient system for preventing anything contrary to the public interest, since an individual usually does not have the control over others to achieve such a result himself. The promotion principle increases the public interest, and there is a good chance that one's ability to fulfill one's self-regarding wants will be increased. The same considerations apply to it as apply to the preservation principles.

While the public interest principles, like the public welfare principles, may be argued for on the basis of self-interest, these considerations alone may not make them acceptable, and, an appeal to benevolence may also be needed. Moreover, the benevolence required for the public interest principles must be stronger than for the public welfare principles. Since the considerations involved in the public interest are less basic than those in welfare, a person must care about what happens to others beyond the mere provision for their welfare. Still, the argument for the acceptability of the public interest principles is not based simply on a concern for others. It may well be that a person would not accept those principles on grounds of benevolence alone; he might accept them only if he too might be expected to benefit. In order to keep the need for benevolence to a minimum, public interest principles may be applied in a more restricted way than welfare principles. For example, one might allow public welfare principles to support a policy providing benefits to only a few, e.g., victims of floods and tornadoes, but one might require that policies for the public interest affect larger groups, e.g., users of public highways. In this way public policies can be based more on the self-interest of many persons than on their benevolence.

Since decreases in one's ability to fulfill self-regarding wants are harms, while increases are benefits, the public interest preservation principles provide stronger reasons than does the promotion principle. Of course, great increases in the public interest provide stronger reasons than small decreases.

One of the most important uses of the public interest and welfare principles pertains to public goods. A good is a public good if it is public and indivisible.[26] Such goods include commodities, services, and other things which people can use to fulfill self-regarding wants. (Of course, there may also be public evils, but no one would contend that political authorities should promote them.) To be public, these goods must be provided for the public rather than for specific individuals. The crucial requirement is that the goods be indivisible. The root notion of an indivisible good is that it cannot practically be provided for one person without providing it for at least one other person. Generally, then, if one provides such a good, one cannot in practice exclude those who refuse to pay for it or otherwise contribute to its provision. Clean air is an example of an indivisible good. It cannot be provided for only the richer members of a community. All persons residing in an area breathe clean air, whether or not they contribute to providing it. However, public goods need not be of the same value to everyone. National defense is often taken as a paradigm of a public good. A plausible argument may be made that the rich have more to protect than the poor and that they therefore receive a greater benefit from national defense, but national defense is still a public good.

There are crucial problems surrounding the provision of public goods which may best be exhibited by a simple example. There is a small lake, and ten families have cottages bordering it. Each empties its raw sewage into it, and as a result the lake has become so polluted as to make it unsafe for swimming and to kill the fish. X owns one of the cottages. It would be in his interest to have the lake free of pollution. However, as things stand it is not in his interest to install a septic tank for his sewage. It would cost him a large sum of money, and the lake would still be unfit for swimming and fishing. Each of the other cottage owners is in the same position. Obviously, what is needed is a group decision or policy to install septic tanks, for if all the cottage owners did so, the pollution of the lake would be halted. Suppose, then, that all ten agree to do so. It is still not in X's interest to do so. If the others do not comply with the policy and he does, he has paid for a septic tank without receiving the benefit of an unpolluted lake. If the other nine cottage owners do install septic tanks and X does not, the lake will be substantially cleaner and X will have saved the price of a septic tank. In this situation the cost of X's pollution is externalized: he does not have to bear all the bad effects of his sewage, for they are distributed among all the cottage owners.

The point is that along with a collective policy for public goods there must also be some assurance that all or most people will comply with it.[27] Without that assurance, it is not in the interest of individuals to comply. Usually this assurance may be achieved by making it in their interest to comply. In the lake example, if each cottage owner were to be fined one-third the price of a septic tank every year, it would be in his interest to install the tank. In four years he would save money. But if the fine were as low as ten dollars annually, it would be cheaper for him to pay the fine.

Provision of public goods is thus an activity which promotes the public interest or welfare depending upon the good in question. A public policy is needed to overcome the isolation of each individual's view of the situation. Further, some form of assurance is needed that others will comply. Only political authority can provide such assurance for large, indeterminate groups. Thus, positive public interest and welfare principles are especially desirable for public goods.

The remaining issues concern the types of legislation which public interest principles support. As with public welfare, the negative public interest preservation principle provides a reason against all legislation contrary to the public interest. Both of the positive principles will support penal legislation if the public interest is sufficiently affected. However, it seems likely that a reasonable person would restrict their use to situations involving public goods, and even then the emphasis would be upon fines rather than incarceration. The risk of incarceration is quite grave compared to the fulfillment of self-regarding wants other than those involved in one's welfare. However, penal sanctions would seem acceptable in order to prevent, for example, long and widespread transportation strikes or increased levels of pollution which do not endanger health.

Traditionally, grievance-remedial legislation has primarily been intended for the benefit of particular persons. However, the public interest preservation principle supports such legislation. (The promotion principle is irrelevant here since grievance-remedial legislation requires a harm or a threat of harm, i.e., something contrary to the public interest.) Public officials or private citizens, through class action suits, might be authorized to sue because of conduct contrary to the public interest. The remedies might be either injunctions to prevent the activity or some form of public compensation. For example, if a strip mine operation results in a mud slide across a highway, the strip mine company might be required to pay to clean it up and even be assessed extra damages to compensate the public for the inconvenience. Of course, usually the benefit to private individuals is so small that it is not worth the cost of initiating a suit unless they stand to gain substantially from it.[28] Moreover, the procedure for class action suits in the Federal Rules of Civil Procedure treat them as something of a mixture between suits by large numbers of specific individuals and suits on behalf of a large, indeterminate number of people.

Both positive public interest principles support administrative-regulatory legislation. Indeed, the public interest principles form the rationale for most regulatory commissions, from wage and price boards to the Federal Communications Commission. Such agencies are empowered to regulate prices, atomic energy, commerce, etc., in the public interest (and also welfare, as here explicated). Sometimes legislative directives to them are phrased in terms of the public interest, although often they are more specific. For example, a price control board could be charged with regulating prices in the public interest or with keeping price increases below a certain level. Many of these matters involve public goods, e.g., keeping the inflation rate down to a certain level. The preservation principle seems to be of more importance for this type of legislation than the promotion principle.

Burden-imposing legislation is also supportable by the public interest principles. There are several interesting applications of them to such legislation. First, special taxes may be imposed upon activities which are contrary to the public interest. Instead of suing companies that pollute the water or the air for compensation, companies may be taxed at a rate proportionate to the amount of pollutants they discharge. This legal technique increases their interest in decreasing the amount of pollutants discharged and also provides government revenues to clean up the environment. In the public interest gasoline taxes and auto license fees are used to build highways. The idea is that while highways may be in the interest of even nonmotoring people, motorists derive more benefit from them than others do and should pay a greater percentage of the cost.

Besides taxes earmarked for specific uses in the public interest, there are general revenues for governmental operations. The government is itself a public good. It cannot be provided for some persons without being provided for all or at least most persons. Further, taxation is a public good problem. It is contrary to an individual's interest to pay taxes if either everyone else or no one else will. Thus, a public policy providing assurance that others will comply, a compulsory taxation system, is needed.

There are two more difficult issues here. One concerns the amount of money which should be raised by tax revenues. The other concerns the appropriate or just scheme for allocating burdens. The obvious solution to the first problem is to say that revenues should be raised for governmental activities until the increased burden out-weighs the increased benefits. What that means in practice is very difficult to determine. Primarily, it must be determined by political authorities and the political process. However, there are clear cases in which the increased benefits are not worth the increased costs, but these cases are unreasonable and are never seriously proposed. For all serious proposals, some people believe that the increased burdens are more than balanced by the increased benefits. For ex-ample, cities could probably plant trees every twenty yards on each side of every street, but the increased cost per taxpayer would not be worth the increased aesthetic beauty. Nonetheless, the planting of some trees is worth a small increase in taxes. The general problem of a just rate for imposing burdens will be taken up under "Social Priorities" in the next chapter.

The public interest promotion principle supports some benefit-con-ferring legislation. The preservation principle is usually irrelevant here, since providing benefits promotes the public interest. The only exception concerns increases in dollar amounts of benefits to cover inflationary losses. Promoting the public interest can cover a lot of matters. Grants of money to large numbers of persons might appear to be in the public interest, but such measures cannot usually be sup-ported by the public interest promotion principle because all such benefits must be paid for, so that at best there is a redistribution of money. Such proposals are more a matter of social justice than of public interest, although some redistribution may be in the public interest so long as those who receive funds are benefited more than those who lose funds are harmed.

More difficult cases concern providing benefits to small numbers of the public, for example, low-cost loans to businesses such as Lock-heed Aircraft or price supports to farmers. As explained earlier, those who directly receive these benefits are not, in that context, members of the public. Farm price supports must be shown to bene-fit non-farmers by helping ensure an adequate food supply, keep-ing prices low, providing goods for export to improve the national balance of payments, etc.

Even more difficult to support are subsidies for the arts—orchestras, operas, theaters, and public television. The employees of these en-terprises benefit directly. The audience for these activities repre-sents only a small percentage of the public. Moreover, those who wish to take advantage of the opportunity for aesthetic enjoyment could perhaps pay higher admission prices (pay TV) to make these enterprises self-supporting. Theoretically, it may be argued that there is some method of distributing costs among those who desire these benefits. Otherwise, it is claimed, the benefits are not really worth the expense.[29] However, such a system is very difficult to carry out in practice. Every time the price goes up, there will be people who decide not to observe such activities; the price will go up again, and more people will drop out.[30] Thus, the arts seem to be public goods for small segments of the population.[31] The public interest promotion principle can support such benefits provided that all other purposes of political authority are being sufficiently pursued and provided that such benefits are available to all segments of the population, so that everyone is likely to receive some benefit of this type which he wants.

The final types of legislation are private-arranging and compulsory treatment. The promotion principle supports private-arranging legislation, while the positive preservation principle supports limits upon the private arrangements made. Thus, the promotion principle supports, for example, marriage laws which are in the public interest. The preservation principle supports legislation prohibiting, or not enforcing, contracts in restraint of trade, etc. Compulsory treatment legislation is not supportable by the public interest principles: the loss of liberty involved is simply too great. Further, the chances for abuse by legislators, even those of good will, is tremendous. One can easily imagine being confined for therapy and "re-education" in the public interest if one happened to oppose the current regime. Thus, the public interest principles are weaker than the public welfare principles, in that the former do not support compulsory treatment while the latter do.

In conclusion, the public interest principles generally provide weaker reasons for and against legislation than the public welfare principles. However, the positive public interest principles do support penal legislation with respect to public goods. They also support all other types of legislation except compulsory treatment. The promotion principle is irrelevant for grievance-remedial legislation. The public welfare and interest principles are basic for supporting taxation, since a public good is involved.

The public welfare and interest principles are based upon aggregative concepts, that is, on the sum of benefits to the members of the public. While the welfare principles have an element of distributive justice built into them because there is an upper limit to a person's welfare, the public interest principles do not. Yet it has often been thought that one major purpose of political authority is to promote social justice, especially equality. The principles developed so far do not seem to do so. Moreover, some philosophers argue that requiring one person to contribute to the welfare of others through taxes is unjust. The next chapter considers social justice and the role of political authority in promoting it.

VIII
SOCIAL JUSTICE

Traditionally, one important purpose of political authority has been to secure justice. While most political philosophers have thought that political authority should ensure justice, they have meant very different things by "justice." Locke, for instance, thought that the justice which political authorities should ensure was primarily impartial enforcement of known laws. This conception of justice has already been discussed as governance by law. More recent political philosophers have had a broader conception.

Most analyses of social justice involve two elements—liberty and equality. Liberty has already been discussed. Freedom from governmental limits to action are provided for by the negative liberty-regarding principles. Liberty from limits imposed by other citizens has not been explicitly considered. However, the private harm principle clearly pertains to the lack of freedom which results from actions by other citizens. If political authorities are to protect citizens from harm caused by other citizens, then they must protect their liberty, for they must protect them from force. While the previous legislative principles explicitly or implicitly provide for liberty, they do not provide for equality. Hence, legislative principles of equality need to be considered.

EQUALITY OF OPPORTUNITY

Many principles of equality have been proposed as essential to social justice. Few people seriously argue for strict equality—identical

164

treatment of everyone—but few deny that some principle of equality is desirable. Between the two extremes there is a large area of disagreement. Nonetheless, there is widespread agreement that justice at least requires equality of opportunity, that everyone should have a fair and equal chance to obtain the good things in life even if some people are more successful in doing so than others.

Perhaps the best way to develop the concept of equality of opportunity is to first consider what it involves in a restricted area, in which its requirements may be clear. The concept can then be expanded to other areas. Equality of opportunity is thought to be very important in filling jobs. A person's share of wealth, power, prestige, and security is largely determined by his job. The following discussion is not meant to provide an analysis sufficient to clarify many current debates about job equality but only to describe the main elements of equality of opportunity in getting a job.

Equality of opportunity in obtaining a job may be analyzed by considering various ways in which it may be denied people. A job may be given to someone who is less well qualified, or the qualifications for a position may not be the basis on which it is filled; favoritism to friends and relatives may play a part. Thus, equality of opportunity involves giving jobs to those who best meet the qualifications. However, it is not always easy to determine who best meets the qualifications. To what extent can one meaningfully compare the competence of several holders of doctoral degrees applying for an assistant professorship?

Equality of opportunity may be denied even though a job is given to the person who best meets the stated qualifications. Qualifications might be that one be white, a Christian, or a Republican. Here the qualifications themselves deny equal opportunity. The objection to these qualifications is that they are not relevant to the performance of most jobs. There are special jobs for which they might be relevant, e.g., being a minister, but usually not. Thus, a second aspect of equality of opportunity is that the qualifications for a job must be relevant to a person's competence to perform the tasks involved.

One criticism of sexism and racism in the United States in recent years has been that stated qualifications for positions are irrelevant to performance of a given task. For example, many states used to require that bartenders be male, and the Supreme Court held that such laws did not deny equal protection.[1] It was claimed that men are better able to handle intoxicated and unruly customers, and the Supreme Court did not consider itself justified in overriding such a legislative judgment. However, even if true, that claim ignores the possibilities of using "bouncers" rather than bartenders to handle unruly customers. In short, it was not obvious that men would be better able to handle unruly customers (since women could be barmaids) nor that doing so was part of a bartender's tasks. This example shows the two distinct considerations which must be made: (1) what are the tasks of a position? and (2) what skills and abilities are needed to perform them?

The analysis of these two factors for specific jobs is often quite difficult. For example, many persons argue that university teachers serve as role models and, consequently, that being female or black may be relevant for such jobs. Moreover, there are problems about the levels of skill needed for various jobs. Are all those trained in American history who hold a doctoral degree competent to fill an assistant professorship in that field? These issues also relate to the requirement that the job be given to the most qualified person. There is now a vast literature addressed to these problems.

Suppose the most qualified applicant is chosen, and the qualifications are in fact all related to competence for the job. There might still be lack of equal opportunity because some people might not be permitted to apply—"No blacks need apply." Thus, a further condition for equality of opportunity is that everyone shall have a chance to apply and demonstrate his competence. For this condition to obtain, people must have access to information about job openings. A widespread practice in university hiring prior to the 1970s (which still exists to some extent) was the "old boy" system. When a department had an opening, a few faculty members would call their friends and ask for recommendations. Job openings were never announced, so unless one knew the right people one had no chance to apply. The availability of information that a job opening exists is thus fundamental.

At least one more condition is necessary for equality of opportunity. Suppose the three above conditions are fulfilled but the structure of society is such that certain people do not receive adequate educational training to qualify for certain jobs. For example, consider a racist society in which members of a particular race cannot get more than an elementary school education. Although accountants are hired strictly on the basis of competence for the task and everybody is permitted to apply, the members of the minority race simply never qualify for such positions. Thus, a final condition for equality of opportunity is that everyone be given an equal chance to develop his capacities.

This last condition is not clear until one knows what counts as denying people an equal chance to develop their capacities. Differences in competence caused by factors which are not under human control, such as inherited differences in capacity, do not deny persons equality of opportunity.[2] If a person cannot develop his capacities because of a social policy which deliberately excludes persons of his race, religion, etc., from certain types of training, then he is being denied equality of opportunity or an equal chance to develop his capacities. Controversial questions concern such factors as the following: a person may not be able to afford to attend a good school, or may receive little encouragement from his parents, or may have to drop out of school in order to work. Do these kinds of factors deprive people of an equal chance to develop their capacities?

While in fact a child's educational and other chances for developing his capacities may depend upon his family's income, wealth should not be a factor. Equality of opportunity requires that children of poor families have access to education equal to that of children of similar ability from wealthier families. However, equality of educational opportunity does not necessarily require equal funding per student. There are obvious economies of scale in larger schools: enough students to fill a Latin class may enable one to provide equal facilities for less money per student. What is more important, to require equal funding is to confuse inputs with outputs. The output should be the development of students' capacities. Students of very good and devoted teachers in schools with poor facilities will do better than students of poor teachers in schools with good facilities. Roughly equal facilities will contribute to equal educational opportunity, but mental challenge and stimulation, the asking of appropriate questions, and logical reasoning may occur quite independent of physical facilities, salaries, etc. In fact, very little is known about the conditions most important for the development of a critical, logically reasoning intellect.

Beyond the schools themselves, there is considerable evidence that children from different social classes receive different kinds of support and encouragement from their parents to attend school and engage in activities. While the attitude may be changing, for many years working-class families were much less inclined to encourage their children to attend college than were upper-income families. Thus, as Plato realized, pushed to its limits, an equal chance to develop one's capacities may require abolition of the family.[3]

There are limits to providing an equal chance to develop one's capacities. Logically, all humanly eliminable factors which might influence a person's development of his capacities should be made equivalent. In practice, however, there will always be some variation in the treatment and conditions of people which may affect their chances for developing their potential. Hence, perfect equality of opportunity is not realizable. Besides this practical point, provision of exactly equal chances in life for all would involve elimination of some factors which may be desirable on other grounds; that is, it would involve nearly identical life experiences, at least in childhood, and most would agree that there is value in variation. Most persons also believe that the family structure is of value and are willing to sacrifice some equality of opportunity in order to maintain it. Furthermore, it is agreed that differential treatment should be provided to persons who have unusual limitations of capacity. For example, children who are born blind or deaf or with other handicaps require special treatment if they are to develop their potential. Were they treated as normal children, they would not develop their abilities nearly as much. Differential treatment is required to provide them an equal chance.

The critical factor is that people not be denied an equal chance to develop their abilities because they are members of a given class. A fundamental objection to discrimination on racial, sexual, religious, and ethnic grounds is that people are not treated as individuals but as fungible members of a class, each replaceable by any other. Although mongoloids as a group have less intellectual capacity than non-mongoloids, their individual capacities differ widely. If the social structure cannot, and perhaps ought not to, provide everyone an equal chance to develop their capacities, it should at least try to randomize people's chances. People can then consider their good or ill fortune to be the result of a fair draw rather than of a stacked deck.

To summarize, there are four requirements for equal job opportunity. (1) Positions must be given to the best-qualified applicants. (2) Job qualifications must be relevant to the performance of the tasks involved. (3) Everyone must have an equal chance to demonstrate his qualifications for a position. (4) Everyone must have a roughly equal chance to develop his capacities so as to achieve competence for the tasks involved.

Since jobs are a primary means of distributing wealth, a brief comment may be made here about wages. A popular slogan of the women's movement is "equal pay for equal work." If this principle is interpreted to mean that the work done is the sole reason for the payment of wages, equal pay is not required to fulfill the goal of equality of opportunity: considerations of seniority and need (dependents) may also be appropriate in fixing wage levels. However, if equal pay is interpreted to mean that whatever criteria are used to determine wages for white males should be applied to females and blacks, then equal pay is required.

This conception of equality of opportunity pertains to jobs. However, social justice demands equality of opportunity for more than jobs. People may be denied equality of opportunity to use or enjoy public parks, transportation, and other facilities. Full equality of opportunity, then, includes equal opportunity to enjoy or take advantage of all public services. 'Public services' does not mean services provided by the public, i.e., those supported by public institutions, although these are of course included. The term means all those services offered to the public—restaurants, stores, and other businesses providing goods and services. The relevant qualifications for these goods and services (the parallel with task competence) are usually simply ability to pay for and use them. Thus, equality of opportunity requires that businesses serve all people regardless of race, creed, etc.

As always with this concept, there are gray areas between that which is public and that which is private. One very difficult area concerns social clubs—country clubs, Elks, Moose, etc.—with exclusionary clauses in their rules preventing people of certain races, religions, etc., from being members or guests. Various considerations are involved. The purpose of such clubs is the promotion of activities with friends. This purpose might be defeated if they were forced to admit people with whom most members did not wish to associate, yet many people believe that considerations of race and religion are not appropriate grounds for liking or disliking people. Hence these considerations are not relevant, or ought not be relevant, to friendships and associations.

Essentially, social clubs involve a conflict between privacy and freedom, and equality of opportunity. Considerations of privacy and freedom allow people to exclude persons from parties in their own homes on grounds of race, etc. The question is whether this privacy and freedom of association should extend to social clubs. The implications of equality of opportunity are not clear in such cases. It may be maintained that if clubs cannot exclude persons on such grounds everyone may still exclude people from their homes and not join clubs. On the other side, it may be maintained that people who are excluded may form their own clubs. Moreover, since membership in clubs is voluntary, those who object to such exclusions need not join them. Consequently, exclusionary social clubs do not clearly deny equality of opportunity. Whether or not they should be legally forbidden, however, rests on the application of various legislative principles.[4]

Equality of opportunity includes the principle of non-discrimination but not what is sometimes called the integration principle. It requires that jobs and public services be distributed on the basis of considerations relevant to task performance or the provision and use of goods and services. A person's race, sex, creed, or national origin is almost always irrelevant to his ability to perform the tasks of a job or to take advantage of goods and services. The integration principle requires a mix of people of different racial, ethnic, religious, sexual, or age classes in various social divisions.[5] In its strong form, the ratio of people of different classes in all social divisions (including types of jobs) is required· to be the same as that in the total population. In its weak form, a proportional mix is not required, only that the different classes be generally mixed in society.

The integration principle (in either form) may be either a fundamental or secondary one. As a fundamental principle, it is not very attractive. It is simply a preference for a socially mixed society independent of the effects of that mix on other social values. It thus appears to be an aesthetic principle which has gotten into politics and morality by mistake, and it is not even a good aesthetic principle. In a representative painting, it is not desirable to have the same colors mixed in the sky and grass.

As a secondary principle, integration is justified by its effects upon society.[6] It may be held that it promotes efficiency and harmony or protects minority groups. The efficiency argument, however, is not plausible insofar as integration requires that someone other than the best qualified person receive a job. The disharmony and minority group protection arguments are similar. Disharmony would probably result from non-integration only if most members of a minority group were in the less desirable positions. Assuming group consciousness, disharmony would result from members of the group being envious or believing that they had been wronged. It is highly questionable that the members of a group should be mixed with members of another group simply because they are envious.[7]

If the group has been wronged (disharmony or non-protection), the wrong must be determined by some independent criterion. The equality of opportunity principle would serve as such a criterion.[8] Further, equality of opportunity would probably result in a social mix which would prevent disharmony.

Providing equality of opportunity includes providing the conditions required by the public welfare principle. People who are cold, hungry, or ill do not have the same chance to develop their capacities as those who are not. Thus, considerations of equality of opportunity and public welfare overlap. However, there is a difference between them. Two policies may provide the same total amount of welfare, but one may distribute it more evenly among the population than the other. While welfare considerations provide no reason for preferring one of these policies to the other, considerations of equality of opportunity do provide a reason for preferring the policy which results in the more even distribution. Because equality of opportunity requires a distribution of goods needed to develop capacities equally, it may entail a relativistic concept of poverty. For example, (although there are some good reasons against it) it might be defined as having less than half the average income. Such a concept does not imply that poor people are below a minimal standard of living or that their relatively low income is the result of unequal opportunities. The point is that in an affluent society, in order to have equal opportunities the worst off must live substantially above the minimal standard of living required for one's welfare.[9]

There are two possible equality of opportunity principles of legislation. The positive principle is that if legislation increases equality of opportunity, that is a reason for it. The negative principle is that if legislation decreases equality of opportunity, that is a reason against it. Thus, the negative principle covers all legislation which discriminates among classes of people on irrelevant grounds. For example, all of the school segregation legislation which once existed in the United States was contrary to the negative principle. The irrelevance of discrimination among classes of people may be determined, at least in the first instance, by noting that since the aim of public schools is to provide education to people, the color of their skin is irrelevant, although their intellectual capacity is not. This issue of relevant factors is discussed further in the next section.

The desirability of the equality of opportunity principles rests upon three major considerations. First, equality of opportunity increases one's freedom by enabling one to engage in various activities if one so desires. Second, equality of opportunity is in one's interest. The development of capacities is essential for one to be able to satisfy self-regarding wants. If one has not had a chance to develop one's capacities at mathematics, one cannot fulfill one's desire to be a computer programmer. A basic self-regarding want of most persons is for a certain type of employment; that is, one of a person's most basic self-regarding desires is to be employed in a job which he finds interesting and satisfying. Equality of opportunity especially pertains to the fulfillment of this desire; however, it does not provide a reason for everything which might be done to fulfill it.[10]

Third, equality of opportunity opens the way for one to engage in activities utilizing one's capacities. John Rawls has suggested what he calls the Aristotelian Principle: "other things equal, human beings enjoy the exercise of their realized capacities (their innate or trained abilities), and this enjoyment increases the more the capacity is realized, or the greater its complexity."[11] This idea is a modern formulation of the claim made by many hedonists such as J. S. Mill that the pleasures consequent on the use of "higher" capacities (usually intellectual ones) are different in kind and preferable to those involved in the use of "lower" capacities. This claim does not appear to be plausible if taken as universal.[12] However, it does appear plausible if restricted to employment: equality of opportunity for jobs will increase satisfaction by making it easier to develop one's capacities and use them in one's work.

These considerations for the desirability of the equality of opportunity principles all rest upon increasing one's opportunities. The difficult point is whether a reasonable person would accept principles which emphasize *equal* opportunities. Would he not prefer a principle which favored himself by granting more opportunities to a class to which he belongs than it does to other classes? Such an argument is not easily refuted. Nonetheless, certain types of unequal opportunity principles would not be accepted. A principle to the effect that political authorities may give greater opportunities to their friends would not be acceptable. A person may not be a friend of certain political authorities, and even if he is at a given moment, he may not still be at a later date. So no principle which lets political authorities decide arbitrarily upon the favored class or membership in it would be acceptable.

However, principles of unequal opportunity which favor classes to which a reasonable person belongs and is almost certain to continue to belong are not ruled out by such considerations.

Moreover, it is certainly in a person's interest to accept such principles. Sometimes it is argued that it is not in a person's long term interest to adopt such principles because those who are excluded may take revenge upon the favored classes.[13] At best, the soundness of these arguments is doubtful. However, it is clear that no one will accept a principle which gives him a less than equal opportunity. Since all other principles favor one class at the expense of another, only equality of opportunity principles can be acceptable to everyone. For a political system to endure, there must be fairly widespread agreement upon acceptable principles. Nevertheless, this consideration would not prevent a large majority from accepting a principle assigning lesser opportunities to a small minority. In such a circumstance, however, the average member of the majority would have little to lose by adopting the equality of opportunity principle because if the minority is small, his loss will be small.

The upshot is that the equality of opportunity principles probably cannot be shown to be acceptable to a reasonable person who is completely self-interested: at least some benevolence is needed. Moreover, such benevolence must be of the stronger sort involved in justifying the acceptability of the public interest principles rather than the weaker sort used for public welfare principles. Still, a person need not have a concern for all others or a concern for them equal to his concern for himself; all he need have is concern that other subjects of the political system to which he belongs shall have an opportunity equal to his, not that they be equally successful. And self-interest still plays a role in accepting the principle that the government shall promote equal opportunities because a person might not accept it unless he thought he would also benefit. Most people appear to have sufficient benevolence to accept such principles, but they backslide when their implementation requires a sacrifice on their part. Backsliding especially occurs when people are deprived of opportunities they previously had so that opportunities for others can be provided.

Consequently, the positive equality of opportunity principle would be more acceptable if its use were restricted to increasing equality of opportunity only when it can be done without decreasing anyone else's opportunities except insofar as they are naturally decreased by the fact that more people have the same opportunities. For example, suppose that only white persons are permitted in national parks. Equality of opportunity can be achieved in two ways— excluding everybody or letting non-whites into the parks. The latter method will decrease the opportunities of white persons to obtain rooms at park lodges and good camping sites because it will result in increased demand for them. By the first method, opportunities of white persons are directly decreased, and not because others now have more opportunities. The restriction upon the use of the positive equality of opportunity principle is meant to exclude the first method, not the second. Also, it is not an absolute restriction. It may be necessary to deprive some people of opportunities in order to increase opportunities of other kinds for disadvantaged persons. But the greater number of people who are deprived of such opportunities, the weaker the reason provided by the equality of opportunity principle. Consequently, a criterion of application for the positive equality of opportunity principle is that the opportunities of others not be decreased as a result.

While one should use the positive equality of opportunity principle sparingly for penal legislation, it does support it. There are clear instances of the denial of equality of opportunity, especially instances of discrimination. Some such denials are so fundamental that the strongest possible measures must be taken to prevent them, for examples, denials of employment and the right to vote. Criminal laws forbidding such discrimination are supported by the equality of opportunity principle. They are most strongly supported when the discrimination is practiced by persons in positions of political authority.

In many areas, administrative-regulatory and grievance-remedial legislation may be more effective than penal legislation in preventing discrimination. Instead of punishing those who deny others equality of opportunity, such bodies can simply be required to make good what they have denied. Thus, the government may set up commissions to ensure that women receive pay and promotion on the same basis as others. Organizations which deny women, blacks, and other minority groups equality of opportunity can be required to provide pay increases, promotions, and perhaps even preferential treatment.[14] Grievance-remedial legislation would permit those discriminated against to sue to recover losses from (and perhaps penal damages for) discrimination. These techniques are combined, for example, in the U.S. Equal Employment Opportunity Commission. There is much to commend the use of grievance-remedial legislation in this way. Without a large bureaucracy, the government cannot monitor practices throughout society to ensure equality of opportunity. If those subject to the practices can sue to obtain it, then many persons (those most concerned) are monitoring them at no increase in governmental expense except the minimal one of providing court facilities.

Equality of opportunity supports benefit-conferring legislation designed to enable people to develop their capacities. Thus, it supports high-quality free or low-cost education at all levels. It supports scholarships and financial aid to give the poor the same opportunities as the rich and preschool programs for disadvantaged children. Further, the positive equality of opportunity principle supports public provision of museums, libraries, and other cultural facilities which are essential for developing one's capacities. The emphasis in benefit-conferring legislation supported by the positive equality of opportunity principle is upon provision of benefits for children. It is primarily in one's youth that capacities are developed, especially capacities which can be utilized in jobs. However, people can develop capacities throughout their lives, so the equality of opportunity principle supports provision for such development, as in adult education programs.

The equality of opportunity principle does not support burden-imposing legislation, except as needed to provide the benefits supported by it, and it is not acceptable for compulsory treatment legislation. The idea of equality of opportunity is to provide the chance to develop capacities, not to require that they be developed. Thus, it does not support legislation requiring those in the upper 5 per cent in mathematical ability to develop their capacity by studying mathematics. It does not support compulsory treatment of those who are inclined to deny others equality of opportunity. Their desires and inclinations to discriminate are their own business so long as they are not acted upon except in private matters such as friendships.

SOCIAL PRIORITIES

Acceptance of the equality of opportunity principles obviously helps account for social justice. However, it may be thought that other principles are needed—that the social justice which political authority should pursue involves more than equality of opportunity. Many writers have argued that the basic formal principle of justice is that like cases be treated alike and different cases be treated differently. Indeed, some argue that this principle, or a very similar one, is a requirement of rationality.[15] However, the principle does not state that cases should be presumed to be alike until shown to be otherwise. This latter principle is a rule of evidence, a presumptivist principle. There is no general requirement of rationality that cases should be presumed to be alike instead of different.[16]

The formal principle of justice is not simply a prescription to comply with general rules.[17] Instead, it prescribes that only relevant considerations be taken into account. If there are no relevant differences, then cases must be treated alike; if there are relevant differences, then they should be treated differently in proportion to their differences. But if the principle is a requirement of rationality, it is only because 'relevant' means providing a good reason for treating cases in some particular way. However, the formal principle does not determine which features are relevant or irrelevant. Indeed, Aristotle recognized that the crucial problem in issues of justice is the determination of what features are relevant.

The issue of relevancy may arise at different levels in a system of political authority.[18] The most concrete level concerns the application of laws to particular cases. Here the criteria of relevancy are specified by the laws. The laws determine classes of people who are to be treated in certain ways. For example, the crime of burglary involves unlawfully entering or remaining in a building with the intent to commit a crime. Two people who meet these conditions are both guilty of burglary. It would be unjust to charge one with the crime and not the other. A person who unlawfully enters or remains in a building without the intent to commit a crime differs from the first two persons in a relevant respect, as defined by the law. It would be unjust to charge him with burglary. He should be treated differently—charged with criminal trespass. Justice at this level, however, is not a matter of legislation but of administration. Thus, although this aspect of justice was discussed under the heading of governance by law, it was not made a legislative principle.

The next level of justice concerns the relevancy of the characteristics specified in the law. For example, although it might be justly administered, a law which granted a right to counsel in criminal trials to the rich but not the poor would be unjust. This basis for selecting people who are entitled to counsel is irrelevant to the immediate aim of the law, which is to ensure that the defendant's position is adequately presented in court. There is no reason to believe that the positions of poor people can be adequately presented without counsel but those of rich people cannot. Justice here concerns properly drafting legislation to achieve the desired aim. The negative equality of opportunity principle covers this sort of situation. To deny counsel to the poor is to deny them an opportunity on grounds irrelevant to the use of the opportunity.

The next level of justice concerns the formulation of the immediate aim of legislation. Its aim may itself be unjust because the legislative purposes or principles which support it are not acceptable ones. For example, since a criminal law prohibiting oral or anal sexual relations between married couples (sodomy) would not be supported by any acceptable principle, the aim of the legislation would not be justifiable. Hence, one may consider the law unjust no matter how carefully it is drafted and how impartial its administration.

There is another way in which the immediate aim of legislation may be considered unjust. Suppose many persons are malnourished and receive inadequate medical services. Further suppose there are several million dollars in the state treasury which the legislature has not yet appropriated. If the legislature appropriates the money to build new state parks, many people would consider the immediate aim of the legislation unjust. The legislature is not pursuing an unacceptable purpose, for presumably state parks are in the public interest. Instead, the claim is that the legislature is promoting the public interest instead of the public welfare, and that the public welfare is a more important purpose. In short, the legislative priorities are wrong.

Not all political philosophers would agree that mistaken priorities are properly considered a matter of justice, but all would consider them to be crucial for the use of political authority. Indeed, in recent years much political discussion in the United States has centered on questions of social priorities. Defense budgets have been criticized because large expenditures of funds provide only negligible increments in national security when similar expenditures could make large improvements in the public welfare. This element of justice may be called putting first things first. It requires establishing some system of priority among legislative principles.

One method of establishing priorities is to rank principles in a lexicographical order so that legislation to achieve one purpose must be passed, or the purpose secured, before legislation to pursue the second is considered.[19] Thus, one might hold that the private harm principle comes before the public interest ones and that no legislation to secure the public interest is justified until citizens are secured as well as they may be from private injury. However, one might be willing to swap some decrease in protection from private injury for a great gain in equality of opportunity or public interest. Further, private harm and public interest considerations vary according to the severity of the injury and the importance of the self-regarding wants being fulfilled.[20] Since principles may support legislation in different degrees, no such lexicographical ordering of them is plausible.

Nonetheless, there is some conception of priority of principles. Considerations of private harm are usually more important than those of public interest. In evaluating the priority of legislation, one should look at which types of principles are involved and at how strongly the legislation pursues the given purposes. Only very affluent societies can pursue all the purposes of political authority simultaneously, and in underdeveloped countries only a few purposes can be pursued with any effectiveness. It is therefore important to have a conception of which purposes should be paramount.

While principles cannot be placed in a lexicographical order, they can still be placed in a partial serial order. If there are principles of similar importance, they can be classed as a group which has greater or lesser importance than other groups. The discussion of the various principles of legislation in the previous chapters has already provided a basis for ranking the principles in importance and has shown that they pertain to more or less basic self-regarding wants. Some positive principles do and others do not override the liberty-regarding considerations against types of legislation. Hence, the positive principles can be partially ranked by the negative liberty-regarding principles they override.

The strongest negative liberty-regarding principle is that against penal legislation. Only five positive principles can frequently override it. Thus they appear to provide the most important purposes for political authority. The first purpose, both historically and as developed here, is protection from injury by others, i.e., the private harm principle. A political system which does not protect citizens from murder, assault, robbery, and theft has failed. Second comes the public harm principle, for it is essential to the pursuit of any other purpose. Third is the public welfare preservation principle. The first three principles thus primarily protect a person's minimal well-being and the social system necessary for such protection. The fourth principle supporting penal legislation is that of equality of opportunity. It primarily supports penal legislation to prevent denial of equal opportunity by political authorities. In effect, it supports penal legislation for equality before the law. Other considerations of equality of opportunity are of lesser importance and may well rank below other principles.

The fifth principle is that of privacy. It may be considerably less important than the others. In many underdeveloped countries, the concern with privacy is much less than it is in developed countries. Hence, one may think that privacy should not be given the importance it is accorded here. The penal legislation which the privacy principle supports concerns only gross violations. However, with the development of many technological devices for invading privacy, this principle will probably assume much more importance in all countries than it has in the past, when protection of privacy was not a major purpose of political authority simply because invasion of privacy was not very easy.

Two other principles support compulsory treatment legislation involving incarceration. Since the liberty-regarding principle against compulsory treatment involving incarceration is almost as strong as that against penal legislation, these principles may be listed next in order of priority. Sixth comes the public welfare promotion principle. Seventh is the weak preservative paternalist principle. Both of these principles are also concerned with rather basic levels of well-being. Equality of opportunity other than that guaranteed by penal legislation probably falls in here. It is basic to one's chances of satisfying self-regarding wants.

The seven principles listed so far provide a reasonable set for political authorities; that is, if a system of political authority is reasonably successful in pursuing these purposes, it will have made society a rather acceptable place in which to live. One will be protected from private injury, will have reasonably good health, will be prevented from injuring oneself, will have an equal opportunity to fulfill one's wants, and will have a minimal amount of privacy. These principles provide an ideal which is sufficiently out of the reach of most underdeveloped countries to be worthy of their most serious efforts.

Affluent, industrially developed countries, however, can set other purposes for political authority to pursue. These purposes consist of the rest of the acceptable principles of legislation. There is little basis for ranking them except that the public interest preservation principle is prior to the public interest promotion principle. The reason for that was discussed in developing the principles. Between these two principles comes the weak promotive paternalist principle. After all of them come the positive liberty-regarding principles for private-arranging and benefit-conferring legislation.

One caveat must be made concerning this ranking of principles. The imposition of taxes falls under the public interest principles as concerned with a public good. Hence, the public interest principles as supporting the public good of financing governmental operations must be accorded sufficient weight to provide adequate taxes for whatever programs are justifiable. The listing of the public interest principles in the third and least important group must then be construed as reflecting matters other than the public good of maintaining adequate governmental financial resources.

The negative legislative principles may also be ranked in categories of general importance. The most weighty negative principle is the liberty-regarding one against penal legislation. In the same group with it and of almost equal weight is the principle against compulsory treatment legislation. Also in this group but perhaps of somewhat lesser importance are the negative public welfare and privacy principles. Decreases in public welfare obviously cause great harm to basic self-regarding wants. Some losses of privacy may not be of sufficient weight to be listed here, but governmental invasion of privacy by wiretaps, searches, and seizures are certainly very difficult to justify.

The negative principles in the second group do not provide as strong reasons against legislation as those in the previous group. The liberty-regarding principles against administrative-regulatory, grievance-remedial, and burden-imposing legislation belong here. Likewise, the negative equality of opportunity principle and the freedom of communication principle belong to this group. The classification of the freedom of communication principle in this group does not imply that legislation abridging freedom of communication is very easy to justify. Where restrictions on freedom of communication by political authority are concerned, one of the other liberty-regarding principles applies as well as the freedom of communication principle. Thus, for example, penal legislation limiting freedom of communication always has two reasons against it, which makes it much more difficult to justify than most other penal legislation.

The establishment of priority among legislative principles thus completes the account of justice at three levels: that of the purpose, the formulation, and the application of legislation. However, a crucial area of social justice concerns the distribution of burdens, especially taxes. A full discussion of justice with respect to taxation would require a complete book. Nevertheless, a brief sketch is needed to indicate how the various principles apply to determining a just method of taxation.

Tax burdens are distributed to support programs pursuing acceptable purposes of political authority. The positive equality of opportunity principle is restricted to making people more equal by increasing, not decreasing, opportunities. All impositions of burdens, including taxes, decrease people's opportunities by depriving them of the means to purchase goods and services. Hence, the positive equality of opportunity principle is not directly relevant to determining tax burdens.

Taxes are also a public good problem. Everyone or nearly everyone benefits, but they cannot do so unless they are sure that enough others will also contribute. Thus, nearly everyone must share in the tax burden. The negative equality of opportunity principle provides a reason against legislation which decreases equality of opportunity. If the tax burden on the rich is smaller than that on the poor, then the taxation decreases equality of opportunity. Consequently, the negative equality of opportunity principle supports the burden on the rich being at least as great as that on the poor, but the positive equality of opportunity principle does not support its being greater.

However, it is not clear what constitutes as great a burden. It may mean either equal quantity of burden or equal percentage of burden.[21] With equal quantity of burden, the point is to ensure that the rich forgo as much interest fulfillment (utility) as the poor. With equal percentage burden, the rich must forgo the same percentage of their total interest fulfillment (utility) as the poor. Since equality of opportunity concerns the relative positions of people, the percentage or proportional burden is the appropriate interpretation. With equal quantity of burden, the relative position of the poor vis-à-vis the rich would become worse. For example, suppose a poor person had 2 units of utility and a rich person 10 units, a relative proportion of 1 to 5. If each had a tax burden of one unit of utility, the after-tax relative proportion would be 1 to 9.

Adoption of the equal percentage burden interpretation does not, by itself, justify a progressive or graduated income tax rate but only a proportional (same percentage) one. In order to support a progressive tax rate, one must accept the principle of diminishing returns for income which states that the utility of money decreases the more of it one has. This principle has intuitive appeal; the utility of fifty dollars to a person with an annual income of three thousand dollars seems greater than its utility to a. person with an annual income of thirty thousand dollars. While there is also some empirical support for this principle, it is at best a statistical generalization.[22] With the principle, however, the rich must pay a higher percentage tax in order to forgo the same percentage of utility.

Nevertheless, there are several difficulties with this justification of progressive taxation.[23] Even at the same level of income, the utility which people derive from money varies enormously. Moreover, even if one uses a reasonable person as a standard for determining the utility of income, there is no strong evidence as to how rapidly utility of income decreases. Without such knowledge, there is no way to determine how progressive tax rates should be. Finally, the principle becomes less intuitively plausible the more rapidly utility of income decreases. For example, to support a 10 percent tax rate for an income of ten thousand dollars and 20 percent for an income of twenty thousand, one must claim that fifty dollars for a person of the lower income has as much utility as one hundred dollars for a person with the higher income. Thus, the reasons for a steeply progressive tax rate are not very persuasive.

However, even use of a proportional tax must take into account other principles. A tax which deprives people of a minimal standard of living would hinder the public welfare purpose. Any goods needed for a minimal standard of living which might be taken away by taxation would have to be made up by returning the money or providing goods and services. Moreover, as noted above, at least in advanced societies equality of opportunity requires a level of well-being considerably above the minimal standard of living, and no one should be deprived of it via tax burdens. Since tax burdens ought not to deprive people of a minimal standard of living or equality of opportunity, people at the lower end of the economic scale might not be taxed at all but might receive net benefits. Such a procedure may save administrative costs of taxing and spending. Whether it is easier to tax them and then return benefits in the form of money, goods, and services or to tax them less or not at all is, in the end, a technical question.

Simple considerations of justice, such as equal burdens, are thus not the only relevant ones in determining tax rates. One must consider their effect upon the achievement of all governmental purposes. Even if one begins with the assumption that the rates should be equal percentages, one may vary them in order to pursue other purposes. For example, one may set lower rates to encourage activities in the public interest and set higher rates to discourage activities contrary to the public interest. Psychologically (and perhaps legally) it is easier for legislators to encourage activities by not taxing them than by providing benefits. Even apart from constitutional problems in the United States, most legislators would find it very difficult to vote funds for churches and non-profit organizations in amounts equal to the taxes forgone by making them tax-exempt. Moreover, it is doubtful that the acceptable legislative principles would support such actions in many cases. In order to keep the reasons for benefit-conferring legislation clear, the collection and expenditure of revenues is preferable to the method of tax exemption. However, other considerations, such as administrative costs, may outweigh this one. What is essential is that in each case one be able to justify the benefits by appropriate legislative principles.

The final problem concerns what wealth should be taxed. The above discussion assumes that it is to be income, but many taxes are not on income. Sales taxes are assessed upon income spent. The underlying principle is that a person does not derive a benefit from wealth until he uses it, and so no burden (tax) should be imposed before then. Indeed, if people save money, they already forgo the benefits they could obtain by spending it. However, one might argue that they receive the benefit of financial security, which to them must be of equal value or they would not save.

One may also consider whether non-investment property such as automobiles, furniture, and homes should be taxed for general revenues. Usually, a sales tax is paid on automobiles and furniture, and a property tax on such items is double taxation, once as purchase and again as property, which is not the case with money spent on such things as entertainment. Indeed, it is a triple tax if the income which paid for them has also been taxed. While there is no sales tax on houses, capital gains from their sale are taxed in the United States. Moreover, with the income tax, money used to purchase the house has usually already been taxed once. One might claim that property tax does not impose an extra burden without an extra benefit because people derive continuing benefit from such property, but this continuing benefit has already been figured into the original cost and decision to buy. Moreover, there is a continuing benefit in the form of fond memories derived from money spent on entertainment. Consequently, in order to provide an equal burden, whether one taxes income or expenditures at proportional or progressive rates, much can be said for having only one form of taxation rather than the plurality of forms which now exists in most countries.

ALTERNATIVE CONCEPTIONS

The foregoing account of the purposes of political authority and justice may be criticized as inadequate from two different perspectives. Some critics will contend that it does not go far enough toward establishing equality. Other critics may contend that the welfare and equality of opportunity principles go too far. In this section, each of these criticisms will be briefly examined. Two recent and impressive arguments for the respective positions are those of John Rawls and Robert Nozick. It would be impossible to analyze and criticize the views of Rawls and Nozick within the compass of a section or even a chapter. The intention here is to use their work as a basis for considering these two possible lines of criticism.

The first line of criticism contends that equality of opportunity, public welfare, and public interest do not sufficiently provide for equality because the benefits attached to positions would be so unequal that justice would not be achieved. Even if everyone has an equal opportunity, some people will fail to obtain the better positions. Their failure will be due, at least in part, to lack of capacity, but according to Rawls, people do not "deserve" their natural capacities and character because capacities and character depend upon factors which they do not control. The notion of desert does not apply to natural endowments or character.[24] Thus, social arrangements which allow the distribution of goods to be determined by them are unjust.

This intuitive basis for Rawls' theory is appealing and widely shared, but it is not obviously true. A couple of points will be suggested which cast some doubt on it (although they hardly refute it).[25] In claiming that natural endowments and character are neither deserved nor undeserved, Rawls is apparently contending that they are irrelevant to how people should be treated. First, this claim seems to be false. As noted at the beginning of this chapter, those born with handicaps deserve extra goods from society in order to receive equal opportunities; of course, one may claim (as was done) that the different treatment is needed to provide equal opportunities and benefits. However, such a reply shifts the concept of "treatment." In short, one must specify which natural endowments and character are irrelevant for what kinds of policies, for in some contexts, some of them are relevant to the distribution of economic goods.

Second, even if natural endowment and character are irrelevant, it does not follow that people should be treated equally. For that to follow, one must take the formal principle of justice to be a presumptivist one. Rawls assumes that people in an original contract position are equal and are essentially impartial (by the veil of ignorance, which prevents knowledge of one's particular situation) and that the problem is to justify inequalities. The method adopted in Chapter II above does not make such assumptions. Indeed, almost the reverse is true. People are taken as they are found in society, and a constant issue has been how to justify equality to people who are not in equal positions and are not impartial. The problem is to justify the exercise of political authority to transfer goods from those with more to those with less.

To prevent the alleged injustice of the distribution of goods and benefits attached to positions being determined by natural endowments and character, Rawls adopts the difference principle. According to it, given the greatest equal liberty and equality of opportunity, inequalities attached to positions are to be arranged so that they are "to the greatest benefit of the least advantaged."[26] Essentially, then, everyone is presumed to be entitled to equal benefits, but this presumption may be overridden if overriding it will benefit the least advantaged. There are many qualifications and assumptions governing the use of this principle which need not be considered here. For present purposes, the difference principle may be used as the basis for suggesting other legislative principles of justice.

The issue, then, is whether a reasonable person would accept the difference principle as a legislative principle. This issue is not the one to which Rawls addresses himself. He argues for the difference principle as part of a moral conception of justice for the basic structure of society rather than for legislation. As argued in Chapter II, legislative and moral principles are distinct. Hence, even if the difference principle is a proper moral account of justice, it does not follow that it should be accepted as a legislative principle. Not all morally good ends should be pursued by political authority.

There would probably be two legislative principles based on the difference principle, a negative and a positive one. The positive principle would state that if legislation increases the well-being of the least advantaged, that is a reason for it. The negative principle would state that if legislation decreases the well-being of the least advantaged, that is a reason against it. Following the general assumption that people are more concerned to prevent decreases in their well-being than to achieve increases, the negative principle would be a stronger one than the positive principle. Hence, one may focus upon it, for if it is unacceptable, the positive one probably is too.

One must consider what legislation the 'difference principles might justify by themselves. Since the claim is that they are needed in addition to the previous principles, their practical function would be for legislation to which the previous principles do not apply. The negative (and positive) public welfare and equality of opportunity principles provide reasons against (for) legislation decreasing the well-being of the least advantaged. So the real issue concerns decreases (increases) in the well-being of the least advantaged other than those required for a minimal standard of living and equality of opportunity. However, the public interest principles pertain to well-being above these levels. Hence, the practical scope of difference principles of legislation would be restricted to providing a reason against legislation in the public interest which does not benefit the least advantaged and a reason in favor of legislation which benefits the least advantaged but does not promote the public interest. Thus, the practical scope for the independent use of difference principles of legislation would be quite limited.

Rawls' argument for the difference principle is based upon acceptance conditions different from those used in this book. Essentially, he contends that a person accepting principles under the conditions he specifies would choose conservatively, using a maximin strategy of choice, i.e., opt for that choice in which the worst outcome is better than for any other choice. For example, if the

worst outcome from one option were a loss of fifty dollars and the
worst outcome from another option were a loss of sixty dollars,
one would choose the first. A maximin strategy ignores the best
outcomes. Thus, one would still choose the first option even if the best
outcome of the second option were much better, e.g., a gain of
three hundred rather than seventy-five dollars. Rawls presents
three conditions which make such a strategy plausible—the probabilities are discounted, one cares very little for the benefits one
might gain above the minimum, and the other choices have unacceptable outcomes.[27]

None of these conditions applies to a person's accepting legislative
principles under the conditions developed in Chapter II, "Acceptance Conditions." No conditions of ignorance were imposed requiring that probabilities should or must be discounted. Even if he
accepts the principle of diminishing returns, a reasonable person
would want any benefits he might receive above the minimum.
Finally, none of the outcomes is totally unacceptable. Given the
public welfare and equality of opportunity principles, no choice will
result in a totally miserable life. Indeed, all choices probably provide a better life than the current minimum in any society.

Consequently, instead of a maximin strategy, a reasonable
person would seek to maximize expectable average utility. The
public interest principles essentially do that. In order to justify
them, it was assumed that a person would usually be a member of
the public benefited by public interest legislation and that he would
have considerable benevolence toward others. It is plausible to assume the first part because the public is a large, indeterminate
group of persons not directly benefited by the legislation. However, one cannot assume that most people will be members of the
class of least advantaged. This contention would only hold for societies with a large poor class (more than 50 percent of the population). But the advanced industrialized societies are not so struc-
tured, and in the underdeveloped countries the public welfare and
equality of opportunity principles are more important and provide
for the poor. Consequently, acceptance of the difference principles
would require complete as opposed to limited benevolence. People
who are not members of the least advantaged class (a majority)
would have to desire that the members of the least advantaged class
be made as well off as possible, no matter what they themselves
might have to give up. If the more advantaged are not completely
benevolent, they will assert that they should receive at least some

benefits in addition to those (if any) which they would receive through making the least advantaged as well off as possible.[28]

Thus, additional principles to provide for more equality do not appear acceptable unless the unrealistic assumption is made that people are completely benevolent. However, it may be argued that the principles already accepted go too far in providing for equality and violate fundamental rights. In particular, the principles that have been developed are what Nozick calls "end-result" or "patterned" principles.[29] End-result principles determine the correctness of the distribution of goods on the basis of a current or series of time slices; that is, they are concerned with the distribution of goods to persons regardless of how that distribution came about historically. In contrast, Nozick opts for historical principles which hold that past circumstances or actions may determine who should have what; that is, the justice of a distribution of goods depends on how the distribution came about. Some historical principles are "patterned"; that is, they specify that distributions are to vary along some natural dimension. The welfare principles are patterned because they prescribe distributions of goods on the basis of the natural characteristics of a minimal standard of living. The public interest and equality of opportunity principles, however, are end-result principles because they support distributions which maximize interest fulfillment and the same opportunities.

Nozick objects to both end-result and patterned principles because they are incompatible with liberty.[30] If people are allowed to make transfers of wealth and goods, the resulting distribution will not be in accordance with that prescribed by a given end-result or patterned principle. Hence, people will have to be prohibited from making exchanges or further transfers will have to be required to establish the prescribed distribution. However, this objection fails to take into account the fact that acceptable principles are founded upon persons' self-regarding wants. If two (or more) people want to exchange goods or money, then presumably both consider it in their interest to do so. A set of such transactions, since each would be to the interest of those involved, would be in the public interest. Hence, the public interest promotion principle supports private-arranging legislation which allows them. Moreover, since welfare and opportunities are in people's basic interests, presumably they will not exchange goods needed for them except for something they want very much. The weak paternalist principles do not support legislation preventing people from making such exchanges unless they are incapable of fully voluntary decisions about them.

Finally, the liberty-regarding principles oppose legislation which would unduly restrict liberty, i.e., restrict it without justification by other acceptable principles.

However, Nozick's more basic argument is based upon his "entitlement" theory of justice. In essence, this view is that the possession of goods (holdings) is just (one is entitled to them) if the goods were justly acquired from someone entitled to them. If one assumes that unowned property was originally acquired in a just manner (as Nozick appears to do, though with some hesitation), and that the subsequent transfers have been just, then each person has a right to the property he has. Political authority must not violate people's rights. A right to property is the right to determine what shall be done with it, subject to the constraints that the rights of others not be violated (essentially determined by the private harm principle).[31] Any legislative principle which requires persons to transfer property (via taxation) contrary to their desires, violates people's rights and is unjust.

This argument is very complex, and only the very bare outlines have been presented to show its basic structure and the difficulties with it. First, it violates the autonomy of political allegiance. The property rights of which Nozick speaks are moral rights. As was indicated early in Chapter II, political theory should proceed independent of moral principles. Second, Nozick assumes there are no obligations which do not have corresponding rights. If there are such obligations, e.g., those of beneficence, then persons with property may have obligations to provide for the well-being of others. Third, Nozick encompasses more in the concept of property rights than has traditionally been included. While he does not spell out precisely what he does include, historically there have been more limits than he implies. People have not been allowed to use their property in ways contrary to the perceived public welfare and interest: tort law has long been concerned with public nuisances. In short, Nozick's conception of a property right is too strong. Even if one accepts a general theory of entitlements, one may accept (and historically there have been) limits upon what a property right involves. Nozick has not shown or attempted to show that his conception of a property right is morally justifiable.[32]

If one drops the natural rights basis for Nozick's claim, there is no basis for criticizing the acceptable legislative principles as violating rights. In particular, if the arguments for the various legislative principles have been sound, a reasonable person would not wish to claim rights contrary to them. The principles were acceptable on the grounds of self-interest and limited benevolence. Of course, if a person knew he was better off than most members of society and did not possess even limited benevolence, he might accept rights which would protect his preferred position, and if a person had complete benevolence, he might accept rights which would establish an even more equal distribution of goods. But if a system of political authority requires a degree of cooperation on the basis of mutually acceptable principles, then neither of these alternatives is really viable. A system of cooperation among completely self-interested persons requires a degree of rationality and knowledge not possessed by the ordinary reasonable person. A system based upon complete benevolence requires a concern for others not found in most human beings. In short, Hume was correct to maintain that for persons of complete benevolence justice is not needed, and that for persons of no benevolence it is not possible.[33]

In conclusion, it may be useful to see what place there is for rights on the basis of the acceptable legislative principles. The point is not to establish any particular rights, but merely to show how rights may be fitted into the general scheme. First, there is obviously no difficulty in establishing ordinary legal rights. These rights are determined by laws, so the legal rights will be those provided by legislation which is justifiable on the basis of acceptable legislative principles.

Constitutional rights present more of a problem. However, the difficulty is extrinsic to the view here, for it concerns the nature of such rights—whether they are absolute or are capable of being overridden in some circumstances. Constitutional rights will be the fundamental ones within a system of law. However, they may be justified by legislative principles. If constitutional rights are absolute, then they must be so strongly supported by principles that they can never be outweighed by contrary principles. For example, one might carefully define a right to free speech such that within the delimited area limitations would never be justified. However, very few such rights could be justified, or if they were, they would be of quite narrow scope.

If constitutional rights are taken as fundamental but capable of being outweighed in some areas by other compelling considerations, then one might establish broader rights in a constitution. Essentially, they would protect values (e.g., privacy) and activities (e.g., free speech) by creating a strong presumption in their favor. However, that presumption could be overridden. Basically, this approach has been taken by the United States Supreme Court in applying the Bill of Rights to the states through the due process clause of the Fourteenth Amendment. The Court has generally held that such rights may be infringed only by legislation reasonably related to a compelling state interest.[34]

Finally, one might speak of political rights which are not legally enforceable. Such rights would be claims which subjects of a political system could make against political authorities. These claims would be founded in the responsibilities and duties of occupiers of positions of political authority to pursue the purposes for which those positions were created. From this perspective, legislative principles state political rights. Thus, one may say subjects have negative political rights—rights that political authorities not enact laws contrary to the principles of privacy, freedom of communication, the public welfare, etc., without reasonable justification on the basis of acceptable positive principles. Similarly, there would be positive political rights to legislation preventing private and public harm, protecting privacy, etc., provided that it does not unjustifiably infringe negative political rights.

In conclusion, the acceptable legislative principles discussed in this and previous chapters provide an adequate account of the purposes of political authority. Of course, further principles may always be proposed and must be considered on their own merits.[35] However, the basic outline of the uses of political authority—the combinations of purposes and types of legislation—has been presented. The remaining task is to return to the issue of political allegiance and consider the implications of these uses for it and its general limits. These issues are considered in the next chapter.

IX
POLITICAL
ALLEGIANCE

In Chapter I it was argued that persons in positions of political authority do not have a right to be obeyed. Rights entail duties, and citizens do not have duties to obey such persons. Nonetheless, it was held that if the rules constituting positions of political authority are justifiable, then a person may have an obligation to comply with the norms issued by political authorities. Whether or not rules constituting positions of political authority are justifiable, it was argued in Chapter II, depends largely upon the purposes which the authorities are to pursue. Subsequent chapters have considered the acceptability of purposes for political authority. Having accepted and rejected various purposes, the nature and limits of political allegiance and of obligations to obey laws may now be more precisely delineated.

LEVELS AND TYPES OF COMMITMENT

The general form of a rule constituting a position of authority is as follows: person X, with qualifications Q, may issue norms N, in manner M, to persons Y, concerning topic T, for the purpose(s) P. Political authority is characterized by the fact that one of the topics for which norms are issued is the direction or use of the supreme coercive power in society. The purposes for exercising political authority have been elucidated and a preference indicated for the issuance of norms which are laws. Of course, even with governance by law various other types of norms will be issued. Controversies concerning what form of government is preferable, e.g., democratic or aristocratic, primarily focus on the qualifications for persons occupying positions of political authority and the manner in which norms are to be issued or made, e.g., by a majority vote of public representatives.

Rules constituting positions of political authority may be specified in more or less detail. The only variables in the rules which have been specified in this book pertain to the type of norms (laws), one topic (use of supreme coercive power), and the purposes. Except for governance by law, no restrictions have been placed upon the form of government. Hence, the acceptable purposes pertain to any form of political authority.

Since there are acceptable purposes for political authority (legislative principles), a reasonable person has a sufficient reason for being committed to some form of political authority. Acceptance of a purpose for political authority commits one to some rule or other constituting political authority. It does not commit one to any particular form—democratic, aristocratic, communist, etc.—or to any particular system of political authority. Acceptance of a legislative principle or purpose for political authority only commits one to having a state of some sort or other. Commitment of this sort is the most general level of political commitment, for it is not to any form of political authority and may be called commitment to political authority in general.

One must distinguish two types of commitment to political authority which one may have—permissible and mandatory. A reasonable person may consider the arguments for, or value of, political authority pursuing acceptable purposes such that it is permissible (and somewhat desirable) but not required to have political authority. He may find political authority permissible because he believes life will be no worse with it, yet he may believe that life will be little better with it than without it. However, he may judge that life for himself and others would be disastrous without some such system. That is, he may consider that the arguments for political authority's pursuing acceptable purposes are so strong, and the value of its doing so is so great, that it is not merely permissible but required. One may then speak of mandatory commitment; in other words, there is no permissible alternative. Thus, there may be permissible or mandatory commitment to political authority in general.

Commitment to political authority in general entails commitment to some form of political authority, which is the second level of commitment. Again, however, one may find several forms of government permissible or only one, so there may be permissible or mandatory commitment at this level as well. Commitment to political authority in general leaves open the type of commitment to the form of political authority. One may believe that there is a mandatory commitment to political authority in general but believe that more than one form is permissible. One may believe that commitment to political authority in general is permissible yet believe that if there be political authority, one form is mandatory.

Commitment to a form of political authority does not entail commitment to any particular system of political authority. There are different possible systems of each form, and some of them may be permissible but not others. Also, among the permissible ones, some may be considered better than others. Commitment to a form of political authority only entails commitment to some particular system of that form. However, one may be committed to one form of political system without being committed to all instances of it. Further, the particular system to which one is committed need not be an existing one: a person may be committed to democratic political authority but not to any existing democratic systems because of a belief that only a fully participatory democracy is permissible. Permissive or mandatory commitment to a particular system of political authority is the third level of political commitment.

These various levels and types of political commitment may be diagrammed as follows (P indicates permissive, M mandatory):

Levels   *Types*

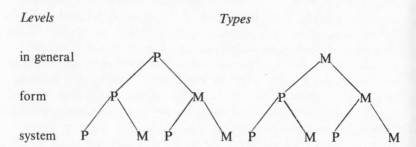

One may thus commit oneself to any hierarchical line of either commitment pyramid.

Each of these levels of political commitment involves different specificity in rules constituting political authority. Rules constituting political authority in general are only specific enough to distinguish political from other types of authority. To distinguish one form of political authority from another requires specification of the types of qualifications for occupying positions of authority and the manner of reaching decisions and issuing norms. Finally, a particular system of political authority requires complete specification in a rule or rules constituting a system of political authority.

A rule constituting a position of authority establishes a decision procedure.[1] The rule entitles a person occupying the position to issue norms in some manner. The person thus entitled to issue norms decides what is to be done, and the norms express this decision. Acceptance of a purpose for political authority, then, commits one to a decision procedure for the use of the supreme coercive power in society.

One logically cannot commit oneself to a decision procedure and yet reserve the right to accept or reject the results of the procedure for any reason whatsoever, ignoring the fact that a policy or norm is the result of the procedure. If one could do so, there would be no difference between commitment and non-commitment. One need not accept a decision which results from the procedure, but the fact that a decision was reached by the procedure must count for something. There must be some possible situations in which one will comply with some norms because they result from the decision procedure.[2] Usually, commitment to a decision procedure at least involves not refusing to comply with a decision merely because it is inconvenient to do so. Hence, commitment to a system of political authority entails that one will act in ways one would not have acted but for that commitment.

This point may appear paradoxical. It seems to imply that one must think that a policy produced by a decision procedure is right even if one opposed the policy before the decision was made. For example, in a majority vote method it seems to imply that those who voted against a policy must, if they lose, think that they were wrong.[3] This paradox vanishes once one notes that commitment to a decision procedure does not imply the belief that the result of the procedure is correct or is the best. Instead, one need only believe that it is better to have a collective policy than not, or that it is better to have a collective method for determining policy than not. One may then comply with the decision even though one thinks it is wrong. In such a case one believes that it is better to have a settled judgment or method of judgment for everyone than to have each person acting on his own.

Decision procedures of political authority involve what has been

called imperfect procedural justice.[4] The term 'justice' may not be
the appropriate one for a political system, in as much as not all
legislative principles concern justice. The idea, however, is the
same. A permissible political system involves a method of decision-
making which is considered at least reasonably satisfactory for producing legislation in accordance with acceptable principles. The
decision procedure may be better than many others because it is
more likely to result in laws justified by acceptable principles. Laws
so adopted will not always be the best according to the principles
of legislation. Indeed, some of them may be contrary to the principles. Since the system does not guarantee that only the best possible laws will be adopted, it is one of imperfect, not perfect, procedural justice.

As legislative principles constitute a standard of good legislation,
they may be used to judge laws better or worse. Overall, a particular
law may be supported by the principles but may not be the best
possible law. When evaluated by all applicable principles of legislation, a given law may be better than no law at all, but there may be
another possible law covering the same matter which would be better
than the given one. The first law is thus in accordance with acceptable legislative principles but is not the best. Evaluation of a
law by the principles may indicate that it would be better to have
no law than the one in question: the reasons against the law may be
stronger than those for it. Such a law is contrary to acceptable
principles.

Political authority decision procedures are imperfect partly because of the imperfection of people. The method used here to determine acceptable legislative principles has taken account of this
source of imperfection. It was not assumed that legislators always
act in accordance with legislative principles. They may make mistakes in evaluating laws by acceptable principles of legislation. Like
other human beings, they may not always act impartially according
to principles. Sometimes they may vote for laws from selfish considerations. So the imperfection of political authority decision procedures does not negate the commitment to political authority in
general.

Consequently, acceptance of a legislative principle entails acceptance of some laws which are not the best possible and perhaps
of some which are contrary to acceptable principles of legislation.
Acceptance of a legislative principle entails commitment to political
authority in general, which in turn entails commitment to some par-

ticular political system. Commitment to a particular political system entails acceptance of, or compliance with, some norms which
are not the best possible. How much less desirable than the best
possible a law may be depends upon the strength of one's commitment to the particular system, and that in turn partly depends upon
the importance one ascribes to the acceptable purposes of political
authority. Nonetheless, the fact that a law results from a permissible
or mandatory decision procedure of political authority provides a
reason for complying with it which may be called the procedural
obligation to obey the law. It is only a prima facie, not an absolute,
obligation and may be outweighed by other considerations.

Ronald Dworkin denies that there is always a prima facie procedural obligation to comply with laws which result from a permissible decision procedure of political authority.[5] He claims there is
no such obligation when the law violates citizens' moral (political)
rights against government because the decision procedure was not
followed, in as much as the decision was on a topic not included in
the power-conferring rule constituting the position of authority.
However, court orders *ultra vires* are binding until overruled; that
is, they are deemed permissible until determined otherwise.

One must distinguish between substantive and procedural limits
to political authority. Procedural limits concern the manner in which
the norm is issued and the qualifications of the person for the position. Substantive limits concern the topics and purposes of norms.
So long as no procedural limits are violated, there is a procedural
obligation to law, although it may be outweighed by substantive
considerations. In legalistic terms, violations of substantive due
process do not remove the procedural obligation to obey the law.

There is also what may be called a substantive obligation to
obey particular laws. It rests entirely upon their evaluation by acceptable principles of legislation. If a particular law is the best
possible one for its subject as determined by the legislative principles, then one has a strong reason for complying with it. This situation may be called one of pure substantive obligation to a particular
law. However, a law may be in accordance with acceptable principles of legislation but not the best one for its topic. In that case,
one has some substantive reason for complying with it but not as
much as though it were the best possible law. In this case, one has
what may be called an impure substantive obligation to a particular
law.

This analysis of the levels and types of commitment to political authority and obligation to laws indicates that questions of political commitment and obligation to law are very complicated. A given system of political authority may be undesirable at various levels. One may believe that the form of political authority is impermissible, permissible, or mandatory. There may be similar considerations with respect to particular systems of each form. For example, one may believe that democracy is the best form and that participatory democracy is better than representative democracy. If one happens to live in a representative democracy, what is the extent of one's commitment to the political authority? Should one foment revolution or attempt peaceful change to a better form of government? When, if ever, are *coups d'état* justifiable? No attempt is made here to settle such questions—another book would be required to sort them all out. Instead, the section below is devoted to a consideration of disobedience to political authority when one is generally committed to the particular system even though it may not be the best. Civil disobedience arises when one's procedural obligation to law conflicts with substantive considerations.

CIVIL DISOBEDIENCE

Many definitions of civil disobedience have been offered by writers on the subject. No definition has emerged which is generally agreed upon. Instead of offering a set of necessary and sufficient conditions for an act to be called civil disobedience, several characteristics of standard or clear examples of civil disobedience will be indicated. One or perhaps more of these features may be lacking and an act may still be civil disobedience. However, if none of the features listed below are present, an act would not be civil disobedience. Whether or not these features provide a precise definition, they focus on a range of conduct which both needs analysis and provokes questions about the strength and limits of obligations to obey laws.

Civil disobedience, then, is typically selective and public performance of actions (either by commission or omission) which the actor believes to be illegal but to be morally or politically justified. The actor must believe his action to be illegal. There are, of course, borderline cases in which one is not sure whether or not an action is illegal, or one may believe it to be illegal when it is not. The puzzles about justifiability arise from the conflict between a procedural obligation and substantive considerations. If a person does not think his act is illegal, then no conflict with procedural obligation arises.

Ronald Dworkin has criticized discussions of civil disobedience for not taking sufficient account of the possibility of doubt about an act's illegality. He contends that it is usually uncertain whether an act of civil disobedience is illegal.[6] His argument rests upon two assumptions not made here: (1) that there is a constitution which incorporates criteria for declaring laws unconstitutional which are contrary to at least some principles of legislation (e.g., the negative equality of opportunity principle), and (2) that the law to be violated is that to which one objects. Consequently, he is led to overestimate grossly the percentage of cases of civil disobedience in which there is doubt of a law's validity. But the problem of obligation only arises if one thinks the law is valid. To the extent that the illegality of an act is in doubt, the weight of the procedural obligation not to perform it is decreased. However, if a person believes that the law is valid, he faces the same problem when deciding to act, whether or not he turns out to have been correct. So there is no point in requiring that the act in fact be illegal.[7]

Civil disobedience is typically public. Such acts are sometimes performed in public, e.g., at mass meetings or on television. They may be public in that no attempt is made to hide one's identity or acts from the authorities, in contrast to an embezzler, who attempts to prevent anyone's knowing that a theft has occurred. A person engaged in civil disobedience may keep his identity hidden by performing an act when no one can observe it, e.g., dumping garbage in front of the entrance to the factory of an industrial polluter in the middle of the night, but he intends the public to be aware of the act.

Civil disobedience must be selective; a person must object to specific norms—laws, regulations, or policies—not to the entire system of political authority. Such a person must be committed to most norms of the existing system. No assumption is made here about the form of that system.[8] However, it will generally be assumed that the principles of governance by law are operative. This assumption does not imply that all norms issued by political authorities are laws. In the following discussion, however, the term 'law' will be used to signify a law, a regulation, or a policy. The object of protest may be any one of the three, but only laws or regulations having the force of law are being violated.

This characterization of civil disobedience includes both violent and non-violent actions. Some philosophers have argued that civil disobedience denotes only *civil*—that is, non-violent—disobedience.[9] To so restrict the term tends to beg the question of the justifiability of violent civil disobedience by implying that violence is never justified except in revolutionary situations. As the problem of justifying the use of violence has great importance, it should be squarely faced and not adroitly defined away. So, while there is some linguistic basis for thus restricting the term, it will not be so restricted here.

Since civil disobedience is selective, the burden of proof—both of production and persuasion—rests upon the one contemplating it. This point follows from the fact that a potential participant in civil disobedience is committed to a particular political system and thus has a procedural obligation to obey particular laws. This procedural obligation must be outweighed by contrary considerations. This point might be taken to imply that such a person must think he has an obligation to disobey the law—that, since conflicting prima facie obligations are being weighed against one another, one has an obligation to act in accordance with the way the weight falls. Such a conclusion does not follow, however. One may decide that conflicting obligations are so closely balanced that there is no obligation to obey or to disobey. Of course, if one believes the prima facie obligations weigh heavily in favor of disobedience, one may conclude that one does have an obligation to disobey.

Two different purposes or intentions may be involved in civil disobedience, and they require different justifications. One type of civil disobedience, which may be called personal civil disobedience or conscientious refusal, is simple refusal to perform an action because doing so is deemed contrary to one's basic obligations (moral, political, or religious). In such a case, one is not primarily concerned with reform or protest but with the preservation of one's rectitude. Socrates' refusal to obey the thirty tyrants' order to arrest Leon the Salaminian provides an example of this sort.[10] He considered that aiding the thirty to execute Leon was an evil action which he could not perform and maintain his moral integrity. In such cases of disobedience, one is not concerned with setting an example for others nor even with their knowledge of one's action. Personal disobedience applies only when the law requires an action which one deems wrong or forbids an action which one believes oneself obligated to perform.[11] It does not pertain if the law requires or prohibits an action only thought to be permissible, for then there is no objection to performing it. This point constitutes a fundamental limitation on the area of personal civil disobedience.

The second purpose of civil disobedience is to change or protest a law thought to be bad, or to protest the absence of one deemed proper. The following discussion leaves open, at least initially, the issue of whether one expects his action to be effective in changing laws; it only assumes that he intends to protest them. This second type of civil disobedience, which may be called social civil disobedience, does not necessarily involve one being legally required to perform an action one deemed wrong or legally forbidden to perform an action deemed obligatory. As a result, it applies to situations to which personal disobedience does not. In particular, it may arise in protesting the absence of laws, regulations, and policies and those which do not require one to perform any specific actions, e.g., foreign policy.

Perhaps the most crucial question concerning civil disobedience pertains to the substantive badness of the law being disobeyed or protested. First, one needs to distinguish between objection to an existing law and objection to the absence of a law. Disobedience aimed at protesting the absence of a law is considered below as a special case, so only existing laws need be considered here. Second, an existing law may be judged to be contrary to the principles of legislation or merely to be not the best. If the law is in accordance with acceptable principles of legislation but is not the best possible, then there is not sufficient warrant for civil disobedience. Not only is there a procedural obligation to the law; there is also an impure substantive obligation to it. The law is not bad but merely not as good as another. Nor, it seems, could such a law require one to perform an action one deems wrong. If the law is so supported by acceptable legislative principles, the conduct it requires should not be judged wrong although it may be less than one considers the best. Consequently, for civil disobedience to be justifiable, the existing law being disobeyed or protested must be contrary to acceptable legislative principles.

Third, an existing law should be clearly contrary to acceptable legislative principles. There must be negative principles against it. It is sometimes difficult to determine whether or not negative principles outweigh the positive ones supporting it. The application of some negative principles is clear, e.g., the liberty-regarding principle against penal legislation. However, the application of other negative principles is sometimes not clear because they require judgments of the effects of legislation upon society concerning which evidence may be lacking. Thus, one should be very cautious in determining that a law is bad on the basis of the negative public welfare and interest principles. However, one cannot assert that they may never provide a sufficient ground for judging a law to be very bad indeed.[12]

In determining the badness of a law, two confusions often occur. First, one may confuse the degree or amount of evil involved if the law is bad with the strength of the reasons for thinking it bad. If regulation of the economy is bad, then the greater the activity of a wages and prices council, the greater the evil. In this case, the evil logically depends on the badness of the activity, so that the mere extent of a wages and prices council activity cannot be a reason for thinking that regulation of the economy is bad. Of course, some evil, such as suffering, does not logically depend on the wrongness of the actions which involve it. For this type of evil, the greater the amount involved, the stronger the reasons needed to show that a law is substantively acceptable. But this evil may be outweighed by other considerations, and its greatness is no proof that other considerations are not more weighty. Second, one may confuse the psychological feeling of certainty with the degree to which reasons warrant a conclusion. Newton was psychologically certain of the law of gravity at an early age, but it took him twenty years to·produce what he believed to be sufficient evidence for it. While this comment does not imply that reasons for the badness of laws are the same as evidence for factual claims, judgments as to the badness of laws do frequently rest upon factual considerations as to what their results will be.

If one does have warranted reasons for thinking a law contrary to acceptable principles of legislation, the second major consideration concerns the use of legal recourses. Obviously, if legal recourse for redress of grievances is available and there is time to use it, then one should do so before engaging in civil disobedience except for a special situation in personal civil disobedience (noted below). However, it is not always clear what constitutes a reasonable effort to change a law by legal methods. For example, how much time should one spend attempting to get legislators to repeal a law before resorting to civil disobedience? No precise criterion is possible for this point. Further, it should be noted that the possible recourses may vary depending upon whether it is a law, a regulation, or a policy which one considers bad. Most laws can be challenged in the courts, although this requires a test case. Appeals concerning regulations usually involve administrative law and requests for reconsideration. Recourse in policy matters generally involves requests for reconsideration or removing the policy's author(s) from office.

The implications of these considerations for civil disobedience of a bad law may now be considered from the viewpoints of the two types of civil disobedience. For personal civil disobedience, a bad law should never be obeyed under any circumstances. One finds oneself legally required to act contrary to one's obligation. One cannot obey the law even while using legal recourses. So long as one is required to perform the action, one must refuse whether or not legal recourse has been used. However, both before and after the situation calling for disobedience arises, one should use all possible legal recourses to avoid the requirement.

The position of a person contemplating social civil disobedience differs from that of one contemplating personal disobedience in important respects. In social disobedience, one's purpose is to change or protest a law one considers bad, so no sufficient grounds for disobedience exist until one has made substantial use of avenues of legal change or protest. It may be urged, however, that occasionally there is no time for legal recourse before the evil effects of a law take place. If so, two considerations are relevant. First, was the law opposed before it was adopted? If not, then unless one was incapable of opposing it (e.g., one was too young or lived elsewhere) or has since changed one's mind, this claim is not a sufficient reason for ignoring legal recourses. Second, as one's purpose is to prevent the evil effects from occurring, the likelihood of disobedience being successful in this respect becomes relevant. If it has little or no chance of success, then disobedience cannot be justified.

Violating a law considered acceptable in itself (either the best possible or in accordance with the acceptable legislative principles) to protest the existence or absence of another law involves special considerations in addition to those above. Such disobedience can never be of the personal sort, for the latter solely concerns not performing an action deemed intrinsically wrong. Social civil disobedience can involve violating a law itself deemed acceptable, although some persons such as retired Supreme Court Justice Abe Fortas claim it is never justifiable in a society which offers legal means of recourse.[13] Violating an acceptable law to protest another law, he claims, constitutes an act of rebellion, not dissent. However, this view overlooks some important considerations. Some laws, many regulations, and most policies cannot be directly violated. To look only at laws, voter qualification tests, for example, are practically impossible to violate; in order to violate them one must register and vote. Laws concerning the use of drugs and alcohol, however, may often be directly disobeyed.

Although it need not be impossible to violate a law deemed bad in order to justify violating another one in protest, it is never justifiable to disobey an acceptable law to protest another one unless it would be justifiable to disobey the bad one if that were possible. There is always a double prima facie obligation to obey an acceptable law. There is a prima facie procedural obligation to obey any law—acceptable or bad. For an acceptable law, there is also at least an impure substantive obligation to obey it. Hence the case against disobeying an acceptable law is always stronger than that against disobeying a substantively bad law, and the strength of the case is proportionate to the strength of the substantive obligation.

One may also engage in social disobedience to protest the absence of a law, in which case it is also impossible to directly violate the condition being protested. In this type of case, it is extremely difficult to determine whether legal recourses have been sufficiently pursued, for they include getting persons in positions of authority to agree with one by lobbying, submitting petitions, etc. However, it seems necessary at least that substantial efforts be made to get the proposed law adopted. The other considerations which may be relevant in protesting the absence of a law are not all clear. It must be the case that it would be possible to justify violating the acceptable law if there were another law requiring the actual conditions which the proposed one would change. For example, suppose one is advocating an open housing law, and the actual condition is one of general discrimination (although this is not required). For disobedience of some law to be justified, one must at least think that such an action would be justifiable if there were a law requiring the actual discriminatory practices. If one is only protesting the absence of any clear law or policy and is not especially concerned with its precise form or content, disobedience probably would not be justifiable. Even this requirement appears to be minimal, however, and usually a stronger justification than this is needed. This requirement at least conceptualizes situations in which laws do not exist as like those in which they do so that similar considerations may be applied. Further considerations in disobeying one law to protest the existence or absence of another law involve a comparison of the value of the two laws.

The ranking of acceptable principles of legislation provides a partial basis for such comparative judgments of the importance of laws. The application of this ranking of principles to particular possible laws provides a priority of legislation. Laws can be roughly ranked on the basis of the weight of the purposes which support them and their effectiveness in pursuing those purposes. Such a classification is, of course, very rough, but there are clear differences of importance between, say, laws prohibiting assault with a deadly weapon and laws banning the use of trucks with loudspeakers after 10:00 P.M. There will be differences of opinion about the priority of various laws, but one need not have every law ranked in order of importance. A general classification as of fundamental, moderate, and minimal importance will be useful.

The use of this classification in conjunction with general rules of evaluation provides some guidance for the justification of the violation of an acceptable law to protest another. A reasonable person prefers a greater to a lesser good or the lesser of two evils. In the present context, this rule implies that it is never right to violate a law of greater importance to protest one of lesser importance. The substantive obligation to it will be greater than the substantive obligation to protest the bad or nonexistent law. It follows that violent civil disobedience, certainly the kind which involves physical injury to persons, is never justifiable. The use of violence except in self-defense or defense of others can probably never be justified. Destruction of property, especially personal property, to protest a law is rarely the least harmful method of making a point, that is, it is rarely the lesser of two evils. Laws prohibiting the exercise of violence (save in defense of self or others) are not bad; hence no grounds exist for violating them because of their badness. The only possible grounds for violating them are to protest some other law. However, violence is contrary to the most important purpose of political authority, namely, that involved in the private harm principle. No other law can pertain to a purpose of greater importance.

If the law being violated is of the same or lesser importance than that being protested, the considerations involved are not as precise as if it were of greater importance. At the same general level of importance, disobedience of an acceptable law to protest another might be justifiable if the violations of the acceptable law were few, for then the general purpose promoted by the law violated might not be frustrated to a very great extent, and considerable good might result. Nonetheless, the actual likelihood of such disobedience being justifiable is small, for choosing the lesser of two evils requires violating the least important law which will make the protest. For example, if one can protest by parading without a permit rather than, say, blocking access to a public building, then (assuming that

access to public buildings is more important than licensed parades—
a questionable assumption) one should resort only to the parade
technique.

Even granted that legal recourses have been utilized and that the
law being protested is more important than the one to be violated,
it does not automatically follow that civil disobedience is justifiable.
As the purpose is to protest, the likelihood of the protest being
effective in producing the desired change is relevant. The degree of
likelihood necessary varies inversely with the importance and badness of the present condition. The efficacy of a protest may depend
upon the closeness of the connection between the law to be violated
and the matter being protested. Hence, the degree to which a law
to be violated contributes to the enforcement or maintenance of the
condition being protested has relevance.

However, the relationship between a law to be violated and the
matter being protested appears even more significant than this. It
seems reasonable to claim that if there is little or no connection
between the two, disobedience is not justified, but the grounds for
this claim are obscure. For example, the connection between muni-
cipal taxes and rags and torn uniforms on clotheslines in the front
yard is minimal, and it seems ridiculous to put up such clotheslines
to protest tax increases.[14] The connection between the Vietnam war
and the draft is closer, making violation of draft laws seem a reasonable form of protest. To some extent this relationship between laws
is contingent and variable. For example, there is no logical or general empirical connection between voting rights and regulations concerning parade permits, but in the southern United States in the
early 1960s one could only peacefully protest bad laws respecting
voting rights by unlawful parades. In these cases, disobeying the
law concerning licenses for parades was surely justifiable, perhaps
because parades exemplify one method of protest no matter what
the law being protested.

Throughout this discussion the question of whether one should
accept legal punishment for one's civil disobedience has been studi-
ously avoided. A few comments on this topic are appropriate. It
would seem paradoxical to maintain that one should think one's
violation of a law justifiable and yet also accept one's punishment
for it as justifiable. It would seem that one must think it a case of
punishing an innocent person, and surely that is contrary to the
principle that only the guilty be punished.

One often hears that such a person should accept legal punishment because it indicates his sincerity, that he should have taken

account of it in his original decision to violate a law, or that the point of disobedience is to persuade others by sacrificing oneself. However, one's sincerity can be demonstrated without suffering, and others can have good reason for believing one to be sincere without it. That one should take the likelihood of being punished into account before violating a law is at least relevant. But if one thinks one's act is justifiable even if one is to be punished, one may think it would be better if one were not punished, for then there would be an even greater balance of good over bad consequences. Finally, giving oneself up to punishment is only a tactic to try to bring about change, and sometimes the tactic may be almost as effective, if not as effective, even if one is not punished.[15] More substantial reasons than these are needed to show that one should accept legal punishment for civil disobedience.

The basis for acceptance of legal punishment lies in the acceptance of governance by law. Unless all persons who it is reasonable to believe violated the law are indicted, 'governance by law' makes no sense. Laws are special types of rules. To apply a rule is to judge all relevant cases in terms of it. Hence equal enforcement of laws is essential to governance by law.[16] This is a question of administrative justice, discussed in the previous chapter. Thus one should usually accept the application of legal punishment to oneself if one is convicted of violating a law. To renounce governance by law is to renounce the basic principles of acceptable political authority. Nonetheless, there may be exceptional cases when it is still justifiable to avoid punishment because the punishment is for violation of a law itself deemed bad on grounds of a legislative principle even more basic than those of governance by law.

An air of paradox may still surround this conclusion, and these final comments may help dispel it. First, the apparent conflict one engaged in civil disobedience faces in accepting punishment is between thinking it proper that all persons who commit a crime (violate a law) be convicted and punished in accordance with the law and thinking it wrong that some or all actions of type A be illegal. There is no logical contradiction between "all laws should be enforced" and "there should be no law prohibiting actions of type A." Second, to think it proper that a person who commits a crime be convicted and subject to legal punishment does not imply that the maximum punishment be applied. For most cases of civil disobedience, a suspended sentence, probation, or a very short sentence is possible. There is no justification for giving a more than usually severe sentence. Third, only when one violates a law deemed bad does one think that the proscribed action is justified regardless of special circumstances. In social civil disobedience of a law deemed acceptable in order to protest another law, one does not believe that ·the action is substantively justifiable regardless of the purpose for which it is performed. But to speak of the purpose for which a person acts is to speak of motives, and the law primarily concerns intentions, not motives.

Thus, even with a commitment to a given system of political authority and with legislators who generally comply with acceptable principles of legislation, situations may well arise in which a reasonable person would think disobedience justified. Men are not perfect, not even legislators. Mistakes are made and laws are adopted for purposes less than the highest. No state or government legislates to the satisfaction of all subjects. But if it is clear what sorts of reasons are acceptable and proper for justifying legislation and what are not, there is a greater chance of achieving good legislation and a better life for all subjects. Clarity about the acceptable purposes of political authority will not prevent abuses and guarantee good government, but good government is much less likely without it. Consequently, the clearer and more widely accepted are the purposes of political authority, the fewer the occasions for justifiable civil disobedience will be.

APPENDIX 1

SUMMARY OF LEGISLATIVE PRINCIPLES

N   negative principle: there is a reason against legislation that . . .
P   positive principle: there is a reason for legislation that . . .

Governance by Law
- (N)   stability: makes the law unstable
- (N)   generality: is not general
- (N)   clarity: is not clear or intelligible
- (N)   consistency: is inconsistent with itself or other legislation
- (N)   retroactivity: is retroactive and imposes harms
- (N)   practicability: requires conduct which the normal person to whom it is intended to apply cannot perform

Liberty-Regarding Principles
- (N)   penal: primarily uses the penal technique
- (N)   compulsory treatment: primarily uses the compulsory treatment technique
- (N)   administrative-regulatory: primarily uses the administrative-regulatory technique
- (N)   grievance-remedial: primarily uses the grievance-remedial technique
- (N)   burden-imposing: primarily uses the burden-imposing technique
- (P)   private-arranging: primarily uses the private-arranging technique
- (P)   benefit-conferring: primarily uses the benefit-conferring technique

Communication and Privacy Principles
  (N)   communication: limits communication (deceit criterion)
  (N)   privacy: invades privacy
  (P)   privacy: protects privacy
Harm Principles
  (P)   private: protects individual persons from injury by others (voluntary act criterion)
  (P)   public: prevents impairment of the operation of public institutions
Paternalist Principles
  (P)   weak promotive: makes a person act to promote his well-being (voluntary act criterion)
  (P)   weak preservative: prevents a person from injuring himself (voluntary act and sacrifice criteria)
Common Good
  (N)   public welfare preservation: will decrease the level of public welfare
  (P)   public welfare preservation: will prevent a decrease in the level of public welfare
  (P)   public welfare promotion: increases the level of public welfare
  (N)   public interest preservation: is contrary to the public interest
  (P)   public interest preservation: will protect the public interest
  (P)   public interest promotion: will promote the public interest
Social Justice Principles
  (N)   equality of opportunity: will decrease equality of opportunity
  (P)   equality of opportunity: will increase equality of opportunity (not decreasing opportunities criterion)

UNACCEPTABLE PRINCIPLES

Paternalist Principles
  (P)   strong promotive: makes a person act to promote his well-being
  (P)   strong preservative: prevents a person from harming himself
Social Justice Principles
  (N)   difference: decreases the well-being of the least advantaged
  (P)   difference: increases the well-being of the least advantaged

APPENDIX 2

PRIORITY OF PRINCIPLES

POSITIVE PRINCIPLES

A. Greatest Weight
    private harm
    public harm
    public welfare preservation
    equality of opportunity
    privacy
B. Moderate Weight
    public welfare promotion
    weak preservative paternalist
C. Least Weight
    public interest preservation
    weak promotive paternalist
    public interest promotion
    private-arranging
    benefit-conferring

NEGATIVE PRINCIPLES

A. Greater Weight
    penal
    compulsory treatment
    public welfare preservation
    privacy
B. Lesser Weight
    administrative-regulatory
    grievance-remedial
    burden-imposing
    equality of opportunity
    communication

NOTES

1. See Robert Nozick, "Coercion," pp. 442, 445-57.
2. For a more detailed discussion, see Michael D. Bayles, "A Concept of Coercion," in *Coercion*, ed. J. Roland Pennock and John W. Chapman, pp. 16-24.
3. See, for example, Virginia Held, "Coercion and Coercive Offers," in *ibid.*, pp. 49-62.
4. For a defense of this approach, see Michael D. Bayles, "Coercive Offers and Public Benefits," *Personalist* 55 (1974): 139-44.
5. See Harry G. Frankfurt, "Coercion and Moral Responsibility," pp. 69-70.
6. Richard B. Friedman, "On the Concept of Authority in Political Philosophy," in *Concepts in Social and Political Philosophy*, ed. Richard E. Flathman, pp. 122-24.
7. Kurt Baier, "The Justification of Governmental Authority," *Journal of Philosophy* 69 (1972):704.
8. H. L. A. Hart, *The Concept of Law*, pp. 27-33.
9. Wesley Newcombe Hohfeld, *Fundamental Legal Conceptions as Applied in Judicial Reasoning*, ed. Walter Wheeler Cook (New Haven: Yale University Press, 1919), pp. 35-64.
10. See, for example, Robert Paul Wolff, *In Defense of Anarchism*, p. 4; D. D. Raphael, *Problems of Political Philosophy*, pp. 68-69; and Louis I. Katzner, *Man in Conflict*, p. 15.
11. R. S. Downie, *Roles and Values*, p. 127.
12. Joel Feinberg, "Duties, Rights and Claims," in *Law and Philosophy*, ed. Edward Allen Kent, pp. 150-51.

13. See Karl N. Llewellyn, *Jurisprudence: Realism in Theory and Practice* (Chicago: University of Chicago Press, 1962), p. 12, for the distinction between paper rules and working or operative rules.
14. "Of the First Principles of Government," *Political Essays*, p. 24.
15. *Leviathan*, ed. Michael Oakeshott (Oxford: Basil Blackwell, n.d.), p. 118 (my italics).
16. "The executive of the modern state is but a committee for managing the common affairs of the whole bourgeoisie" (Karl Marx and Friedrich Engels, "Manifesto of the Communist Party," in *Basic Writings on Politics and Philosophy*, ed. Lewis S. Feuer [Garden City, N.Y.: Doubleday and Co., Anchor Books, 1959], p. 9). More precisely, for Marx and Engels the state is the organized power of the ruling class. "The march of God in the world, that is what the state is," said G. W. F. Hegel (*Hegel's Philosophy of Right*, trans. T. M. Knox [London: Oxford University Press, 1952], p. 279).

CHAPTER II

1. See John Ladd, "Legal and Moral Obligation," and Jeffrie G. Murphy, "In Defense of Obligation," both in *Political and Legal Obligation*, ed. J. Roland Pennock and John W. Chapman, pp. 3-35, 36-45, respectively.
2. Ladd, "Legal and Moral Obligation," pp. 5-6.
3. *Ibid.*, p. 6. Most of the other contributors to this volume share Ladd's assumption.
4. *Anarchy, State, and Utopia*, pp. 6, xiv.
5. "On the Justification of Political Authority," in *Authority*, ed. R. Baine Harris, pp. 54-75.
6. Nannerl O. Henry, "Political Obligation and Collective Goods," in *Political and Legal Obligation*, pp. 265-67.
7. "Of the Original Contract," in *Political Essays*, pp. 43-61, esp. p. 56; see also Hume's *A Treatise of Human Nature*, ed. L. A. Selby-Bigge (Oxford: Clarendon Press, 1888), pp. 539-49.
8. Hanna Pitkin, "Obligation and Consent," in *Philosophy, Politics and Society*, ed. Peter Laslett, W. G. Runciman, and Quentin Skinner, pp. 45-85. See also Russell Grice, *The Grounds of Moral Judgment* (Cambridge: University Press, 1967); David A. J. Richards, *A Theory of Reasons for Action* (Oxford: Clarendon Press, 1971); and John Rawls, *A Theory of Justice*.
9. Paul W. Taylor, *Normative Discourse* (Englewood Cliffs, N.J.: Prentice-Hall, 1961), ch. 1.

10. See Ronald M. Dworkin, "The Model of Rules," *University of Chicago Law Review* 35 (1967):25-29.

11. Cf. Note, "Understanding the Model of Rules: Toward a Reconciliation of Dworkin and Positivism," *Yale Law Journal* 81 (1972):938-42.

12. E.g., Marcus G. Singer, "Moral Rules and Principles," in *Essays in Moral Philosophy*, ed. A. I. Melden (Seattle: University of Washington Press, 1958), p. 160; Joseph Raz, "Legal Principles and the Limits of Law," *Yale Law Journal* 81 (1972): 838; and R. A. Samek, *The Legal Point of View* (New York: Philosophical Library, 1974), pp. 292-93. Raz's criticisms of the distinction between rules and principles as drawn here are effectively rebutted by Ronald M. Dworkin, "Social Rules and Legal Theory," *Yale Law Journal* 81 (1972):882-90. For a brief criticism of Samek, see Michael D. Bayles, Book Review, *Wayne Law Review* 21 (1974):200-201.

13. Cf. "Understanding the Model of Rules," pp. 917-18. There are really three questions here. (1) Is the rule relevant? (2) Is this rule the one which governs the case? (3) Is the governing rule in fact applied?

14. Cf. Alan Donagan, "Is There a Credible Form of Utilitarianism?" in *Contemporary Utilitarianism*, ed. Michael D. Bayles (Garden City, N.Y.: Doubleday Anchor Books, 1968), pp. 192-93; Rawls, *Theory of Justice*, p. 133.

15. The conditions of generality and finality are taken from Rawls, *Theory of Justice*, pp. 131, 135.

16. Cf. H. J. McCloskey, "Liberalism," *Philosophy* 49 (1974):13, 17-18.

17. *Theory of Justice*, pp. 20-21, 48-52; see also Joel Feinberg, *Social Philosophy*, pp. 3, 34-35.

18. Rawls, of course, does not use it as the sole method; he also uses a hypothetical contract. However, he does evaluate the adequacy of the contract conditions (original position) by the contractor's adopting principles which are in reflective equilibrium. Hence, this method is his ultimate test. Feinberg applies this method directly, without any intervening hypothetical contract.

19. Immanuel Kant, *Foundations of the Metaphysics of Morals*, trans. Lewis White Beck (Indianapolis: Bobbs-Merrill, 1959), p. 25 (pp. 408-9 in the Akademie edition).

20. *Theory of Justice*, p. 121. For his view of rationality in choosing one's own plan of life, see pp. 416-24.

21. Rawls assumes that one does not know one's own personal goals or situation (*ibid.*, p. 137).

22. Rolf E. Sartorius, *Individual Conduct and Social Norms*, p. 122.

23. "Self-selection has produced a world in which the majority of its members at any moment in history are ego-centered. Theory must be built around the behavior of the majority type, for it persists" (Garrett Hardin, *Exploring New Ethics for Survival: The Voyage of the Spaceship Beagle* [New York: Viking Press, 1972], p. 116).

24. Rawls calls such goods "primary goods"; these are what a person wants whatever else he may want. The list here differs from Rawls' by adding security and omitting liberty and self-respect. Moreover, the ultimate basis of judgment is the satisfaction of a person's desires, not simply his possession of these goods. See Rawls, *Theory of Justice*, p. 92, and the comments by Brian Barry, *The Liberal Theory of Justice*, pp. 30-31, 54-57.
25. Cf. R. B. Brandt, "Some Merits of One Form of Rule Utilitarianism," *University of Colorado Studies*, Series in Philosophy, no. 3 (1967), pp. 49-50; H. L. A. Hart, *The Concept of Law*, pp. 86-88, 98-99.
26. *Liberal Theory of Justice*, pp. 118-19.
27. *Ibid.*, pp. 125-26.

CHAPTER III

1. *The Morality of Law*, ch. 2. See also John Rawls, *A Theory of Justice*, pp. 235-40, and Louis I. Katzner, *Man in Conflict*, pp. 48-50.
2. Thomas Mautner, "Flaws in Laws," *Philosophical Review* 82 (1973): pp. 83-98. One must distinguish between situations in which two mutually inconsistent rules are relevant to a case and those in which two mutually inconsistent rules both apply to or govern the decision in a case. While situations of the first sort are possible, those of the second sort are not. Only one of two mutually inconsistent rules can be followed in a particular case.
3. Review of Fuller, *The Morality of Law, Harvard Law Review* 78 (1965): 1284, 1286-88.
4. *Morality of Law*, pp. 205-6.
5. *Ibid.*, p. 211.
6. Graham Hughes, "Rules, Policy and Decision-Making," in *Law, Reason, and Justice,* ed. Graham Hughes, pp. 104-7.
7. This classification basically follows Robert S. Summers, "The Technique Element in Law," *California Law Review* 59 (1971):733-51. The major difference is the addition of the burden-imposing and compulsory treatment techniques.
8. H. L. A. Hart, *Punishment and Responsibility* (Oxford: Clarendon Press, 1968), pp. 4-5; Antony Flew, "The Justification of Punishment," in *The Philosophy of Punishment*, ed. H. B. Acton (New York: St. Martin's Press, 1969), pp. 85-87.
9. For further discussion of the difference between punishment and treatment, see Michael D. Bayles, "Dismantling the Criminal Law System," *Wayne Law Review* 19 (1973):828-30, 834; Herbert L. Packer, *The Limits of the Criminal Sanction*, pp. 21-26.

CHAPTER IV

1. Gerald C. MacCallum, Jr., "Negative and Positive Freedom," *Philosophical Review* 76 (1967):314.
2. *Ibid.*, pp. 319-28.
3. MacCallum suggests that proponents of positive freedom emphasize conditions of character more than actions as what one is free to do or to be (*ibid.*, pp. 326-27).
4. S. I. Benn and W. L. Weinstein, "Being Free To Act and Being a Free Man," *Mind* 80 (1971):207, 209.
5. Joel Feinberg, *Social Philosophy*, pp. 12-13; MacCallum, "Negative and Positive Freedom," pp. 320-21.
6. Feinberg, *Social Philosophy*, pp. 11-12. Louis I. Katzner takes this to be the distinction between positive and negative freedom (*Man in Conflict*, pp. 32-33).
7. See Benn and Weinstein, "Being Free," p. 199.
8. Feinberg, *Social Philosophy*, pp. 5-6.
9. Benn and Weinstein, "Being Free," p. 197.
10. *Ibid.*, pp. 206-9. This point and the point made in the next paragraph of the text underlie H. J. McCloskey's contention that the concept of liberty is based upon rights and values; see his "Liberalism," *Philosophy* 49 (1974):16-17.
11. Feinberg, *Social Philosophy*, p. 24; H. L. A. Hart, "Rawls on Liberty and Its Priority," *University of Chicago Law Review* 40 (1973):550-51. Katzner calls a conflict of freedoms between persons "the paradox of freedom"; he fails to see the stronger "paradox" that one's freedom to do A may conflict with one's freedom to do B., see his *Man in Conflict*, p. 31.
12. Feinberg, *Social Philosophy*, p. 18.
13. For example, *ibid.*, p. 22.
14. On the difference between taxation and punishment or penalties, see Benn and Weinstein, "Being Free," pp. 204-5; H. L. A. Hart, *The Concept of Law*, p. 39.
15. Other principles may be involved, such as all being "fundamental conditions of self-government"; see Frank A. Morrow, "Speech, Expression, and the Constitution," *Ethics* 85 (1975):239.
16. Thomas Scanlon, "A Theory of Freedom of Expression," *Philosophy and Public Affairs* 1 (1972):206; see also Morrow, "Speech, Expression," p. 236.
17. Various reasons have been offered by political philosophers as to why communication is an important topic for freedom. It would take a book in itself to consider them adequately. Fortunately, the issue here is whether there are adequate reasons for a reasonable person to accept a special negative liberty-regarding principle for speech or communication.
18. *Political Freedom*; this point also applies to Morrow's essay.

19. Scanlon, "Freedom of Expression," p. 213.
20. *On Liberty*, ch. 2.
21. H. L. A. Hart and A. M. Honoré, *Causation in the Law* (Oxford: Clarendon Press, 1959), p. 129.
22. See Wayne R. LaFave and Austin W. Scott, Jr., *Handbook on Criminal Law* (St. Paul, Minn.: West Publishing Co., 1972), pp. 453, 502.
23. See Joel Feinberg, "Limits to the Free Expression of Opinion," in *Philosophy of Law*, ed. Joel Feinberg and Hyman Gross, 135-51.
24. For a comparison of privacy in the United States, England, and Germany, see Herbert J. Spiro, "Privacy in Comparative Perspective," in *Privacy*, ed. J. Roland Pennock and John W. Chapman, pp. 121-48.
25. John M. Roberts and Thomas Gregor, "Privacy: A Cultural View," in *ibid.*, pp. 199-225; Alan F. Westin, *Privacy and Freedom*, pp. 11-21.
26. *Privacy and Freedom*, p. 7. H. J. McCloskey notes that privacy is distinct from freedom, but he does not note that it involves control over some freedom of others. His definition is further vitiated by his consideration of obviously justified invasions of privacy as not involving invasion at all. See his "The Political Ideal of Privacy," *Philosophical Quarterly* 21 (1971):304-11.
27. "On Privacy," in *Privacy*, pp. 149, 152.
28. S. I. Benn, "Privacy, Freedom, and Respect for Persons," in *ibid.*, p. 2.
29. W. L. Weinstein, "The Private and the Free: A Conceptual Inquiry," in *ibid.*, p. 33.
30. See Westin, *Privacy and Freedom*, p. 34.
31. "Privacy," in *Law, Reason, and Justice,* ed. Graham Hughes, pp. 45-69. Cf. McCloskey, "Political Ideal of Privacy," p. 312.
32. "Why Privacy Is Important," *Philosophy and Public Affairs* 4 (1975): 329.
33. "The Right to Privacy," *ibid.*, pp. 295-322, esp. pp. 313, 307.
34. See Hyman Gross, "Privacy and Autonomy," in *Privacy*, pp. 171-72.
35. 385 U.S. 374 (1967).

CHAPTER V

1. *On Liberty*, p. 13.
2. *Ibid.*, pp. 115-16; Mill, *Principles of Political Economy with Some of Their Applications to Social Philosophy*, ed. Donald Winch (Harmondsworth: Penguin Books, 1970), bk. 5, chs. 10-11.
3. *Ibid.*, p. 91. For an interpretation of Mill's doctrine as it concerns preventing damage to the interests of others, see J. C. Rees, "A Re-Reading of Mill on Liberty," in *Limits of Liberty*, ed. Peter Radcliff, pp. 87-107.
4. *Political Argument*, p. 175.
5. *The Public Interest and Individual Interests*, p. 31.
6. This definition is similar to Barry's (*Political Argument*, p. 176).

7. *Public Interest*, pp. 22-23.

8. See *Dillon* v. *Legg*, 68 Cal. 2d 728, 441 P.2d 912, 69 Cal. Rptr. 72 (1968), for an extended discussion of such a case.

9. *Political Argument*, p. 180; Barry, "The Public Interest," *Proceedings of the Aristotelian Society*, sup. vol., 38 (1964):5.

10. *Political Argument*, p. 195; Barry, "The Public Interest," pp. 7-8.

11. Joel Feinberg, *Social Philosophy*, p. 26.

12. Cf. *ibid.*, pp. 47-48; see also his "Legal Paternalism," *Canadian Journal of Philosophy* 1 (1971):109-10.

13. "Utilitarianism," in *Mill's Ethical Writings*, ed. J. B. Schneewind (New York: Collier Books, 1965), p. 330.

14. *Liberty*, p. 16.

15. Feinberg, *Social Philosophy*, p. 48; Feinberg, "Legal Paternalism," pp. 110-11.

16. Feinberg, "Legal Paternalism," pp. 106-7.

17. *Social Philosophy*, pp. 30, 111. He uses the term 'harm' instead of 'injury'. Louis I. Katzner (*Man in Conflict*, p. 71) provides a similar definition of 'need'.

18. This approach has been suggested by John Kleinig in "Good Samaritanism," *Philosophy and Public Affairs* 5 (1976):385, n. 7, 393; and in another journal article, "Crime and the Concept of Harm," *American Philosophical Quarterly* 15 (1978):27-36. His analysis of Good Samaritanism reaches a conclusion opposite to that put forth in the following discussion.

19. *Freedom, Anarchy, and the Law*, pp. 61-62.

20. *Ibid.*, p. 64.

21. See A. M. Honoré, "Ownership," in *Oxford Essays in Jurisprudence*, ed. A. G. Guest, pp. 108-10.

22. See J. R. Lucas, *The Principles of Politics*, pp. 62-66.

23. For example, while he does not distinguish between positive and negative principles, Feinberg writes of using the private and public harm principles to provide reasons *against* legislation; see " 'Harmless Immoralities' and Offensive Nuisances," in *Issues in Law and Morality*, ed. Norman S. Care and Thomas K. Trelogan, p. 89.

24. *Liberty*, p. 91.

25. *Social Philosophy*, pp. 33, 52-54.

26. *Moose Lodge No. 107* v. *Irvis*, 407 U.S. 163 (1972).

27. Art. 3, sec. 3.

CHAPTER VI

1. Nicholas N. Kittrie, *The Right To Be Different* (Baltimore: Johns Hopkins Press, 1971), p. 9.

2. For example, Gerald Dworkin, "Paternalism," in *Morality and the Law*, ed. Richard A. Wasserstrom, pp. 108, 110; and Bernard Gert and Charles M. Culver, "Paternalistic Behavior," *Philosophy and Public Affairs* 6 (1976):45-57. The definition of Gert and Culver is further vitiated for present purposes because it assumes a particular ethical theory.

3. "Paternalism," p. 111. Without argument, C. L. Ten also allows such restrictions as paternalistic; see "Paternalism and Morality," *Ratio* 13 (1971):65-66.

4. "Justifications for Paternalism," in *The Limits of Law*, ed. J. Roland Pennock and John W. Chapman, pp. 203-6.

5. For a general discussion of the two main views of identity, see Saul A. Kripke, "Naming and Necessity," in *Semantics of Natural Language*, ed. Gilbert Harman and Donald Davidson, 2d ed. (Dordrecht: Reidel, 1972), pp. 253-355.

6. *The Enforcement of Morals*, pp. 132-36.

7. For an extended discussion of legal moralism, see Michael D. Bayles, "Legislating Morality," *Wayne Law Review* 22 (1976):759-80.

8. See Basil Mitchell, *Law, Morality, and Religion in a Secular Society*, pp. 71-72; Ten, "Paternalism," pp. 63-64, whose discussion is limited to weak paternalism.

9. *Law, Liberty and Morality*, pp. 32-33.

10. Dworkin, "Paternalism," pp. 119-20.

11. *Ibid.*, pp. 122-23, 121-22, 124.

12. "Justifications," pp. 192-96.

13. "Paternalism," pp. 120-21, 125-26.

14. Cf. John Stuart Mill, *On Liberty*, p. 102.

15. Joel Feinberg, "Legal Paternalism," *Canadian Journal of Philosophy* 1 (1971):116-19.

16. Paternalism thus maximizes freedom, to the extent that it removes limits on fully voluntary choices and actions.

17. Cf. Ten, "Paternalism," p. 65. His examples of impaired decision—force and fraud—are not relevant to paternalism but to private harm.

18. *Ibid.*

19. Dworkin, "Paternalism," p. 126.

20. Hart, *Law, Liberty and Morality*, pp. 30-34; Dworkin, "Paternalism," p. 109.

21. "Paternalism," p. 126. Regan's reasoning is that such a prohibition decreases freedom because it coerces the person into doing something with his life ("Justifications," pp. 198-99). However, Regan must assume that the life is short; otherwise, on his view, the individual's character may change so that it is the life of another person which is saved.

22. American Law Institute, *Model Penal Code: Proposed Official Draft* (Philadelphia: American Law Institute, 1962), sec. 210.5.

23. Dworkin, "Paternalism," pp. 125-26.

24. The Supreme Court has held that it is unconstitutional to confine a person who is not dangerous and is capable of living in society on his own or with the willing help of family or friends; see *O'Connor* v. *Donaldson*, 422 U.S. 563 (1975).

25. See *Wisconsin* v. *Yoder*, 406 U.S. 205 (1972).

CHAPTER VII

1. *Political Argument*, pp. 188, 225.
2. *Three Tests for Democracy*, p. 143.
3. *Welfare*, pp. 11, 48, 57, 88.
4. *Ibid.*, pp. 3, 6.
5. This conception is of a subsistence standard of living. Cf. *ibid.*, pp. 4, 8, 94.
6. This conception of amounts is not a straightforward averaging but closer to what Rescher calls a profile. However, it is not true, as Rescher suggests (*ibid.*, p. 5), that a person's level of welfare is determined by the area in which he has the fewest goods. Nonetheless, since there is an upper limit to the ability to provide for each interest, one cannot compensate for deficiency in one aspect, e.g., health, by providing more than is needed in another area, e.g., wealth.
7. *Ibid.*, pp. 85-86.
8. Norman E. Bowie, *Towards a New Theory of Distributive Justice*, pp. 122-23.
9. Art. 25, sec. 1.
10. Rescher, *Welfare*, p. 33.
11. See Joseph L. Sax, *Defending the Environment* (New York: Alfred A. Knopf, 1971).
12. Frank J. Sorauf, "The Conceptual Muddle," in *The Public Interest*, ed. Carl J. Friedrich, pp. 183-90.
13. *Ibid.*, p. 188; David Braybrooke, "The Public Interest: The Present and Future of the Concept," in *ibid.*, pp. 134-35. While not denying more specific uses, Richard E. Flathman emphasizes the use of 'public interest' as a general term of commendation; see his *The Public Interest*, pp. 4, 12.
14. *The Public Interest and Individual Interests*, p. 167.
15. *Political Argument*, pp. 190, 195, 196.
16. See also Theodore M. Benditt, "The Public Interest," *Philosophy and Public Affairs* 2 (1973):296, n. 9.
17. *Ibid.*, pp. 297-99.
18. See B. J. Diggs, "The Common Good as Reason for Political Action," *Ethics* 83 (1973):285.

19. "The Public Interest," pp. 299, 305, 307.
20. *Ibid.*, p. 309. Benditt apparently welcomes this result.
21. Cf. Rescher, *Welfare*, p. 65. The interests included in public interest include those which Rescher calls trans-welfare values.
22. Cf. *ibid.*, p. 165.
23. Braybrooke, "The Public Interest," pp. 130-31; Barry, *Political Argument*, pp. 190-92.
24. Since deaf-mutes do not have an interest in telephones, on Benditt's definition telephone rates are not a public interest.
25. Rescher convincingly argues that the concept of poverty in the United States is based upon considerations of distributive justice (*Welfare*, pp. 103-5).
26. John Rawls, *A Theory of Justice*, p. 266; Mancur Olson, Jr., *The Logic of Collective Action*, Harvard Economic Studies 124 (Cambridge, Mass.: Harvard University Press, 1965), p. 14; Rolf E. Sartorius, *Individual Conduct and Social Norms*, p. 74; cf. Bowie, *Distributive Justice*, p. 45.
27. Rescher shows that in some cases, if people have some concern for others, they may be motivated to perform actions in the public interest without such an assurance (*Welfare*, pp. 31-32).
28. In *Eisen* v. *Carlisle & Jacquelin*, 419 U.S. 815 (1974), the Supreme Court held that the plaintiffs must pay the costs of notifying all members of the class. The costs of sending the notice were so high that the suit had to be dropped, despite the trial judge's opinion that the plaintiffs were very likely to win on the merits of the case.
29. Rawls, *Theory of Justice*, pp. 282-83.
30. Joel Feinberg, *Social Philosophy*, p. 52.
31. Rescher, *Welfare*, p. 177.

CHAPTER VIII

1. *Goesaert* v. *Cleary*, 335 U.S. 464 (1948). But see *Sail'er Inn, Inc.* v. *Kirby*, 5 Cal. 3d 1, 485 P.2d 529, 95 Cal. Rptr. 329 (1971).
2. See Bernard Williams, "The Idea of Equality," in *Philosophy, Politics and Society*, ed. Peter Laslett and W. G. Runciman, 2d ser., pp. 128-29, for speculation as to what an appropriate attitude would be if (when) such genetic limitations are alterable. See also Michael D. Bayles, "Genetic Equality and Freedom of Reproduction: A Philosophical Survey," *Journal of Value Inquiry* 11 (1977):190.
3. John Rawls agrees (*A Theory of Justice*, p. 74).
4. For an insightful discussion of this issue, centering on privacy and

freedom, see W. L. Weinstein, "The Private and the Free: A Conceptual Inquiry," in *Privacy*, ed. J. Roland Pennock and John W. Chapman, pp. 42-46. The United States Supreme Court has held that such exclusion from social clubs does not violate the equal protection clause of the Fourteenth Amendment because it does not constitute state action; see *Moose Lodge No. 107* v. *Irvis*, 407 U.S. 163 (1972).

5. Brian Barry, *Political Argument*, pp. 122-24.

6. *Ibid.*, p. 133-35.

7. See the definition of envy in Rawls, *Theory of Justice*, p. 532.

8. Barry's second and third arguments to justify the integration principle seem to rest upon the assumption that equality of opportunity has been denied; see *Political Argument*, p. 134.

9. Nicholas Rescher, *Welfare*, pp. 103-5.

10. See Brian Barry, *The Liberal Theory of Justice*, pp. 164-65.

11. *Theory of Justice*, p. 426.

12. Barry, *Liberal Theory of Justice*, p. 28.

13. See, e.g., Michael Scriven, *Primary Philosophy* (New York: McGraw-Hill, 1966), p. 253.

14. See Michael D. Bayles, "Compensatory Reverse Discrimination in Hiring," *Social Theory and Practice* 2 (1973): 301-12.

15. Isaiah Berlin, "Equality," in *The Concept of Equality*, ed. William T. Blackstone, pp. 15-16; J. R. Lucas, *The Principles of Politics*, pp. 128-29.

16. Joel Feinberg, *Social Philosophy*, pp. 100-101; Louis I. Katzner, "Presumptivist and Nonpresumptivist Principles of Formal Justice," *Ethics* 81 (1971):253-58.

17. Louis I. Katzner, *Man in Conflict*, p. 65.

18. See Feinberg, *Social Philosophy*, pp. 103-7.

19. Rawls, *Theory of Justice*, pp. 42-43.

20. Thus, general indifference curves showing a willingness to trade equality for utility are not adequate for legislative decisions; it is necessary to know what sort of equality is being traded and to know the nature of the utility or productivity received. However, they can provide a general idea of the type of priority developed below. Cf. Barry, *Political Argument*, pp. 6-8.

21. Walter J. Blum and Harry Kalven, Jr., *The Uneasy Case for Progressive Taxation*, p. 41.

22. For studies supporting the notion of diminishing marginal utility of income, see Frederick Mosteller and Philip Nogee, "An Experimental Measurement of Utility," *Journal of Political Economy* 59 (1951):371-404; and Charles Jackson Grayson, Jr., *Decisions under Uncertainty: Drilling Decisions by Oil and Gas Operators* (Boston: Harvard University, Division of Research, Graduate School of Business Administration, 1960), ch. 10.

23. See Blum and Kalven, *Uneasy Case for Progressive Taxation*, pp. 43-49.

24. Rawls, *Theory of Justice*, p. 104.
25. For a more detailed criticism, see Robert Nozick, *Anarchy, State, and Utopia*, pp. 213-27.
26. *Theory of Justice*, p. 302.
27. *Ibid.*, p. 154. Barry has forcefully argued that even in the situation which Rawls assumes, these conditions either do not obtain or do not justify the adoption of the difference principle; see *Liberal Theory of Justice*, pp. 87-107.
28. See Nozick, *Anarchy, State, and Utopia*, pp. 189-97.
29. *Ibid.*, pp. 155-56.
30. *Ibid.*, pp. 160-64, esp. p. 163. See also David Hume, *An Inquiry Concerning the Principles of Morals*, ed. Charles W. Hendel (New York: Bobbs-Merrill, 1957), p. 25.
31. *Ibid.*, p. 171.
32. This general criticism has been more adequately developed by A. M. Honoré, "Property, Title and Redistribution," in *Equality and Freedom: Past, Present and Future*, ed. Carl Wellman, Archives for Philosophy of Law and Social Philosophy, suppl. 10, IVR IX (Wiesbaden: Franz Steiner Verlag, 1977), pp. 107-15.
33. *Inquiry Concerning the Principles of Morals*, pp. 16, 18.
34. See, among many discussions, *Roe* v. *Wade*, 410 U.S. 113 (1973); *Kramer* v. *Union Free School District*, 395 U.S. 621 (1969); *Griswold* v. *Connecticut*, 381 U.S. 479 (1965).
35. Offense and legal moralist principles are discussed and rejected in my "Comments: Offensive Conduct and the Law," in *Issues in Law and Morality*, ed. Norman S. Care and Thomas K. Trelogan, pp. 111-26; and in "Legislating Morality," *Wayne Law Review* 22 (1976): 759-80.

CHAPTER IX

1. J. R. Lucas, *The Principles of Politics*, pp. 13-14.
2. Richard A. Wasserstrom, "The Obligation To Obey the Law," in *Essays in Legal Philosophy*, ed. Robert S. Summers, p. 296.
3. See Richard Wollheim, "A Paradox in the Theory of Democracy," in *Philosophy, Politics and Society*, ed. Peter Laslett and W. G. Runciman, 2d ser., pp. 71-87, for a formulation of this point. The paradox can be derived from any decision procedure except unanimous consent.
4. John Rawls, *A Theory of Justice*, p. 85.
5. "Taking Rights Seriously," in *Oxford Essays in Jurisprudence*, ed. A. W. B. Simpson, pp. 202-27, esp. 205, 216. See also M. B. E. Smith, "Is

There a Prima Facie Obligation To Obey the Law," *Yale Law Journal* 83 (1973):950-76.

6. "A Theory of Civil Disobedience," pp. 225-26.

7. Cf. Carl Cohen, *Civil Disobedience*, pp. 97-98.

8. It is frequently claimed that civil disobedience is more difficult to justify in democracies than in other forms of· government. Whether or not this claim is true, at most it means that the procedural obligation to comply is stronger in democracies than in other forms of government. For an excellent discussion of the claim about democracies, see Peter Singer, *Democracy and Disobedience*.

9. See, for example, Richard Wasserstrom, in *Civil Disobedience*, ed. H. A. Freeman et al. (Santa Barbara, Calif.: Center for the Study of Democratic Institutions, 1966), p. 18.

10. Plato *Apology* 32.

11. Cf. Cohen, *Civil Disobedience*, pp. 57-58, 71-72. His concept of moral civil disobedience, while similar, is not identical with personal civil disobedience since it includes disobedience in protest.

12. Cf. Rawls, *Theory of Justice*, pp. 371-73; Rawls, "The Justification of Civil Disobedience," in *Civil Disobedience: Theory and Practice*, ed. Hugo Adam Bedau, pp. 249-50. Rawls' view is criticized in Brian Barry, *The Liberal Theory of Justice*, pp. 151-52; Singer, *Democracy and Disobedience*, pp. 86-92.

13. Abe Fortas, *Concerning Dissent and Civil Disobedience*, p. 63.

14. *People* v. *Stover*, 12 N.Y. 2d 462, 191 N.E. 2d 272, 240 N.Y.S. 2d 734 (1963), *appeal dismissed*, 375 U.S. 42 (1963).

15. Cohen, for example, claims that avoidance of punishment is inconsistent with the whole enterprise of civil disobedience but then presents an argument similar to the one presented here; see *Civil Disobedience*, pp. 88, 91.

16. Dworkin urges leniency by prosecutors in the exercise of their discretion, but his argument only pertains to instances where the law being protested is the same as that disobeyed and is of questionable constitutionality; see "A Theory of Civil Disobedience," pp. 237-38. There has been considerable recent concern over prosecutorial discretion leading to administrative injustice. Dworkin's proposal might well increase such injustice.

SELECTED BIBLIOGRAPHY

Baier, Kurt. "The Justification of Governmental Authority." *Journal of Philosophy* 69 (1972):700-716.

Barry, Brian. *The Liberal Theory of Justice: A Critical Examination of the Principal Doctrines in "A Theory of Justice" by John Rawls.* Oxford: Clarendon Press, 1973.

———. *Political Argument.* London: Routledge and Kegan Paul, 1965.

———. "The Public Interest." *Proceedings of the Aristotelian Society,* suppl. vol. 38 (1964):1-18.

Bay, Christian. *The Structure of Freedom.* Rev. ed. Stanford, Calif.: Stanford University Press, 1970.

Bayles, Michael D. "Harm to the Unconceived." *Philosophy and Public Affairs* 5 (1976): 292-304.

———. "Legislating Morality." *Wayne Law Review* 22 (1976):759-80.

Bedau, Hugo Adam, ed. ,*Civil Disobedience: Theory and Practice.* New York: Pegasus, 1969.

———. *Justice and Equality.* Englewood Cliffs, N.J.: Prentice-Hall, 1971.

Benditt, Theodore M. "The Concept of Interest in Political Theory." *Political Theory* 3 (1975):245-58.

———. "The Public Interest." *Philosophy and Public Affairs* 2 (1973):291-311.

Benn, Stanley I., and Peters, Richard S. *The Principles of Political Thought.* New York: Macmillan Co., 1964.

Benn, S. I., and Weinstein, W. L. "Being Free To Act and Being a Free Man." *Mind* 80 (1971):194-211.

Berlin, Isaiah. *Four Essays on Liberty.* New York: Oxford University Press, 1969.

Blackstone, William T,, ed. *The Concept of Equality.* Minneapolis: Burgess Publishing Co., 1969.

Blum, Walter J., and Kalven, Harry, Jr. *The Uneasy Case for Progressive Taxation.* Chicago: University of Chicago Press, Phoenix Books, 1963.

Bowie, Norman E. *Towards a New Theory of Distributive Justice.* Amherst: University of Massachusetts Press, 1971.

Brandt, Richard B., ed. *Social Justice*. Englewood Cliffs, N.J.: Prentice-Hall, 1962.

Braybrooke, David. *Three Tests for Democracy: Personal Rights, Human Welfare, Collective Preference*. New York: Random House, 1968.

Care, Norman S., and Trelogan, Thomas K., eds. *Issues in Law and Morality*. Cleveland: The Press of Case Western Reserve University, 1973.

Chapman, John C., and Friedrich, Carl J., eds. *Justice: Nomos VI*. New York: Atherton Press, 1963.

Clor, Harry M. *Obscenity and Public Morality*. Chicago: University of Chicago Press, 1969.

Cohen, Carl. *Civil Disobedience: Conscience, Tactics, and the Law*. New York: Columbia University Press, 1971.

Daniels, Norman, ed. *Reading Rawls*. New York: Basic Books, 1975.

Devlin, Patrick. *The Enforcement of Morals*. London: Oxford University Press, 1965.

Dorsey, Gray, ed. *Equality & Freedom: International and Comparative Jurisprudence*. 3 vols. Dobbs Ferry, N.Y.: Oceana Publications, 1977.

Downie, R. S. *Roles and Values: An Introduction to Social Ethics*. London: Methuen and Co., 1971.

Dworkin, Ronald. *Taking Rights Seriously*. Cambridge, Mass.: Harvard University Press. 1977

——— "A Theory of Civil Disobedience." In *Ethics and Social Justice*, edited by Howard E. Kiefer and Milton K. Munitz. Albany: State University of New York Press, 1970.

Feinberg, Joel. "Duty and Obligation in the Non-Ideal World." *Journal of Philosophy* 70 (1973):263-75.

——— "Legal Paternalism." *Canadian Journal of Philosophy* 1 (1971):105-24.

——— *Social Philosophy*. Englewood Cliffs, N.J.: Prentice-Hall, 1973.

——— and Gross, Hyman, eds. *Philosophy of Law*. Encino, Calif.: Dickenson Publishing Co., 1975.

Flathman, Richard E. *Political Obligation*. New York: Atheneum, 1972.

——— *The Public Interest: An Essay Concerning the Normative Discourse of Politics*. New York: John Wiley and Sons, 1966.

———, ed. *Concepts in Social and Political Philosophy*. New York: Macmillan Co., 1973.

Fortas, Abe. *Concerning Dissent and Civil Disobedience*. New York: Signet Books, 1968.

Frankfurt, Harry G. "Coercion and Moral Responsibility." In *Essays on Freedom of Action*, edited by Ted Honderich. London: Routledge and Kegan Paul, 1973.

Friedrich, Carl J., ed. *Liberty: Nomos IV*. New York: Atherton Press, 1962.

———, ed. *The Public Interest: Nomos V*. New York: Atherton Press, 1962.

Fuller, Lon L. *The Morality of Law*. Rev. ed. New Haven: Yale University Press, 1969.

Gert, Bernard, and Culver, Charles M. "The Definition of Paternalism." *Philosophy and Public Affairs* 6 (1976):45-57.

Golding, Martin P. *Philosophy of Law*. Englewood Cliffs, N.J.: Prentice-Hall, 1975.

Guest, A. G., ed. *Oxford Essays in Jurisprudence*. 1st ser. Oxford: Clarendon Press, 1961.

Hacker, P. M. S., and Raz, J., eds. *Law, Morality, and Society: Essays in Honour of H. L. A. Hart*. Oxford: Clarendon Press, 1977.

Hall, Robert T. *The Morality of Civil Disobedience*. New York: Harper Torchbooks, 1971.

Harris, R. Baine, ed. *Authority: A Philosophical Analysis*. University: University of Alabama Press, 1976.

Hart, H. L. A. *The Concept of Law*. Oxford: Clarendon Press, 1961.

————. *Law, Liberty and Morality*. Stanford, Calif.: Stanford University Press, 1963.

Hayek, Friedrich August von. *The Constitution of Liberty*. Chicago: University of Chicago Press, 1960.

Held, Virginia. *The Public Interest and Individual Interests*. New York: Basic Books, 1970.

Hook, Sidney, ed. *Law and Philosophy*. New York: New York University Press, 1964.

Hospers. John. *Libertarianism*. Santa Barbara, Calif.: Reason Press, 1971.

Hughes, Graham, ed. *Law, Reason, and Justice: Essays in Legal Philosophy*. New York: New York University Press, 1969.

Hume, David. *Political Essays*. Edited by Charles W. Hendel. New York: Liberal Arts Press, 1953.

Jouvenel, Bertrand de. *Sovereignty: An Enquiry into Political Good*. Translated by J. F. Huntington. Chicago: University of Chicago Press, Phoenix Books, 1963.

Katzner, Louis I. *Man in Conflict: Traditions in Social and Political Thought*. Encino, Calif.: Dickenson Publishing Co., 1975.

————. "Presumptivist and Nonpresumptivist Principles of Formal Justice." *Ethics* 81 (1971):253-58.

Kent, Edward Allen, ed. *Law and Philosophy: Readings in Legal Philosophy*. New York: Appleton-Century-Crofts, 1970.

Kleinig, John. "Good Samaritanism." *Philosophy and Public Affairs* 5 (1976):382-407.

Lakoff, Sanford A. *Equality in Political Philosophy*. Cambridge, Mass.: Harvard University Press, 1964.

Laslett, Peter, ed. *Philosophy, Politics and Society*. 1st ser. Oxford: Basil Blackwell, 1956.

Laslett, Peter, and Runciman, W. G., eds. *Philosophy, Politics and Society*. 2d ser. Oxford: Basil Blackwell, 1962.

————. *Philosophy, Politics and Society*. 3d ser. Oxford: Basil Blackwell, 1967.

Laslett, Peter; Runciman, W. G.; and Skinner, Quentin, eds. *Philosophy, Politics and Society*. 4th ser. New York: Barnes and Noble, 1972.

"Legal Obligation and Civil Disobedience." *Monist* 54 (1970):469-624.

Leiser, Burton M. *Liberty, Justice, and Morals.* New York: Macmillan Co., 1973.

Lucas, J. R. *The Principles of Politics.* Oxford: Clarendon Press, 1966.

Mabbott, J. D. *State and the Citizen: An Introduction to Political Philosophy.* 2d ed. New York: Humanities Press, 1967.

MacCallum, Gerald C., Jr. "Negative and Positive Freedom." *Philosophical Review* 76 (1967):312-34.

McCloskey, H. J. "Liberalism." *Philosophy* 49 (1974):13-32.

Manicas, Peter T. *The Death of the State.* New York: G. P. Putnam's Sons, Capricorn Books, 1974.

Meiklejohn, Alexander. *Political Freedom: The Constitutional Powers of the People.* New York: Oxford University Press, Galaxy Books, 1965.

Mermin, Samuel. *Law and the Legal System—An Introduction.* Boston: Little, Brown and Co., 1973.

Mill, John S. *On Liberty.* Edited by Currin V. Shields. Indianapolis: Liberal Arts Press, 1956.

Mitchell, Basil. *Law, Morality and Religion in a Secular Society.* London: Oxford University Press, 1967.

Morrow, Frank A. "Speech, Expression, and the Constitution." *Ethics* 85 (1975):235-42.

Nozick, Robert. *Anarchy, State, and Utopia.* New York: Basic Books, 1974.

———. "Coercion." In *Philosophy, Science and Method,* edited by Sidney Morgenbesser, Patrick Suppes, and Morton White. New York: St. Martin's Press, 1969.

Oppenheim, Felix A. *Dimensions of Freedom.* New York: St. Martin's Press, 1961.

Packer, Herbert L. *The Limits of the Criminal Sanction.* Stanford, Calif.: Stanford University Press, 1968.

Pennock, J. Roland, and Chapman, John W., eds. *Coercion: Nomos XIV.* Chicago: Aldine-Atherton, 1972.

———. *Equality: Nomos IX.* New York: Atherton Press, 1967.

———. *The Limits of Law: Nomos XV.* New York: Lieber-Atherton, 1974.

———. *Political and Legal Obligation: Nomos XII.* New York: Atherton Press, 1970.

———. *Privacy: Nomos XIII.* New York: Atherton Press, 1971.

Perelman, Chaim. *The Idea of Justice and the Problem of Argument.* London: Routledge and Kegan Paul, 1963.

———. *Justice.* New York: Random House, 1967.

Plamenatz, John P. *Consent, Freedom and Political Obligation.* London: Oxford University Press, 1968.

———. *Man in Society.* 2 vols. New York: McGraw-Hill, 1963.

Quinton, Anthony, ed. *Political Philosophy.* Oxford: Oxford University Press, 1967.

Rachels, James. "Why Privacy Is Important." *Philosophy and Public Affairs* 4 (1975):323-33.

Radcliff, Peter, ed. *Limits of Liberty: Studies of Mill's "On Liberty."* Belmont, Calif.: Wadsworth Publishing Co., 1966.

Raphael, David D. *Problems of Political Philosophy.* New York: Praeger, 1970.

Rawls, John. *A Theory of Justice.* Cambridge: Harvard University Press, Belknap Press, 1971.

Raz, Joseph. "Legal Principles and the Limits of Law." *Yale Law Journal* 81 (1972):823-54.

Reiman, Jeffrey H. *In Defense of Political Philosophy: A Reply to Robert Paul Wolff's "In Defense of Anarchism."* New York: Harper and Row, 1972.

Rescher, Nicholas. *Distributive Justice.* Indianapolis: Bobbs-Merrill, 1966.

————. *Welfare: The Social Issues in Philosophical Perspective.* Pittsburgh: University of Pittsburgh Press, 1972.

Richards, David A. J. *The Moral Criticism of Law.* Encino, Calif.: Dickenson Publishing Co., 1977.

Sartorius, Rolf E. *Individual Conduct and Social Norms: A Utilitarian Account of Social Norms and the Rule of Law.* Encino, Calif.: Dickenson Publishing Co., 1975.

Scanlon, Thomas. "A Theory of Freedom of Expression." *Philosophy and Public Affairs* 1 (1972):204-26.

Simpson, A. W. B., ed. *Oxford Essays in Jurisprudence.* 2d ser. Oxford: Clarendon Press, 1973.

Singer, Peter. *Democracy and Disobedience.* Oxford: Clarendon Press, 1973.

Smith, M. B. E. "Is There a Prima Facie Obligation To Obey the Law?" *Yale Law Journal* 82 (1973):950-76.

Stephen, James Fitzjames. *Liberty, Equality, Fraternity.* Edited by R. J. White. Cambridge: Cambridge University Press, 1967.

Summers, Robert S. "The Technique Element in Law." *California Law Review* 59 (1971):733-51.

————, ed. *Essays in Legal Philosophy.* Berkeley and Los Angeles: University of California Press, 1968.

————. *More Essays in Legal Philosophy.* Berkeley and Los Angeles: University of California Press, 1971.

Taylor, Richard. *Freedom, Anarchy, and the Law: An Introduction to Political Philosophy.* Englewood Cliffs, N.J.: Prentice-Hall, 1973.

Thomas, Larry L. "To *A Theory of Justice*: An Epilogue." *Philosophical Forum* 5-6 (1973-75):244-53.

Thomson, Judith Jarvis. "The Right to Privacy." *Philosophy and Public Affairs* 4 (1975):295-314.

Tussman, Joseph. *Obligation and the Body Politic.* New York: Oxford University Press, 1960.

Unger, Roberto Mangabeira. *Knowledge & Politics.* New York: Free Press, 1975.

————. *Law in Modern Society: Toward a Criticism of Social Theory.* New York: Free Press, 1976.

Walzer, Michael. *Obligations: Essays on Disobedience, War & Citizenship.* Cambridge, Mass.: Harvard University Press, 1970.

Wasserstrom, Richard A., ed. *Morality and the Law.* Belmont, Calif.: Wadsworth Publishing Co., 1971.

Westin, Alan F. *Privacy and Freedom.* New York: Atheneum, 1967.

Wolff, Robert Paul. *In Defense of Anarchism.* New York: Harper and Row, 1970.

Zinn, Howard. *Disobedience and Democracy: Nine Fallacies on Law and Order.* New York: Random House, 1968.

INDEX

Ability, 100-101
Acceptance, 57
Accomplice before the fact, 87, 88
Actions, 72
Administrative-regulatory legislation: defined, 67-68; distinguished from compulsory treatment, 69; mentioned, 133-34, 135; principle against, 80-81, 180; principles supporting, 92, 112, 118, 136-37, 148, 160, 174
Advocacy, 86-87, 88
Allegiance, 12, 13; autonomy of, 12, 38-42, 50, 55, 189; justifications of, 38-42; to power-conferring rules, 38. *See also* Commitment; Obligation: political
Anarchists, 95
Authority, 23-30; acceptance of, 25; basic and delegated, 34; crisis of, 11; effective, 28; efficiency of, 22, 33; justifiable, 30; legitimate and illegitimate, 28-29; over conduct or belief, 23; positions of, 25-27; possessive and active senses of, 16; and power, 22, 32-33. *See also* Political authority

Barry, Brian, 57-58, 98, 103, 142, 143, 152, 153
Benditt, Theodore, 152-53
Benefit: defined, 17-18; legitimately expected, 19-20
Benefit-conferring legislation: defined,

68; distinguished from compulsory treatment, 69; principle for, 82, 180; principles supporting, 92, 112, 118, 137-38, 149, 161-62, 175
Benevolence: complete, 50, 187; limited, 54, 147, 157, 173, 187-88, 189-90; of reasonable person, 54
Bodily integrity, 108-9
Braybrooke, David, 142-43
Burden-imposing legislation: defined, 68; mentioned, 133-34; principle against, 81-82, 344; principles supporting, 92, 112, 118, 137-38, 149, 160-61, 175
Burden of proof: in civil disobedience, 200; for limiting liberty, 79-80, 128-29

Children: benefits for, 168, 175; consent of, 123-24; educational opportunity for, 167; parental power over, 31
Chinese revolution, 30-31
Civil disobedience, 198-208; defined, 198-99; legal recourse before, 202, 203, 206; personal, 200, 203; to protest absence of law, 204; punishment for, 206-8; social, 201, 203-6, 208; violent, 199-200, 205
Class actions, 149, 159
Coercion: adjectival use of, 22; defined, 18-19, 20-21; and government policy, 20, 21-22
Commitment: to a decision procedure, 195; mandatory and permissible, 193; political, 192-98; to a power-conferring

232

*Michael D. Bayles, professor of philosophy
at the University of Kentucky, received the
Ph.D. degree (1967) from Indiana University
and has been a Fellow in Law and Philosophy
at Harvard Law School. He edited*
Contemporary Utilitarianism *(1968) and* Ethics
and Population *(1976) and has written many
scholarly articles.*

*The manuscript was edited by Jean Owen.
The book was designed by Mary Primeau.
The typeface for the text is Times Roman,
designed under the supervision of Stanley
Morison, and the display face is Bodoni Ultra,
based on an original design by Giambattista
Bodoni.*

*The text is printed on International Bookmark
paper and the book is bound in Holliston's
Kingston Natural Finish cloth over binder's
boards. Manufactured in the United States of
America.*